a very large soul

a very large Soul

Selected Letters from Margaret Laurence to Canadian Writers

edited with a preface
and introduction
by J.A. Wainwright

CORMORANT
BOOKS

The publisher wishes to gratefully acknowledge the financial assistance of the Canada Council, the Ontario Arts Council, the Government of Ontario through the Ministry of Culture and Communications, and the Department of Canadian Heritage.

"For Margaret" from *Woman on the Shore* by Al Purdy. Used by permission of the Canadian Publishers, McClelland & Stewart, Toronto.

Cover photograph © Beverley Rockett, courtesy of the Scott Library Archives at York University.

Author photograph © Beverley Rockett.

Cover design is by Artcetera Graphics in Dunvegan, Ontario.

Published by Cormorant Books Inc.,
RR 1, Dunvegan, Ontario, Canada, K0C 1J0.

Printed and bound in Canada.

CANADIAN CATALOGUING IN PUBLICATION DATA
Laurence, Margaret, 1926-1987
    A very large soul : selected letters from Margaret
Laurence to Canadian writers

ISBN 0-920953-87-5

    1. Laurence, Margaret, 1926-1987--Correspondence.
2. Novelists, Canadian (English)--20th century--
Correspondence. I. Wainwright, Andy, 1946-
II. Title.

PS8523.A86Z54 1995   C813'.54   C95-90029208
PR9199.3.L38Z48 1995

for Malcolm Ross
mentor and friend to Margaret Laurence
and to so many Canadian writers

ACKNOWLEDGEMENTS

Jocelyn and David Laurence gave their support to this project from the very beginning. Without them it would have been impossible, and I am deeply appreciative of the freedom they gave me to proceed and of their commitment throughout.

I would like to thank all of the writers in this volume who granted me their permission to use these edited letters from Margaret Laurence, and especially those who gave of their time during my interviews with them. I would also like to thank the literary executors of the estates of Ernest Buckler, Marian Engel, Hubert Evans, Hugh MacLennan, and Gabrielle Roy for their co-operation.

I am grateful to the Canada Council for providing the funds necessary for me to meet with so many Laurence correspondents, and to the Office of Research and Development at Dalhousie University for additional funding.

Thank you as well to library archivists Charlotte Stewart (McMaster University), Appollonia Lang Steele (University of Calgary), George Henderson (Queen's University), and Phyllis Platnick and Heather Pitka (York University), who, with friendly suggestions and much practical help, made me feel they were doing more than mere professional duty.

A special thanks to John Wadland at Trent University, who knew Margaret Laurence when she lived in Lakefield and was associated with Trent. He was always there in the distance and when I visited Peterborough to listen to my ideas and concerns about the project.

Malcolm Ross inspired me and kept the faith when completion and publication seemed a long way off. I greatly value his friendship and cultural expertise.

As always, my wife and colleague, Marjorie Stone, "heard Jimi" when he tried to sing.

TABLE OF CONTENTS

PREFACE

Margaret Laurence was born in Neepawa, Manitoba, on July 18, 1926, the daughter of Verna Simpson Wemyss and Robert Harrison Wemyss. Her maternal grandmother's family had been United Empire Loyalists who came to Upper Canada during the American Revolution and later moved to Manitoba. Her paternal grandfather had emigrated from Scotland to Manitoba during the 1870s. Both of Laurence's parents died when she was quite young, and she was raised by her stepmother, about whom she writes with great love and respect in her memoir *Dance on the Earth* (1989). She attended public and high schools in Neepawa and then went to United College in Winnipeg, where she was taught English literature by Arthur Phelps and Malcolm Ross and met her lifelong friend Adele Wiseman. Here she wrote poems and short stories which were published in the student newspaper. In her final year she met Jack Laurence, a hydraulic engineer; she married him in 1947.

After a year at the co-operative daily the *Winnipeg Citizen*, Laurence moved to England with her husband, and then to Somaliland in 1950 and the Gold Coast (soon to be Ghana) in 1952, where Jack worked as a dam builder with the British Overseas Development Service. Their daughter, Jocelyn, was born while they were on leave in England, and their son, David, in the Gold Coast. Africa changed Laurence; her youthful Western idealism was modified as she encountered the life experience, the history, and the literature of peoples emerging from the long shadows of colonial rule. Tangible evidence of her development is found in her translations of Somali folk tales and poetry, *A Tree for Poverty* (1954); her first novel, set in Ghana, *This Side Jordan* (1960); and her collection of short stories, with its variety of African settings, *The Tomorrow-Tamer* (1963). These latter two books were written in Vancouver after the family had returned to Canada in 1957. Laurence also turned her diaries from Somaliland into a memoir, *The Prophet's Camel Bell* (1963).

While in Vancouver, Laurence also worked on the first draft of *The Stone Angel*, set in the fictional town of Manawaka, Manitoba. She took the manuscript with her to England in 1962 and rewrote it substantially while living in London. In the fall of 1963 she moved with her two children into Elm Cottage in Penn, Buckinghamshire, where she was to live for the next twelve years and to continue writing her Manawaka cycle of fiction, *A Jest of God* (1966), *The Fire-Dwellers* (1969), most of the stories in *A Bird in the House* (1970), and parts of *The Diviners* (1974).[1] Laurence's reputation in Canada was established with her portrait of one of the most remarkable figures in Canadian literature, Hagar Shipley, in *The Stone Angel* (1964), and confirmed when she won the Governor General's Award for fiction for her next novel in 1966. She visited Canada on publicity trips for the novels and in 1969–70 was writer-in-residence at the University of Toronto. Her eventual full-time return to Canada was prefigured by her purchase of a cottage on the Otonabee River near Peterborough, Ontario, in the fall of 1969, after she and Jack Laurence were divorced. It was at "the shack", as she called it, that she lived by the "river of now and then" so prominent in Morag Gunn's creative life in *The Diviners*.

In 1974 Laurence settled in Lakefield, Ontario, a few miles from Peterborough. She was by this time *the* Canadian literary matriarch, whose life and work were profound influences on more than one generation of writers and readers. As W.H. New has said, the Manawaka cycle "altered how Canadian writers responded to words. Through her, Canadian cadences became a language of art, rooted in place, yet shared. . . . Canadian readers recognized themselves in her works." New also emphasizes how in life "she was there: there in imagination, there to reach, there as encouragement."[2]

Although she wrote no other adult fiction during the last twelve years of her life, Laurence did gather personal and more literary essays into the collection *Heart of a Stranger* (1976), and she published three books for children in 1979–80. When she died of cancer on January 5, 1987, Margaret Laurence was mourned not only by those who had known and worked with her, but also by critics, academics, and the general reading public alike. "She is unforgettable," said Marian Engel, "because she is us."[3]

This book originated in conversations about Margaret Laurence with Malcolm Ross, who not only taught her at United College but also published her "first real story", "The Drummer of All the World", as editor of *Queen's Quarterly* in 1956.[4] Ross told me of Laurence's correspondence with a number of writers. He was sure, for instance, that she and Hugh MacLennan had exchanged letters over a period of years and that in them there was likely to be some important discussion of Canadian writing. Subsequent discussions with writers such as Al Purdy and Silver Donald

Cameron suggested to me that Laurence's chief contact with creative associates was through letter-writing. It kept her in touch with those near and far in geographical terms, and let her communicate to them her complex thoughts and feelings about their work, her work, and Canadian cultural matters in general.

In 1989 I had my initial look at the Laurence papers in the Scott Library Archives at York University in Toronto. In later years Laurence began to keep copies of letters she wrote to friends and colleagues, but it was the letters she had received that allowed me to begin to compile a list of her correspondents. I wrote to Jocelyn Laurence, who is her mother's literary executor along with her brother, David, and she gave me her approval of the project, provided she and David could read my proposed text of edited letters before any publication. Subsequently I wrote to various archives—at the University of Calgary, for example, for any letters to Hugh MacLennan—and to individual writers such as Silver Donald Cameron who still had personal possession of their Laurence material. There were a few exceptions, but nearly all of those approached enthusiastically supported the idea of a Laurence book of letters which would focus on creative and cultural matters, and indeed made many helpful suggestions about whom and what to look for. With the aid of a Canada Council grant in the spring of 1991, I was able to interview two dozen of these writers about their relationship and correspondence with Laurence.

Essentially the same set of primary questions was put to each writer. By and large these dealt with the following: first encounters with Laurence, in actual meetings, in letters, or through her works; the development of the relationship between Laurence and established/aspiring writers, and in particular what she had to say to writers about their own work and how she influenced them; how she influenced the "tribe" of Canadian writers to whom she apparently meant so much; the substance and quality of her fiction and what she would say about her work in progress and published work; the question of appropriation of voice in *The Diviners*; her return to Canada in 1974 and the fact that she did not write any more adult fiction after that date; her cultural legacy and her more personal impact, given that her life and art were so closely bound up together (though not in predictable or conventional ways, as is the case for many of those interviewed). I also asked questions that arose out of specific letters. With George Bowering, for example, I discussed Laurence's response to his 1971 article in *Canadian Literature* on

A Jest of God, and his addressing her in one letter as "My dear soul. . . ." Selected excerpts from the interviews are placed in italics among the relevant letters. This book is meant to reveal Margaret Laurence's voice, and so the thoughts and feelings of her correspondents, while significant, are limited in comparison.

Since I was aware that John Lennox at York University was editing the Laurence–Al Purdy letters, I decided to include only interview material with Purdy in my volume. There is, it seems, only one available letter from Laurence to Robert Kroetsch, but Kroetsch's response to Laurence as a writer and Canadian cultural figure is profound; hence his interview remarks are present. Farley Mowat and I could not track down any of his exchanges with Laurence, but he was a close friend so his voice is heard as well. I have tried to include Canadian writers with whom Laurence had a sustained correspondence over a period of time (between the early 1960s and the mid-1980s), and whom she considered close to her for a number of different reasons. The actual number of letters to each person varies widely and, while sometimes an indicator of intense involvement for a few years (as with Ernest Buckler and Gabrielle Roy), is in no way a proper basis for discerning between relationships. The integrity of Laurence's expression should be a guide, rather than the amount she wrote.

As for who is obviously not here, I spoke on several occasions with Adele Wiseman about including at least some of Laurence's letters to her in this volume. Although she was very interested in the project, offered the names of several other correspondents, and promised that she would soon sort through the "boxes of letters in my basement", Wiseman never did provide me with any selections. In the end, it seemed to me better that she did not. She was Laurence's oldest and closest friend, and Laurence wrote extensively to her over the years. Their correspondence is voluminous and significant in its own right, and deserves a publication of its own.

The writers in this volume are presented in alphabetical order. Chronological ordering would have allowed readers to focus on what Laurence was saying to more than one person at any particular time (for example, on the censorship issue in 1976); however, it would have diminished the perception of the relationships she sustained with various individuals (the power of her words to Ernest Buckler can be best appreciated if her letters to him are read as a unit). Readers can easily check letter dates for each writer to discover whether Laurence wrote to more than one person about a given issue.

I have not changed Laurence's use of punctuation in her letters, including her rather curious use of the two-dot ellipse (..) throughout. (Marjorie Stone, Elizabeth Barrett Browning scholar, has told me that E.B.B. employed the same form of ellipse in her letters.[5]) Conventional three- or four-dot ellipses are my own, to indicate that material has been omitted. Although obvious spelling slips have been corrected, consistent idiosyncrasies and shortcuts have been retained, without the distracting *sic* notation; the anomalies in these letters are part of their character.

PREFACE NOTES

1. All of the books in Laurence's Manawaka cycle were published in Canada by McClelland & Stewart.

2. W.H. New, *Canadian Literature* 112 (Spring 1987), pp. 222–223.

3. Quoted in W.H. New, p. 221.

4. "The Drummer of All the World," *Queen's Quarterly* 63 (Winter 1956), pp. 487–504.

5. See Marjorie Stone, *Elizabeth Barrett Browning* (London: Macmillan Women's Writers Series, 1995).

INTRODUCTION

It is no exaggeration to suggest that Margaret Laurence is the most significant creative writer in Canadian literature. This statement is not meant to spark any debate about the merits and deficiencies of her work compared to that of others. One could point to Canadian novelists who are her equal or better as writers. Nor is the statement meant to posit a hierarchy of literary figures with Laurence at the pinnacle; a writer's worth is not determined through competition with her/his colleagues. But when the profound effect of Margaret Laurence's fiction and of Margaret Laurence herself combine, the result is an unparalleled influence on Canadian writers and readers, as is evident from the testimony of those with whom she corresponded through three decades.

Laurence's Manawaka world is imaginary, but the experiences and voices of its women and men are so intrinsically a part of Canadian experience and voice that they have become what Morag Gunn, in *The Diviners*, called "fiction more true than fact". Writing to Ernest Buckler about his Annapolis Valley-based fiction, Laurence told him that he had done what Mordecai Richler once said about his own writing and Montreal: "It was my time and my place, and I have set myself to get it exactly right."[1] Richler's claim can be applied to Laurence and her art, as Dennis Lee explains:

> There were just people who found that she spoke for them. . . . People who'd have roots in small towns, who were intelligent, who were no longer just constrained within small-town Puritan Upper Canada. . . . I think [they found] that decency and compassion could come together and not be bad writing and be rooted where they lived.[2]

Lee emphasizes the strong presence of such decency and compassion in Laurence's character as well:

> . . . it would be sentimentality just to say that ego played no part in her life. But in the chief and obvious ways, it did not play an important part . . . I knew some generous and warm people who were good writers at that point. I'd never met such a concentration of those things in one person before.[3]

For Laurence there was little separation between art and life, though this does not mean she was an autobiographical novelist. As she wrote to Will Ready about Morag—and, really, all her female protagonists—"[She] . . . is NOT (repeat, NOT) me, but we are, as usual, spiritually related."[4] Robert Kroetsch recognizes this distinction/connection when he perceptively and precisely joins Laurence, her writing, and her readers: "She doesn't make a very deliberate attempt to separate texts from life. . . . Instead of mirroring Canadian life . . . she became a mirror for us. And so, in a way, she became artwork."[5] Laurence's letters to other Canadian writers allow us, to some degree, to step through the looking-glass and encounter the matrix of her life-text as it developed over a quarter of a century that was certainly one of the most vital periods in Canadian cultural history.

"It's easier for me than for her because she was the beginning of everything," says Alice Munro. Margaret Atwood states, "There were very few books by Canadian writers at that time. [*The Stone Angel*] was the first book by a Canadian writer, almost, that I had read."[6] Of course, every writer has role models, precursors who blazed the literary trail in one way or another. Laurence herself told Ernest Buckler, Hugh MacLennan, Sinclair Ross, and Ethel Wilson how important their creative expression had been to her. As she emphasized to Buckler, "You told us where we really lived":

It might interest you to know that when I first read *The Mountain and the Valley*, my first novel had recently come out [*This Side Jordan*, which was set in West Africa], and I was beginning to think seriously abut how I could return (in the deepest ways—because physically I was living in Vancouver but I hadn't yet returned home in my writing) to the background which was truly my own. Your novel both scared and heartened me—the power and scope of it. . . . I thought it was easily the most powerful Canadian novel ever written, and one of the most powerful I'd ever read from any country or culture.[7]

Writing to the young poet Dale Zieroth in 1971, Laurence told him,

when I first read Sinclair Ross's novel *As for Me and My House*, I must have been about 17 or 18, and it was the first thing I had ever read which was deeply out of a background similar to my own. The first time it ever occurred to me that maybe you did not have to have been born in London Eng[land] or New York USA or the Amer[ican] Deep South, to write a novel which people would read with comprehension.[8]

Both Munro and Atwood had read Buckler's and Ross's novels and other Canadian fiction before they read Margaret Laurence's work, yet her impact upon them was deep and original, as it was on many other Canadian writers who came to the fore during the decade that followed publication of *The Stone Angel* in 1964.

The "beginning" made by Margaret Laurence, to which Alice Munro refers, was a remarkable, sustained creative output of Canadian-based and gender-inclusive material over a number of years. Munro had been writing and publishing stories for a decade by the time her first book, *Dance of the Happy Shades*, appeared in 1968. Atwood, already an accomplished poet, published her first novel, *The Edible Woman*, the following year. In the five years after *The Stone Angel*, Laurence published two more Manawaka novels, *A Jest of God* (1966), and *The Fire-Dwellers* (1969). She went on to complete the Manawaka cycle with *A Bird in the House* (1970) and *The Diviners* (1974). Morley Callaghan and Hugh MacLennan had similar outputs in the 1930s and 1940s, but their protagonists were exclusively male and Callaghan would not designate his urban settings as Canadian.

The main figures of *A Jest of God* and *The Fire-Dwellers* are women in their thirties, and Laurence wrote about their hearts and minds with contemporary insight and in contemporary language, revealing aspects of female experience in terms of family, sexual relationships, and self-perception that had never been dealt with in Canadian fiction. She also wrote in the same way about ninety-year-old Hagar Shipley in *The Stone Angel*, a novel, Atwood says, "closer to my generation" than any written previously in Canada. While the female characters in much if not all of Callaghan's and MacLennan's fiction are handmaidens to the male protagonists,[9] female-male relations in Laurence's novels reveal the complexities of gender difference and human similitude. Thus poet/novelists George Bowering and Robert Kroetsch respond to her work as immediately and powerfully as Munro and Atwood. Bowering wrote an essay on *A Jest of God* that remained Laurence's favourite critical commentary on the novel. In a recent interview he called Laurence "rough and dirty and truly experimental."[10] Kroetsch picks up on another basic quality of Laurence's writing, the utterance of place:

Both she and I begin from geography. . . . we really felt life was a literal place in the world, on the Prairies. We'd work out of that place, and I think we would both feel that silence in our generation, as writers on the Prairies, a kind of wrestling with that silence, which I think went on until the end of life. . . . To resist the silence, in resisting it through story.[11]

Laurence's letters to her Canadian publisher, Jack McClelland, indicate that she was working on *The Stone Angel* (which she was then calling *Hagar*) in the fall of 1962. There is not much in these letters that explains why she turned from her African fiction to the first Manawaka novel, but in June of 1963 she suggested to McClelland that the writing of the novel and her sense of Canada were bound up together:

I have just received the page proofs from Macmillan's [her English publisher], and re-reading the novel, I suddenly felt I had given you a wrong impression in my last letter when I said I liked my home and native land best when I was away from it. Actually, that is not true, as I see now when I read HAGAR. Perhaps reading it again has made me feel homesick—I don't know. But when the chips are down, there is only one country in the world that I really give a damn about, and I see now how right it was to stop writing about any people other than my own. I will be intensely interested to know your reaction to HAGAR, Jack, because it seems to me to be the only really true thing I have ever written—this is because it is the only thing written entirely from the inside with the kind of knowledge that one can only have of one's own people. . . . Anyway, for better or worse, the voice in which [Hagar] speaks is all her own, and I think now that I can't ever again be content to write in anything except this idiom, which is of course mine.[12]

The Stone Angel appeared in print as a brave new era in Canadian writing and publishing was beginning. McClelland & Stewart's New Canadian Library series, edited by a Laurence mentor, Malcolm Ross, was seven years old and had forty titles. The Canada Council was the same age as the NCL, and in 1964, when its original endowment fund was deemed insufficient, the federal government decided to provide annual funds to cover the organization's growing needs—for example, aids to publication and grants to individual artists. The founding of numerous small presses, such as Coach House, Anansi, Oberon, and Talonbooks, was in the offing, and the Independent Publishers Association, including many of these presses, was formed in 1969. New writers, and established ones as well, were able to submit poetry and short fiction to an increasing number of literary journals and magazines. Laurence's idiom was her own, but it seemed to embody the full-scale voicing of Canada that was taking place in fiction and poetry. Her Manawaka world was at the centre of national literary expression during its extraordinary development between the mid-1960s and mid-1970s. Towards the end of this period, and after, when she wrote no more about Manawaka and indeed no more adult fiction, Laurence herself became the embodiment of that voicing, the Canadian literary matriarch and our most revered cultural figure. Her letters to other writers, those she considered her colleagues and friends, reveal the range and depth of the creative issues that concerned her, and the price she paid as she inscribed her time and place, and was inscribed by the variable country of the Canadian mind.

The earliest letter in this collection, to George Woodcock, is dated November 29, 1962, and the latest, to Margaret Atwood, was written November 13, 1986. In that twenty-four-year period, Margaret Laurence published four novels, two collections of short stories, a book of memoirs, two collections of essays, and four children's books, and became a household word in Canada—a considerable achievement for a writer of serious literature.[13] When she first wrote to Woodcock, she had just moved to England with her husband. Most of her fiction about Canada was written there, though much of *The Diviners* was composed during the summers of 1971 and 1972 at her cottage on the Otonabee River near Peterborough, Ontario. Even in 1962, she indicated strong feelings about the interference of domestic and social demands on her time as a writer.

> The great difficulty with life at home, from a writer's point of view, seems to me to be the inevitable involvement with a relatively large number of activities—whether these are worthy causes or community responsibilities, each may be rewarding in itself but taken as a whole they seem to diminish one's time to a point where one can begin to feel a little desperate.[14]

Alice Munro had met Laurence in Vancouver before the move to England, and felt "an immediate rapport" with another woman who was attempting to write while "trying to be a good housewife and mother". Years later, Laurence told Marian Engel, "So many of us, women writers, have chosen to be married, at least for a time, and to have our kids and do our work. I often think of us as heroines."[15] It was, by her own admission, partly the tension between domestic and creative expression that made her the writer she was and, in later life, a feminist.

When Laurence returned to Canada for good in 1974, her own children were grown and she was living alone, but she took on an enormous "mothering" role, according to Andreas Schroeder and others, in her visible support of the fledgling Writers' Union of Canada.[16] Timothy Findley has said, "The impact [of the Union] was that it altered every Canadian writer's attitude to what they were doing. Not utterly defined, and not defined alone by Margaret Laurence, but clarified by Margaret Laurence's presence."[17] During the 1970s and 1980s, Laurence also became heavily involved in the anti-nuclear and environmental movements, but for David Williams there was no dichotomy between Laurence's artistic expression and her increasing social and political activity:

When she came back [from England] she found that the country itself had changed, that there was an emergence from [a] colonial mentality, and as she had been growing and changing the country was different too. . . . I think the general purpose of poststructuralism is freedom, pure and simple. I think she saw a social purpose to that kind of freedom. She was arguing not only for female characters, not only for the country itself, [because] her whole attempt to empower others was also related to her political campaign against old, autocratic governments, against old ways of nuclear thinking and military thinking.[18]

Her commitment to such empowerment and to the writing community on an individual and organizational level took up an enormous amount of her time. Cutting short a letter to Silver Donald Cameron in 1974, Laurence told him, "Must go. I have 70 letters to reply to. . . . "[19]

The correspondence from Laurence to other Canadian writers, those she called her "spiritual kinfolk", essentially articulates two main periods in her life: the very creative years

1962–1974, from the beginnings of her work on *The Stone Angel* to the publication of *The Diviners*; and the years 1975–1986, a time of high public profile and social activism when she struggled to write another novel, making a number of false starts and in the end abandoning the project.

It was during the first period, when she was living at Elm Cottage ("Elmcot", as she wrote on her letterhead), Buckinghamshire, that she befriended and began exchanges with so many emerging Canadian writers, including Timothy Findley, Don Bailey, Silver Donald Cameron, Janis Rapoport, Dale Zieroth, David Watmough, and Myrna Kostash. Her correspondence with more established literary figures began with Adele Wiseman, whom Laurence had known since their days together at the University of Winnipeg and whose novel *The Sacrifice* had been published in 1956. The first of her many letters over fourteen years to Al Purdy dates from January 1967,[20] and those to Hugh MacLennan, also beginning a fourteen-year exchange, from February 1970. She wrote occasionally to Mordecai Richler between 1965 and 1972, and her several letters to Norman Levine span 1966–1973. Much of her letter-writing energy was poured into intense and detailed missives to Ernest Buckler between 1975 and 1978 and to Gabrielle Roy between 1976 and 1983, as she provided comfort to the former in his darker hours and, in large part, sought solace from the latter in her own times of need.

Although she accepted the necessity of working alone as a creative writer, Margaret Laurence always insisted that she was not lonely. Some of her fellow writers have disputed this in my interviews with them—Don Bailey asks movingly, "But who nurtured Margaret? Who nurtured her?"; Andreas Schroeder insists, "So here was an immensely tragic figure, one of the best-loved writers in the country, who was lonely as hell."[21] It is undeniable, however, from what she said in her letters, that Laurence considered her creative colleagues her "tribe" and that she took a great deal of emotional and spiritual sustenance from her correspondence with them. During the eleven years she lived in England, she returned periodically to Canada, sometimes for extended periods as a university writer-in-residence,[22] but she quite naturally relied on transatlantic letters for much information about who was writing what and the specifics of Canada's cultural state. Even so, as early as 1967 she wrote to Silver Donald Cameron about her desire to return to Canada to live: "If I don't, I can't go on writing, because I shall have forgotten how the voices sound."[23]

Despite the sheer number of letters, Laurence did know about what might be called "professional" loneliness, not that of the writer writing, but that which concerned the writer *and* writing. She gave a great deal of support to other writers in regard to their sense of self-worth and belief in their craft. Frank Paci says, "It's almost as if she had this tremendous sense of who and what a writer is and she took it from herself and she gave it to you."[24] John Metcalf adds, "I've never forgotten her kindness either, and the care she would take with younger writers and the time with unknown people. . . . her impact was huge."[25] Time and again Laurence encouraged new poets and novelists. She read their work, either when it was sent to her in manuscript form or upon publication, and she provided positive feedback, since she was aware of how difficult it was to get published and to receive fair reviews.

Her strong sense of loyalty to the members of her tribe, and her awareness of the need to nurture Canada's literary future, may sometimes have prevented Laurence from being objectively critical. But she was not blindly sentimental, and knew how to stress the necessity of revision while praising achievement. Anyone wishing to dismiss her critical commentaries as friendly backslapping should read her analyses of Timothy Findley's *The Butterfly Plague* and *Famous Last Words*.[26] Here her careful and perceptive reading of literature is evident, as well as her ability to probe sensitively and acutely a writer's intentions and results. It is clear from her replies to younger writers such as Bailey, Paci, and Zieroth that they were approaching her as an intelligent authority figure with a heart, and that they gained immeasurably from what she was able to give. John Metcalf says:

> I certainly learned from her and feel that older writers have to take care of younger writers and have to bring them along and help them and do all kinds of things for them, because that's the only way in which we will build and continue a possible literary tradition in this country. . . . That's something I got directly from Margaret.[27]

She was also very open and honest about her creative life with those born a generation after her, and whom she in so many ways considered her peers. She told them of her struggles with her writing, especially about the difficulties of beginning a new novel ("I had to discard 8 months' work and years of brooding on the novel I hoped to do"); about her need, while in

England, for the Canadian experience ("sometimes in sleep I am in my shack on the Otonabee and wake up with a sense of loss"); and about her foresight as to the end of her talent ("I'll quit writing when it quits me, not before. That will happen someday, too. And I'll feel like hell about it, for awhile at least")[28] Most of all she talked to them as equals, as a colleague who was interested in what they were doing and naturally assumed they wanted to know what she was up to as far as her creative activity was concerned. On a personal level she was valuable to them, but as a writer she embodied not only the rewards of public and critical approval, and some apparent financial solvency,[29] but also the integral aspects of artistic success. Laurence represented and communicated essential Canadian experience that took younger writers back into their lives and on into their art. Dale Zieroth emphasizes, "One of the wonderful things about reading [her] books is recognition, recognizing states of being and people. . . . That was the kind of thing that said my life was legitimate."[30]

She could be even more direct with older, established writers about her creative difficulties. "Every time I start a book I'm terrified," she told Ernest Buckler in 1974, and to George Woodcock she wrote in 1981, "if one thinks of the critics, the reviewers, and even God bless them the readers, one is *paralysed*. . . . Pray for me, please, as I know you do."[31] But she did want to let her literary precursors know what they and their work meant to her. She wrote many letters of great encouragement and support to a self-deprecating Buckler, and told an ageing Hugh MacLennan, "It was really only through your novels, and those of Ethel Wilson, and Sinclair Ross, and very few others, that I came to an understanding of the simple fact that novels could be written *here*, out of one's own background, and that in fact this was the only true soil for me to write out of."[32]

Although Gabrielle Roy was seventeen years her senior, Laurence felt a strong affinity with her and her work. Roy was French-Canadian, but was born in St. Boniface, Manitoba, and both women considered themselves prairie writers, even though they had written of other places. Laurence took great delight in Roy's children's and animal stories, especially since during their seven-year correspondence Laurence produced three children's books of her own, and had already, in 1970, combined the two genres in *Jason's Quest*. She was troubled by her inability to express herself in French, and was appreciative of Roy's bilingualism, which led them into some discussion of the importance of literary translations in Canada. By 1976 Roy had seven titles in the NCL,[33] and Laurence was very pleased to be able to tell her that both *The Stone Angel* and *The Diviners* were being translated into French by a Montreal publishing company (*The Fire-Dwellers* had already been translated and published in France). As she struggled with her own writing, Laurence was comforted by and somewhat in awe of Roy's continued output of fiction even as she moved into her seventies. Perhaps one of Laurence's most poignant and telling commentaries on her own creative troubles came in her last letter to Roy in January 1983:

> I have spent the past two years in trying, without much success, to write the novel I have been attempting to do for so long. Maybe I will do it—maybe not. . . . It has been a good time for me, in terms of my own life and friends and children, but not such a good time in terms of my work, which still seems to evade me, much as I try. I do not tell many people about this anguish, because they would not understand and because it is my own private concern. . . . I am not without work or without concerns. But my writing seems to puzzle and foil me. . . . I seem to stand in need of grace.[34]

Laurence insisted to Roy and several other writers that she was not in despair, and there is some disagreement among her correspondents as to the bases of her writing difficulties after her permanent return to Canada and the publication of *The Diviners* in 1974. She had told some people that this was her last Manawaka novel, and others that it might be her last novel altogether. There is division as to whether her public service—as chancellor of Trent University, spokesperson for various causes, speaker in classrooms and elsewhere on Canadian literature, for example—interfered with her writing or whether she took on such responsibilities because she was not writing anyway. Certainly she was slowing down; as she told Frank Paci in 1981, "I can still only work about 3 or 4 hours on weekdays. I'm then exhausted."[35] David Watmough believes firmly that she had more adult fiction to write, while Andreas Schroeder suggests that she did not know how to turn away from that vital "mothering" role she provided for the Canadian literary community, and thus find time for herself. George Woodcock, however, allows her that grace she sought when he says in an interview that her life and work after *The Diviners* "all comes together in a Christian context. It's very much like the progressions of religious people. They create when they reach the end of youth or in middle age; then in their later years they go into devotional exercises. Hers is the classic pattern."[36]

There is little doubt that the attacks against *The Diviners* by Christian fundamentalists in 1976 and again in 1985 took their toll on Laurence. In 1976 the Citizens in Defence of Decency group was formed in Peterborough, near Laurence's home in Lakefield, because the Peterborough Board of Education had approved the use of *The Diviners* for a Grade 13 English course, despite a school administrator's complaint about the book. The CIDD felt the novel was replete with pornographic passages and blasphemies, and the minister who headed the group urged people to sign a petition to force the board to back down (4,385 persons apparently did sign). Meanwhile, at another Peterborough high school, the principal made a personal decision to ban Alice Munro's novel *Lives of Girls and Women*, even though most of his staff and the students opposed his move. The extreme hostility to Laurence's fiction is displayed in a public statement to the school board about *The Diviners* by a member of the Peterborough Council of Women: "The only purpose that this novel could serve in the field of education for students of any age would be for the promotion of degradation, the promotion of indecency and immorality, the knowledge of unsavoury pornography and gutter language spawned in warped minds."[37] Despite such pressure, the board continued to support the teaching of the novel.

In 1985 a local municipal councillor, the mother of three high school students, objected to the Peterborough School Board about the presence in the curriculum of three Laurence novels, *The Diviners, The Stone Angel,* and *A Jest of God.* Once again, after some debate, the board upheld the teaching of Laurence's fiction. Laurence had maintained a fairly low profile during the 1976 controversy, but this time she leapt into the heat of the debate, meeting with students and speaking out in interviews. She told the Peterborough *Examiner* that pornography speaks of hate, while "My books profoundly speak of love. Love between members of family, between different generations, between friends, even, frankly, the Holy Spirit."[38] This echoes what she had written to Gabrielle Roy nine years previously: "In fact, at its deepest level [*The Diviners*] is a novel about God's grace."[39]

In 1976 Laurence wrote to Ernest Buckler that she was "somewhat depressed" by the vitriolic nature of the attacks, and Silver Donald Cameron stresses that she was "deeply offended at the suggestion that somehow her work was not moral."[40] Timothy Findley, who knew how hard she worked "to achieve articulation that was as precise as the voice inside her", emphasizes that the effect of both censorship struggles was "devastating" to Laurence, while Andreas Schroeder insists that "maximum damage" was done to her.[41] George Woodcock puts things simply, but effectively: "She didn't have the life-saving ability to shut off what other people said. She took everything to heart."[42] If this is true, it is also true that she fought the attacks on her work with eloquence and courage, and with the belief that she was also defending the work of her colleagues. She was a figure of moral conscience to her fellow writers, and a spokesperson for the integrity and efficacy of art in our society.

Margaret Laurence had what Harry T. Moore attributed to D.H. Lawrence—an "intelligent heart"[43]—and if it was sometimes easily wounded, its strength of conviction was nonetheless always passed on to others. While the image of the heart perhaps explains her interaction with others, a further image is needed to convey her inherent *presence* in Canada, not only while she was alive but even yet, because of who she was and what she wrote. Her letters, like her fiction, reveal a figure whom Silver Donald Cameron calls "a very large soul".[44] Cameron, unknowingly, echoes what George Bowering told Laurence in a letter to her in 1977. He addressed her as "My dear soul—" and then added: "I say soul because that is the image that yr [sic] achievement brings forth."[45] It is Margaret Laurence's achievement as "writer, but also citizen, parent, friend"[46] that underlies so much of our Canadian cultural conviction, the essence of ourselves as a voiced and voicing people. Like Manawaka with Morag Gunn, she goes with us wherever we go.

J.A. Wainwright

INTRODUCTION NOTES

1. ML to Ernest Buckler, Oct. 3, 1974.

2. Interview with Dennis Lee, June 11, 1991.

3. Interview with Lee.

4. ML to Will Ready, Feb. 8, 1973.

5. Interview with Robert Kroetsch, May 6, 1991.

6. Interview with Alice Munro, June 4, 1991; interview with Margaret Atwood, June 10, 1991.

7. ML to Ernest Buckler, Aug. 30, 1974.

8. ML to Dale Zieroth, Aug. 3, 1971.

9. An exception might be Peggy Sanderson in Callaghan's *The Loved and the Lost* (1951), but this story is told entirely from Jim McAlpine's perspective, and it is his response to Peggy's experience that is emphasized in the novel.

10. George Bowering, "That Fool of a Fear: Notes on *A Jest of God, Canadian Literature* 50 (Autumn 1971), pp. 41–56; interview with Bowering, May 11, 1991.

11. Interview with Robert Kroetsch, May 6, 1991.

12. ML to Jack McClelland, June 29, 1963.

13. The two collections of stories were *A Bird in the House* (1970) and *The Tomorrow-Tamer* (1963); the African memoir was *The Prophet's Camel Bell* (1963); the collections of essays were *Long Drums and Cannons: Nigerian Dramatists and Novelists 1952–1968* (1968) and *Heart of a Stranger* (1976); and the four children's books were *Jason's Quest* (1970), *Six Darn Cows* (1979), *The Olden Days Coat* (1979), and *The Christmas Birthday Story* (1980).

14. ML to George Woodcock, Nov. 29, 1962.

15. Interview with Alice Munro, June 4, 1991; ML to Marian Engel, June 28, 1984.

16. Interview with Andreas Schroeder, May 14, 1991. The Writers' Union of Canada was officially founded in November 1973.

17. Interview with Timothy Findley, April 4, 1991.

18. Interview with David Williams, May 7, 1991.

19. ML to Silver Donald Cameron, April 9, 1974.

20. John Lennox has edited *Margaret Laurence–Al Purdy: A Friendship in Letters* (Toronto: McClelland & Stewart, 1993).

21. Interview with Don Bailey, May 7, 1991; interview with Andreas Schroeder, May 14, 1991.

22. Laurence was writer-in-residence at the University of Toronto in the fall term of 1969, at the University of Western Ontario, in London, in the fall term of 1973, and at Trent University in Peterborough, Ontario, in the winter-spring term of 1974.

23. ML to Silver Donald Cameron, Oct. 11, 1967.

24. Interview with Frank Paci, April 30, 1991.

25. Interview with John Metcalf, March 19, 1991.

26. ML to Timothy Findley, Oct. 26, 1970 and Nov. 5, 1981.

27. Interview with Metcalf.

28. ML to Don Bailey, April 24, 1971 and Aug. 12, 1970; ML to Dale Zieroth, March 24, 1973.

29. Laurence did not have much time for reviewers who were not themselves creative writers; one exception was William French of the Toronto *Globe and Mail*. As for her financial state, she told George Woodcock on June 5, 1980, "for about 5 years my income was nearly that of a full professor of English", but in the last eight years of her life she had to write articles for newspapers, magazines, and journals to support herself.

30. Interview with Dale Zieroth, May 13, 1991.

31. ML to Ernest Buckler, Aug. 30, 1974; ML to George Woodcock, March 26, 1981.

32. ML to Hugh MacLennan, Feb. 16, 1970.

33. *The Tin Flute, Where Nests the Water Hen, The Cashier, Street of Riches, The Hidden Mountain, Windflower, The Road past Altamont.*

34. ML to Gabrielle Roy, Jan. 9, 1983.

35. ML to Frank Paci, Sept. 5, 1981.

36. Interview with George Woodcock, May 9, 1991.

37. As reported by John Ayre, *Weekend Magazine*, Aug. 28, 1976.

38. Peterborough *Examiner*, Jan. 17, 1985.

39. ML to Gabrielle Roy, March 23, 1976.

40. ML to Ernest Buckler, June 9, 1976; interview with Silver Donald Cameron, June 14, 1992.

41. Interview with Timothy Findley, April 4, 1991; interview with Andreas Schroeder, May 14, 1991.

42. Interview with George Woodcock, May 9, 1991.

43. Harry T. Moore, *The Intelligent Heart: The Story of D.H. Lawrence* (New York: Farrar, Straus, and Young, 1954).

44. Interview with Silver Donald Cameron, June 14, 1992.

45. George Bowering to ML, Feb. 24, 1977.

46. ML's description of herself in a letter to Timothy Findley, Nov. 9, 1983.

LETTERS

MARGARET ATWOOD

I first met Margaret Laurence in the washroom of the place where the Governor General's Awards were awarded in 1967, because we both won the Governor General's Award at that time. And I had my first contact lenses. I made it through the awards and then we [all] went to dinner; I mean, it was going to be a long night. I didn't know how to take the lenses out at that point without a mirror, so I sat there and started to cry, and these two lovely Francophones on either side, older men with moustaches, thought that I was overcome with emotion. I was probably too embarrassed to tell them what it really was. As soon as I had a chance I rushed into the washroom, and there was Margaret Laurence having a bit of the shakes, she was so nervous about the whole thing. And that was how I first met her. We were both washroom casualties.

Elm Cottage,
10 Jan 71

Dear Peggy—

Very many thanks for sending me the Women's Lib publication and the poems of bill bissett. Haven't read the poems yet, but read some of the Women's Lib this morning. I guess I really do not have an ambiguous attitude to Women's Lib this morning— basically, I am in great agreement. I can't go along with some of the attitudes, but probably quite a few women in the movement can't, either. I'm not a joiner in the sense that I shall never find a cause with which I agree over detailed beliefs 100%, but of course that isn't so important. I thought "The Politics of Housework" was great! I recognized all the arguments from way back, of course. Except that in my case, I was too naive and uncertain (yeh, even at 34) to do much more than argue sporadically or resent silently. I suppose I do find it emotionally trying to read the Women's Lib stuff, not because I disagree with most of it, but because in many ways I wish so profoundly that such a general movement had existed let's say 15 years ago. I feel as tho I have in fact fought every single one of these issues, but alone and therefore not effectually from the point of view of relationships.

1

The only solution for me, therefore, was to take off and learn to accept the fact that at 44, now, and considering the men of my generation, and also considering that my own work is of enormous overwhelming importance to me, there's no way of having a partnership on the only terms I could now bear. Odd . . I remember figuring it all out about 1962 when I was 36, and on my own for the first time in my life, but with 2 kids, whose presence saves me from despair, and when I got to England, thinking "the only relationship I could possibly now maintain would be a relationship of equals." It seems almost spooky to see the same things now being written about and yelled out loud . . one really wants to say hurrah! Personally, from that point of view, I wish I were 15 yrs younger or else that there were a few more men of my own age or older who cottoned on to these views. They are, however, scarce as hen's teeth. Luckily, the acts of "managing" a household and its economy no longer scare me, as I found I could really do all that without much trouble when I had to, and that I wasn't a financial nitwit after all, as I had always somehow believed.

You know, I think a lot of girls in Women's Lib nowadays tend to resent women like myself who have to some extent or other made their own professional lives, as this is like saying "I'll make it for myself, never mind about the rest," but of course when I set about my own mini-revolution, I didn't know there were so many others who felt the same way. And that was less than ten years ago. Have noticed v[ery] sharply in those years, however, that after I'd had a couple of books published, my relationships with men always fell into 1 of 2 categories . . . those who saw me as a woman and would rather not know about my writing, and those who accepted me as a writer and equal (mostly writers these guys) but kind of a quasi-male figure or sort of neuter, and who would cringe slightly if I mentioned, e.g., my children.

The whole colonial situation, of course (i.e. the woman as black) I not unnaturally figured out years ago when living in Africa, helped somewhat by the French psychologist Mannoni, whose book "Prospero & Caliban: The Psychology of Colonization"[1] for a time was my bible.

Well. Didn't mean to go on like this, but all this is so damn relevant to what I'm praying for the grace to be able to write, but of course the character is not myself, altho also is myself, and the dilemma is also slightly different. (Like Stacey in *The Fire-Dwellers* is both me and not me). But how to *listen* enough to be able to set

2

people down and not theories? Real dilemmas (and god knows they are real) and not diatribes? That is one reason I probably won't read all the articles in the Women's Lib thing. I only want to rely on the sight of my own eyes. I remember refusing to read *The Feminine Mystique* by Betty Friedan,[2] some years ago, because I thought the novel which was brewing might be kind of related, and I thought that reading a whole lot of stuff which might agree but was doing it from the journalistic angle, *not* fiction (which tries to approach by being, not talking) might screw me up. I feel kind of choked with this damn novel, but to do it only on one level—well, one might as well not bother. . . .

I feel kind of embarrassed saying anything about PROCEDURES FOR UNDERGROUND,[3] after your good and encouraging comments on JASON [*Jason's Quest*] and BIRD [*A Bird in the House*]. Will you believe me? Yes, I guess you know it's an area where lies aren't permitted. I like especially the way you have, in quite a few of the poems, of catching a moment in the past, with all its paradox, and suggesting that in some subtle way the past is never over—the photographs, held forever in that one stance, and yet by their very nature of rigidity implying the next moment that happened *then*, the changes that encompass all the intervening years and even the years not yet lived. I find this the most moving thing of all, in your work. One of my favourite poems in the book was FISHING FOR EEL TOTEMS . . this possibly tells you something about me. I pointed this one out especially to Jocelyn, and she said, "Yes, I can see why you like it." I said Why? And she said, "Because of the totem symbol bit, related to the ancestors." I didn't know she knew me that well. It *was* that, but also the feeling of caring about creatures, the planet's inhabitants. . . . I often wonder if this could be conveyed in prose, or if only poetry will convey it truly. I mean, our enormous power to destroy. It may be that God will feel more anguish about the destruction of fishes and birds than about our destruction of ourselves. And yet one's strongest feelings have to relate to the naked ape. Anyway, thank you for the poems, for their strangeness, and (to use a word I hardly ever use, because like "love" the currency has been devalued) their beauty. . . .

Incidentally . . . one point with which I took issue, re: some of the Women's Lib articles [was] the feeling on the part of some women that it was kind of unnatural for women to want to have kids. I would say that if a woman doesn't want to have kids, that is her business and hers only. But if she deeply does, that does not mean she is not interested in anything else. I don't really feel

I have to analyse my own motives in wanting children. . . . It's like (to me) asking why you want to write. Who cares? You have to, and that's that. But the kids, like the writing, belong ultimately to themselves, and not to you. In fact, they're very like the writing. A gift, given to you by life, undeserved like all grace is undeserved by its very nature, and not to be owned. . . .

Love to you and Jim,[4] and please come out again soon.

There were very few books by Canadian writers at that time. . . . [The Stone Angel] was the first book by a Canadian writer, almost, that I had read. It was a novel closer to my generation. In other words, it wasn't Ernest Buckler, whom I had read earlier. So forget there being a Canadian literature at that time [or] just another book by a Canadian writer. Well, there was Mordecai Richler. I read Mordecai, but apart from him, Alice Munro was not on the scene, Marian [Engel] wasn't. Almost nobody you can think of was published yet.

Elmcot,
15 Nov 71

Dear Peggy—

A brief note to re-establish contact. I was sorry not to get together with you this summer, for many reasons, one of them being that I never did tell you what I thought about *Power Politics*.[5] When I last wrote to you, when you were in Europe, I was considerably hassled and trying to get organized to go to Canada, and so didn't say anything about the poems, which had, as a matter of fact, hit me like the spirit of god between the eyes. The very very short beginning one . . "You fit into me like a hook into an eye . . " was, I felt, absolutely stunning because it expressed in hardly any words the whole man-woman thing in its painful essence or perhaps I mean in the essence of the pain which can be involved in it. I think the same is true of a great many of the poems in the book. They aren't bitter, which is good. They are sometimes vicious, as those who know about traps sometimes are. They also imply an enormous need of one another, a belief that men and women do not necessarily have to vitiate one another even tho they so often do. Some of them remind me of Sylvia Plath, but

4

you are much tougher (in the survival sense). . . .

Go back and read the biographies of women writers that were around during the first fifty years of this century. Because I got the same mythology, and it was: they all die young, never get married, live in closets, like Emily Dickinson; they look at life through the wormholes in a shroud. It was built into the idea of being a woman and a writer. It wasn't just Margaret. She was picking up on something that was very much there.* And I think we all did, under a certain age, because the only role models that we had for women who were writers and did get married and did all that were Mrs. Gaskell and Harriet Beecher Stowe. Everybody else had an anomalous life.

Elm Cottage,
3 Dec 72

Dear Peggy—

Thanks so much for yr letter of 21 Nov. By now you will have had my letter, full of astound, re: SURVIVAL.[6] As I said therein, how profoundly glad I am that I had written this novel of mine [*The Diviners*] before I read yr book—which is not to say that such books are dangerous to the writer, but only that if the shock of recognition occurs, better it should occur when the book is shaped. Of course, after a time span, one would not be at all threatened by any analysis, but if one read it when *writing* . . hm . . I wonder. Which is to say only that yr analysis really struck me, probably because it seemed to me the first attempt, EVER, to state why Can[adian] writing is not the same as Amer[ican] or Eng[lish]. I could see, finishing the book, your worry that (a) teachers might think—Aha! This is Everything We Need To Know About Can Writing; and (b) writers might think—Have I A Suitable Victim, Human Or Animal, And If Not, What In Hell Is The Matter With Me? But worry not. These are chances we have to take. No real writer is ever affected by outer comment, and possibly no real teacher is, too. But the book is good, provocative, and (I think) true. . . .

Dear Peggy—

Sorry I've been so long in replying to your letter. The reason is
that I have done nothing for a few months (with time out for
Christmas) except work on the novel. Which—wait for it!—is
now FINISHED. Hallelujah. Or, at least, modified jubilation. I
know quite well that it will need some more work. It has gone
through 3 drafts, and my daughter is now typing a fair copy....
I can see much of what is not yet right with the novel, but feel I
cannot do more until I can get myself distanced from it. Would
also like the views of one or two editors whom I trust—I know
almost for sure that their views will only serve to confirm my
own, and that they will suggest some areas which still need work,
and that these areas will be the ones I myself know about, but
nevertheless, it is better for now to have it out of my hands,
temporarily, and for me to attempt to surface after about 3 years
of being inside this book. I have a sense of release and freedom
and hope and happiness, despite the future work which I know
will have to be done on the thing. Maybe I can complete the final
revisions in my shack this summer—I hope so; actually, I *know* I
can. I have great doubts about the novel, but not basic doubts, if
you see what I mean. I know that even when it is completed, it
will not be the book which was in my head, but then it never is,
is it? It's the last of the Manawaka fiction, if one can call it that
without sounding pretentious, and so I feel a kind of relief at
having brought the wheel full circle, as it were, and also a kind
of loneliness, as I have lived with all those people for a long time,
about 12 years or more, and will miss them. Guess they will still
be there, in me, tho, like one's childhood home or anything else
one has loved but has to leave and move on. I'm a bit afraid of
the editorial comment, Peggy, and also a bit afraid of the
reviewers, and yet, in another way, not afraid at all, because I
know that this is what had to be done, and it ain't done perfectly
but it will be done as well as I can do it at this point in my life,
and I would stand behind it, and risk my life upon it, so one
cannot do more or differently. I could be accused (and no doubt
will be) of dealing with topical themes—Women; Métis; New
Pioneers; etc. All rubbish—I'm dealing with things close to my
own psyche and heart, that is all. And one main theme seems to
be Fiction—which could be called Legend, Myth, or History, just

as well. How we make myths of our own lives, and our parents, and our ancestors, etc. Fiction as History. History as Fiction. Ambiguity is everywhere. But mainly, I get this sense of a continuum—even in our chaos, there still seems to me to be a very real way in which the past is always the present, and the present is always both the past and the future. Like my beloved river, it all flows both ways. It is harder to write about a true affirmation which one has come to, painfully and through many years, than about despair, which by its dramatic nature is convincing. This is no hand-in-hand-into-the-sunset, Peggy, I need hardly say. But it *is* a different and new thing, for me, because it deals not only with survival but with freedom. By *freedom* I do not mean any Garden of Eden, of course, which we must learn to relinquish along with our damaging innocence. My only regret (and it's an unreal one, I know, because all we can do is the best we can with what we have) is that I did not have more talent to convey the characters, to do justice to them, to get them across in as real and living a way as I know them. But we're not God, thank God. Sometimes it seems to me that the most important thing a writer learns is what they *can't* do; only by knowing that can one know what one can do, I think. . . .

[In regard] to the Métis question: the literary truism in Canada between about 1955 and 1970 anyway, and probably beyond, was that Canadian literature would not really come of age until it had come to terms with indigenous presence. That was just repeated ad infinitum in practically every critical article that talked about Canadian literary identity in those years. It was an accepted thing. And I think that one of the reasons Jules [Tonnerre] is a Métis was that. I think it's something that should be brought into that discussion [of appropriation of voice]. So all those [earlier writers who created aboriginal characters] didn't think that they were stealing something; they thought they were giving voice to and connecting with [the indigenous presence].

Lakefield, Ontario,
12 May 81

Dear Peggy—

Many many congratulations on winning the Molson Award!!![7] I wish I could be there for the ceremony, but I'm afraid I just am not going to be able to go. I'm trying to conserve my every ounce of energy for the Trent Convocation in a couple of weeks, and also, our buses are on strike—the first time this has happened in the years I've lived here. But I'm truly delighted at the news. You really deserve it—you've made a fantastic contribution to this country's writing. Enjoy, enjoy! What I think is so great about the actual money is that it is tax free!

Love to you all. . . .

Lakefield,
15 Oct 81

Dear Peggy—

As you probably recall, recently a group of Canadian writers (Alice Munro, Adele Wiseman, Bob Kroetsch, Gary Geddes, Pat Lane, Geoff Hancock, and a Quebec woman writer[8] whose name I'm ashamed to say I can't remember) went on a visit to China. Among the writers they met was Ding Ling, who is China's most famous (and possibly oldest) woman writer.[9] Her career began in the 20's, and she has gone through periods of being a heroine of the revolution, then out of favour, and is now apparently the senior stateswoman of writers. Anyway, Adele had wanted to meet her for years, and this was finally realized. Ding Ling will be visiting Canada briefly in November, and Adele and I are organizing a reception for her at York University on Saturday the 28th of Nov. You and Graeme [Gibson] will be receiving invitations in due course. But a few of us (Adele, me, Clara Thomas, Alice M, Gary Geddes) will be taking Ding Ling, her husband and a young writer (and translator) Richard Liu, out for a quiet dinner beforehand. We wondered if you and Graeme would care to join us for the dinner. We'd let you know the time and place a bit later. . . .

8

Dear Peggy—

Thanks so much for your letter. I'm not answering many these days, but do want to let you know that I was cheering madly for you & Rob [Robertson Davies—he and Atwood were both shortlisted for the Booker Prize]—well, at least the Brits are beginning to realize that we are not just a bunch of wild colonial girls & boys! I loved your description of the event. . . . [10]

I managed to get my so-called memoirs into 3rd draft— truly they still need a lot of work, and I'm still not sure I can manage any more. Anyway, I'm glad I did them. Really, they're sort of a memoir of my 3 mothers (my birth mother, my stepmother, my mother-in-law) and myself as mother/writer. It is frustrating, because I know *exactly* what the manuscript needs, to make a book of it—mainly additions which only I could do— & I don't think I will be able to. If ever published, Joc[elyn] will be my main editor before the thing is ever sent to a publisher ("a" publisher, indeed! Of course I mean M&S). As you well know, the problem of a well-known writer (not only in Mordecai's immortal phrase, "world-famous throughout Canada") is the reverse of a beginning writer. I would only *ever* consider these memoirs being submitted to a publisher *in Canada*, but of course M&S would publish them even if they are garbage, because they (it—a book) would sell. A good enough reason for a publisher, but *not* for a writer at this point in her life. Hence I rely on my daughter's judgement—an unfair burden on her, but I *trust* her *professional* opinion. . . .

Love to you all. . . .

Massey College,
26 Jan 69

Dear Don—

It's MUCH better in the most important way . . ie. you've gone deeper this time, and you're levelling much more.[1] I think the way you manage the back-and-forth swings in time works very well, and nothing is unnecessarily explained. I can begin to see what you meant the other evening when you said it was being written in no chronological order but *you* knew where it all fitted in. I can see "Hum me a few bars . . " fitting in somewhere, even tho I don't know where, naturally. I think the slightly bitter humour of the tone of this excerpt is good—gives a nice acid (oops, sorry—I mean acid in its old-fashioned lemon sense!) bite to the whole thing. But the main thing is that it comes across as much more incisive than most of the first excerpt I read; much less evasive, and that is GOOD. Only thing I felt pretty uncertain about is the way you bring in Trudeau and Dief's name, etc, as these may date it more than it ought to be dated, but I'm not sure—this may just be a very personal prejudice of mine. Art is, of course, ephemeral, but not as ephemeral as politicians! Anyway, that's a detail. Also, I hope you will not scrap the first excerpt I saw—some of it should be kept. And I hope you will include the Saint Anne poems, which I now see in more dimensions than I did at first. They're essential.

Anyway, as Jack McClelland always says to me—Back to your typewriter, slob! . . .

All the best. . . .

Elm Cottage,
12 Aug 70

Dear Don—

. . . Thanks for poem, which does say something which must be pertinent, surely, to all writers—not knowing as a way of knowing. I know about that. And thanks, too, for your letter—the part about seeing each other's insanity, especially. Yeh, I know about that, too, and I agree with you about it. Actually, no one *is* supposed to see another's insanity, in terms of socially accepted values, but I don't believe that, either, and I don't believe a lot of people really believe it—they're simply frightened to reveal their insanity (in case it turns out to be a kind of Pandora's box, the contents of which will overwhelm them?). I only reveal mine (a) when with someone I feel is a real member of my tribe, or (b) when drunk with someone whom I feel is a real member of my tribe. . . . I suppose the greatest thing about writing is that one can say—indeed, *must* say—what you really feel, not what you are supposed to feel. Or think. I remember once getting a letter from Al Purdy, asking me to come and see them at Ameliasburg (I being in Toronto at the time), and he said "I need the sanity of your insanity" . . which is, I think, exactly what you meant. I can sometimes, also, level in letters, in fact quite often . . typewriter being my transmitter through which I tap out my little messages to my spiritual kinfolk, I think. Migawd, were it not for writer-friends, I really would've gone off my rocker years ago! So please keep writing letters, eh, when you can and when you feel like it.

Great to hear about all the writing you've been doing, especially the stories. Articles good news, too, tho, for money and also getting known, etc, sounds cold I expect but you know what I mean. Yeh, the novel. You won't be able to evade it much longer, I guess. Starting the real long haul is terrible and never gets less terrible. But once it is a total commitment, then that is the best part, only comparable to really good lovemaking, most other things being somewhat paler in comparison. That is why I feel so goddamn low about this novel of mine—I think it's going to be the last one. It doesn't matter, in a sense, if only I could receive from somewhere the grace to do this one. Dunno if I will or not. Feel it is very faraway at the moment, and this breaks me up every time I think of it, but maybe it will come. Also, am DETERMINED not to think of its being last novel until it is finished. Don't intend to slit throat even then, even if it *is* last novel, but it is a sad thought nonetheless. But I'm buggered if I'll ever write a mockup of a novel only in order to go on writing. If it isn't really there any more, at whatever point, may God give me the strength to quit without self-dramatization or malice. It'll be others' turn then—the thing itself goes on; or so I believe. I think what I'll do with the rest of my life is to whomp up a living some-

11

how and to run (here and in Canada) a kind of unofficial hostel for young writers who need sometimes a place to go. I'm pretty good at that, actually, and it would only be a natural carrying on from the kind of house that Elm Cottage has always been—sometimes I think I'm running a bloody low-class hotel here, but I love it, actually. My daughter says it fulfils my mother-earth self-image and probably she is right. The damn place is always full of Canadians! I really love this place, but am missing Canada unbelievably and sometimes in sleep I am in my shack on the Otonabee and wake up with a sense of loss. . . .

Love to you and Anne. . . .

Margaret wrote a lot of things between 1975 and 1979 that I saw, that I read. Some of them were stories, some of them were vignettes, and they were as good as anything that she ever wrote in her life. They were moving, they were passionate. . . . I can attribute some of it to the controversy that went [on] around The Diviners. *But she destroyed that work. . . . At my house one night, she had written a story, read it to Anne (who was my wife at the time) and I, and it was a beautiful story, and then threw it in the fireplace.*

Elm Cottage,
24 April 71

Dear Don—

. . . I'm glad you've applied for a Can Council and hope to heaven you get it. But you are doing okay, also, in finding out about where to place the articles you are writing, and stories, etc. Main thing is to get on with the novel. Which you will. Problem of how a man can express his incoherence without destroying himself is one of many problems of fiction, I guess. One discovers some of the things you can do, and also discovers in the process that there are some things you can't do, which is a knowledge of one's limitations and does not matter, because the only thing that really matters, by me, is to go ahead and do what is given to you to do, whatever that turns out to be. And it always exacts a greater price from you than you were originally willing to pay. But it is never a price which you cannot pay. Whatever god we serve probably knows what it is doing. So yr novel will be okay, finally, with or without the Can Council.

Glad you spent that time with Jane [Rule] and Helen. Yeh, they are very good human beings. And yes, Jane's novel THIS IS NOT FOR YOU is an incredible piece of work.[2] Heard from her not long ago, and apparently the next novel will be published fairly soon. She's had a rough deal from critics, who refuse to understand what she is trying to do. . . .

I had to discard 8 months work and years of brooding on the novel I hoped to do, because it turned out I had outgrown it and did not really want to write it. I think another novel is growing under the surface. It is all an odd experience, and although I felt well-nigh suicidal when I had to throw out that novel, I now feel a kind of liberation. It was a great theory, but a novel it wasn't. If there *is* the one there that I think may be there, may it reveal itself in its own time, without my trying to force anything. We will see. . . .

Elm Cottage,
15 Nov 71

Dear Don—

. . . I have been knocking myself out to get 8 articles done for *Maclean's*, Vancouver *Sun*, etc. All promised some time ago. Have done 6 now, and 2 more to go. Short articles on various not-too-serious topics. For bread. Have to get them done before getting back to novel, and then can relax knowing we will not starve in coming year.

Good luck, and much love to you and Anne. . . .

Elmcot,
2 Dec 71

NOW LISTEN HERE DON DEAR—

Novel progressing, by which I mean I am putting down a whole lot of words. When I get ensconced in a part of it, I have no doubts and am happy as anything. Then I think—my God, it is a zillion times too long. But don't care at the moment. Am just doing it the way it wants to be done—probably not publishable. But when inside it, a kind of euphoria—mad, likely. God bless and love to you both. . . .

Always you have characters who are dealing with what might be described as ordinary problems, ordinary kinds of distress, who manage to wilfully pull themselves up, but always, always, there is the shadow of the spirit of what you might call God. . . . And that's what makes her such, for me, an unusual writer. Her characters have their own profile. And then they have a shadow, like you and I do when we stand in the sun. But that shadow [is] not quite just the shadow that we perceive it to be. Within that shadow is some kind of almost mystical, magical power that, again depending on who we are and what kind of faith, program, or background we come from, we identify [with] in that particular way. And that is part of the power of what Margaret did, and her writing continues to be.

Elm Cottage,
25 Jan 72

Dear Don—

Thanks much for your letter and Christmas card-poem and the book. I'd read some of the poems in the book, although not all. It's a *good* book, Don, and I was really so damn pleased to see it. Also touched that you had included the one to M.L.![3] . . . let me say how much I like it, and especially all the series of St. Anne poems. The production job was nice, I thought, and I really liked Sue's drawing for the cover. You are damn good on titles, incidentally, for both book and poems.

    I'm glad the novel is nearly finished. It's hell trying to write and also do a thousand other things. But good to know you are on the home stretch. Wish I could say the same. My novel (?) grows and grows, and is nowhere nearly finished. . . .

Dear Don—

. . . Plans for me—I go to Can [ada] about May 15. In Tor [onto]
for about a week, when hope to see you if you're there, then out
to shack on 20th. Trent U is giving me an honorary D.Litt on
May 26th. Then to Montreal May 30th for a meeting of Can Univ
teachers of Eng, at which I'm on a panel or something. Then Tor
for June 1st, when U of T is giving me an honorary D.Litt (this is
getting embarrassing; also, I wish there were some $$$ attached.)
I have to give the convocation talk, which will be pure hell. I've
now written it, this week. The staff will think it's too radical and
the kids will think it's too conservative, but the hell with them
all. Then, June 2nd, out to shack to work until at least beginning
of Sept, maybe longer if I can arrange it. . . .
        Don—I'm sorry re: your [writing] crisis. Maybe it was
about to happen, whatever brought it on. Yeh, I know about the
Run Run Run bit—did it for years. Now I am writing this novel
slowly, and am suddenly not worried. But for ages I felt abso-
lutely choked up with what I had to express. And also, I felt ter-
ribly split . . needed to relate to husband and kids, and all that
work to be done in the domestic line, and the writing as well.
Role conflict. Tensions. How to live and write at the same time?
This is the eternal problem. . . .

Dear Don—

. . . Okay here, or mostly. Part III finished in rough draft. Only 2
more Parts to go. This novel is getting quite insane, but that is
okay. I just have to see it through the way it wants to go, then see
if we can pare it down to something reasonable. When I'm in-
side it, I am so much inside that I feel a bit crazy re: the outer
world; feel that the fictional world has taken me over; feel that it
is not possible to live in 2 worlds at the same time. Then I finish
one part, and come out again, and find the outer world still there,
with all its hangups and also all its goodnesses—the kids, both

15

my own blood children and the other kids who are young writers and seem to be my family. . . . I have a sense of community, Don, not a community which is together physically all the time (altho that would be good if it were ever possible) but a kind of community which keeps in *touch* (that is a good word; means so many things) through messages and through seeing one another when possible and through thinking and caring about one another. Hoping for the people you love. Praying, even. As I do for you and Anne, and as I know very well you do for me. And there are others. What is a good realization is to know that however the dark cave within oneself threatens, *we are not alone.* I begin now to explore this feeling and to have much more faith in it than once I had. . . . I sit here at my radio transmitter, sending out messages. . . . and you hear them . . . and send back messages. . . .

I need to talk to you, Don, and maybe you need to talk to me. We will. This is what tribe means. . . .

Love—and I mean it, very simply—

Margaret was like, if we can use the image of the tribe, Margaret was the shaman. I mean, she had the magic. She brought the people together. And we were all bewildered and flabbergasted and astonished by her magic, and left refreshed and nourished, forgetting of course old times, how much the shaman had put into the performance, into the myth-making that nourished us.

R.R. 11, Peterborough, Ont.
17 Aug 72

Dear Don—

. . . My correspondence gets done in between chapters . . . as I have just finished a chapter, but MUST begin the next this week. Have got 2 more long chapters to go. Don, this christly novel will be longer than War and Peace, although hardly of comparable quality! I now have the equivalent of about 570 typewritten pages, which is really terrible. I will have to cut it ruthlessly. A lot of it is garbage, actually, so the cutting may not be too difficult. It is very repetitive, but the problem is that part of the point

16

is the repetition of themes; how to repeat without being repetitive, that is the question.

[Somebody] wants to do a book . . . on Frederick Philip Grove, Sinclair Ross, and me. For 10 to 15 year olds; the real true Life Stories!! ye gods. Grove is safely dead; Jim Ross is in Spain; and here I am, vulnerable as a fish on a dock. I got the letter from her yesterday. Natch, she wants to question me about My Life! What to do? I have the feeling that my Real True Life Story would not make such suitable reading for 10 to 15 year olds. And yet if I see her and talk about all the acceptable things, it will make me sound a real schmuck. And if I don't see her, will seem aloof and stand-offish, and she will look up old buddies of mine, who will be conned by her into talking about me and who will be so discreet that I will end up sounding like a plaster saint of the worst variety. Life's tiny problems. . . . Actually, it could be hilarious, but I know I won't end up playing it that way. . . .

Much love to you both. . . .

Elm Cottage,
18 Feb 73

Dear Don—

Sorry to have been so long in replying to your letter—I've been doing nothing except work on novel, and it is now FINISHED!! At least, having gone through 3 drafts, it is finished for the moment. . . . I know I'll have to do more work later, but feel I cannot do more right now—I have to get at least one editor's opinion, and I have to distance myself from the thing. I'm hoping I'll be able to get the further rewriting done this summer at the shack. . . .

Hope you and Anne are surviving the horrible and ghastly Winnipeg winter. . . . When I was in third year university, I had a boarding house in the North End, about a mile past the end of the Selkirk Avenue streetcar line. Whenever I had a date that winter, and the guy discovered where I lived, and in those days it was considered necessary for a man to pick up the girl and take her home later, I rarely had a date with the same boy twice. Flounder-flounder-flounder through a mile of snowdrifts, and at the end of it, a chilly necking session on the *front porch*, at 30

17

below zero. It would have cooled the hottest ardour, believe you me. Finally my girlfriend and I moved from this northerly accommodation and got a small flat on Broadway, after which our social life improved considerably.

Dunno if I told you my long-range forecast—all being well, I shall go in Sept of this year to Western U in London Ont, as writer-in-res for 1 term; then to Trent U in Peterborough for the winter-spring term, and during that time I will look for a house in Peterborough. Then (God willing) back to England to sell Elmcot and move back permanently to the land of my fathers, which I now perceive to be Canada. . . .

My morale is high, but I feel kind of tired—I am surfacing for the first time, really, in about 3 years, as have been into this novel for that length of time. Even tho I will have to do more work, it will be done in my editorial persona, not as a writer, so that will be somewhat easier, I hope. I have a great desire to go places and see things, all the kinds of stuff I haven't wanted to do for 3 years on account of all I really wanted to do was the novel. I may go to northern Manitoba in August. . . . I want to see the place where the first Selkirk settlers landed—erroneously, as they should have set down at York factory, but the Captain of their ship did not have such a good sense of direction. For me it's a pilgrimage. . . .

8 Regent Street,
Lakefield, Ont.
13 Nov 74

Dear George Bowering—

I've just bought a copy of FLYCATCHER,[1] and was very touched to see that you dedicated the book to me. Many many thanks. The stories are very good—*really* good—and you obviously know awfully well that "how is what". The narrative voice in each strikes me as absolutely authentic and right. And you get the sense of place beautifully, in each of the settings. The title story was stunning .. it reminded me of an old man who lived in a brokendown shack in the valley below our town. He was slightly crazy, I guess, and was known as Andy Gump. Some of the kids used to bait him, as though he were an old and bewildered bear. Anything that happens anywhere in the world, in some way happens in one's own town. Anyway, thanks for the stories, for writing them.

I always meant to write, and never did, to tell you how much I appreciate that article you wrote on A JEST OF GOD in Canadian Lit several years ago.[2] I was astounded, because you pointed out things about the use of language that I'd given up hope of anyone ever seeing. It's really nice when someone notices what it is you've been trying to do. So thanks for that as well, belatedly. . . .

All the best. . . .

ps. would you consider joining the Writers' Union of Canada? If you'd let me know, I could get our secretary to send you an application form. Please don't think I'm pressuring you. I'm not normally a joiner, myself, but am pissed off at the way writers get short-changed, financially.

When I was in the airforce in Manitoba . . . I was nineteen to twenty-one, and we normally went to booze it up and have fun and go to dances in Portage la Prairie. But sometimes we would go to . . . Neepawa . . .

and then we would go to the Chinese café. And that Chinese café shows up again in the Manawaka stories. . . . I presumed it was the same café. So it was a double, [and] I attended to her sense of place, which I was all involved with at the time. . . . It wasn't just like it was a place, a fictional place . . . I could see it working and I could see the place that I had been and the place that she was talking about. That and the language were the two most important things. So I was really glad to see it, because before that I had been moved around by American writers who developed over a series of books. A Faulknerian sort of thing. . . . It's like a text that is bigger than a book.

Lakefield,
24 Dec 74

Dear George—

I wish you'd call me Margaret. It's the only name I have which is truly mine, so I really prefer people to call me that—it's not just some North American phoney informality with me; it's a feeling about names, I guess. Anyway, it doesn't piss me off re: your saying about having a kind of awe re: me, but it does just make me hope you won't feel it any more, now that I have, so to speak, materialized, even if only through letters. I am not ferocious! I am not formal nor ladylike nor any of those things! I swear it! Actually, I know that's not what you meant—it was re: my books, and I appreciate your feeling for them, I really do. . . .

I would guess it's just as well you didn't introduce yrself to me at McGill—I always like to think my public and private selves are the same self, but they never are, quite. And at those things a person never has a chance to talk—it's just literary chitchat, really. Better we should meet at a time when we can talk. . . .

Re: smalltown you—hell, where do you think I came from? There is a very considerable portion of my psyche which is still Neepawa, Manitoba. When I first left town, many many years ago (migawd, 30 years ago . . I was 18) I wanted to have no part of small towns, ever again, and disliked my smalltown-ness. In those days I thought Winnipeg was the hub of the universe. Now I realize that it's really Neepawa which is the hub of the universe, or mine, anyway, and don't mind that my outlook is still smalltown. Peggy Atwood once said about me that cities make me uneasy, but so does the wilderness. That's absolutely accurate. As witness the fact that I've settled now in a village, which is just about my speed. . . . Actually, the stories in Flycatcher which dealt with that small Okanagan town were some of the best, I thought. You genuinely got the whole feeling of the place and people across.

The 550 pp novel in 11 months sounds like a marathon. It's a wonder you survived it. I took 3 years to write a 382 pp novel (*The Diviners*) and I'm not quite sure yet if I have survived it . . it damn near killed me. People say, "What are you working on now?" My heavens, I'm not working on *anything*. It's all I can do to write my name on cheques, when necessary. I bat off the odd article and review, but they're far from deathless prose, although I sweat blood over the damn things, I must admit. I always tell people that I'm working on a kids' book, tho. They don't like to be told you're not working on anything. They think that's unbearably lazy, or immoral, or something of the sort.

I liked the film of *A Jest of God* [*Rachel, Rachel*] pretty well, altho there were quite a few things I'd have done differently. At least it bore some resemblance to the novel, and [Joanne] Woodward was good as Rachel, I thought. Yeh, the setting [New England]. Partly my fault, perhaps, altho perhaps it wouldn't have made any difference. They wrote to me and asked me if there was a small prairie town which resembled Manawaka, and which they might consider using as a setting. I wrote back and said NO. I've always wondered if I did the right thing. But all those cameras and film idiots in Neepawa—I just could not do it. No doubt if the Neepawa Board of Trade knew this, they would be furious at me. But I thought it would be an awful thing to do. Anyway, they wouldn't have understood that setting, or so I thought.

All the best. . . .

She seemed to have this sensibility, the confidence to talk like a man, sort of. Not to have to apologize for taking up the space, but just assuming the space. . . . So I was taken by the forcefulness of her presence, the confidence and power and so forth that she came to have. And yet, one knew also that . . . when she had to give a public speech, she was scared shitless.

Dear George—

This is both a reply to yr letter of March 2nd and a response to having met you at long last in Van[couver] at the WUC party. . . . I was really glad to meet you—odd that one wants when writing to someone, to be able to visualize what they look like, and photos are no good at all in this way. From yr photos I sort of thought you would be quite slight and even skinny. I mean, natch, I would've liked you as much if you'd been a 4 foot hunchback or whatever, but interesting that photos are so inaccurate. I don't think I asked you about the photo on FLYCATCHER . . I thought it must have been taken when you were in High School. Hopefully, my next book will be a kids' book—I think I'll have a pic of me at three, in overalls, with hair cut in a fringe on forehead, looking incredibly pugnacious. Anyway, I thought it was a really good evening. I was so glad to see Jane Rule again. . . . Also Audrey [Thomas], whose new novel![3] I tried to review for the Globe. . . .

Re: [Angela Bowering's] editing the western section of Boundary 2. . . .[4] Bob Kroetsch sent it to me. The BC parts were by far the most interesting, I thought. Strange . . those mountains have made a lot of difference in making BC somehow more related to the Amer[ican] west coast poets. I wonder if that sense of being in a separate country, in BC, is lessening. I think at least part of that may be due to the union meetings. . . .

Have you seen [George] Woodcock's collection in the new NCL—THE CANADIAN NOVEL IN THE TWENTIETH CENTURY?[5] Pieces from Canadian Literature over the years, including yr article on A JEST OF GOD, which I think is the best single article ever written thus far on my work. It's a pretty good collection, altho some of the earlier ones from the 60's read a bit timidly, I think. . . .

She never, ever doubted the seriousness of what she was doing. . . . And she had done it in terms of language from the very beginning. . . . She was rough and dirty and truly experimental. She tried things out and sometimes they didn't work.

Dear George—

. . . So now to the essence of your letter, namely and i.e., what *The Fire-Dwellers* is all about. Wa-a-al, now, George, there's this middle-aged broad, see, and she sez to herself, like, life ain't no goddamn bowl of cherries. Life, she sez to herself (and to some off-stage character she sometimes calls God), life, she reiterates, ain't no bunch of roses. But on the other hand, hm hm, what else is there? There, prof. I've done all your work for you. My fee is modest. I'll send the bill at the end of the month.

I liked yr Post-Darwinian [Robert] Herrick [17th century English lyric poet]. You must've had fun writing it. How I envy poets this thing about being able to enclose a short poem in a letter to friends. I may have said this before—I've often said it to Purdy. Imagine enclosing a short 90 pp chapter of a novel. Ye gods.

. . . Re: Audrey's novel [*Blown Figures*]—I'm really glad you did a review, and I look forward to reading it in about five years time. I reviewed Jane Rule's THEMES FOR DIVERSE INSTRUMENTS (review in the *Globe*),[5] and did a paragraph about what interesting books Talonbooks is coming out with (true), and mentioned in passing, as it were, Audrey Thomas's "fascinating new novel, BLOWN FIGURES . . "

I am out at my shack on the river, and am almost sane again after all the running around hither and thither to public occasions which I went through for about a month. Mind you, the money was very acceptable, for both the Gov-Gen and the Molson's, and actually, naive tho I may be, I was glad to get the Gov-Gen's, really. Last chance, sort of. But it took a lot out of me. I felt totally exhausted when it was all over.

. . . Revenue Canada, George, if you haven't already discovered it, *hates writers*. They are *out to get us*. Not caring about the many years we have battled with the chequebook, sitting up nites wondering how to pay the next month's rent, they come down like several tons of brick in the one year we make as much as a full professor or a plumber. I am having a running battle with an idiot lady in Rev Can . . . who doesn't want to give me a 3 yr spreadback on royalties for *The Diviners*, for my 1973 (yep, 1973) income tax, because she says I wasn't living in Can all the time during the 3 years I wrote it and anyway how does *she* know it really took 3 years to write. . . .

ps. did you know that Purdy, that invincible fellow, is going to be w-in-r at the Univ of Manitoba this coming academic year? The thought of another Winnipeg winter is enough to chill the blood instantly. . . . My daughter works at M&S, and when Al was in the office awhile ago, he mentioned to her that he and Eurithe never seem to persuade me to visit them; it's always the other way around. My daughter said, in jest, "I don't think she likes your plumbing arrangements." Which is true, of course; I don't. So Al wrote me a letter saying he was damned if he'd install plumbing with velvet-covered toilet seat just for me! So now I gotta go, in whichever way you like to interpret that. . . .

I think she really reminds a reader . . . especially a person from the rural small town west . . . of somebody, of people you knew. Somebody smart and sensitive from a part of the country that you came from. . . . She has these tools that reach into the experience that you shared with her. What it's like to go to an outhouse in the winter and stuff like that. And the other part has to do with analysing that, which most people who shared that first experience never do.

Lakefield, Ontario,
28 July 74

Dear Ernest Buckler—

Thanks so very much, first for your good letter of 10th June, and secondly for sending me a signed copy of *The Cruelest Month*.[1] I can't tell you how pleased I am to have it. I had a copy, of course, but to have one signed by you means a lot. I'm sure your message in the inscription is a bit inaccurate, to say the least—what's all this nonsense about your being a journeyman carpenter?? You're one of the very best writers this country has ever had, that's all.

I'm really delighted to think that M&S is going to do a collection of your short stories—about time, too. It came up in conversation between myself and Bob Chambers, a professor of English at Trent in Peterborough, who has been writing a book on the writings of Ernest Buckler and Sinclair Ross.[2] We agreed that it was a damn crime that your stories had never come out in a collection, and when I talked to J.G. McClelland about it, Jack thought it was a great idea. I think his idea is to put it out in hard-cover, then a bit later in the New Canadian Library . . is that right? I hope so, because it should be available to students. Lots of kids are really keen on Canadian literature, and are so much more aware of it than they were even a few years ago. Who knows, at some point we may even get CanLit courses in all our high schools, not just a few Can books tacked onto a Contemporary Lit course.

I really wish I could meet you—it would be good to be able to talk with you. I don't suppose you're in this part of the world much, but if you ever are, the red carpet is out for you at any time here.

Again, thanks.

Love and best wishes. . . .

Lakefield, Ontario,
30 Aug 74

Dear Ernie (as you sign yourself that, and presumably that's what
your friends call you I hope you won't mind if that's what I call
you)

. . . Listen, Ernie, I am not a literary giant—migawd! the very
idea! Nor am I a tremendous personality, etc etc. If that's my
public image in Canada at this moment then that's too bad. *The
Diviners* got a lot of publicity—lucky me, I suppose, simply that
I happened along with my first Can book (*The Stone Angel*) at
just the moment when Canadians were beginning to notice that
they had a literature after all. It was very much tougher for you
and Sinclair Ross; even for MacLennan and Callaghan. It was
worse than for me, just because of an accident of history, that's
why. My "public image" . . . how I hate to think that I *have* a
public image! . . . I'm as ordinary and extraordinary as every other
person the length and breadth (sp?) of this land. So let's get that
straight, eh? It might interest you to know that when I first read
The Mountain and the Valley,[3] my first novel had recently come
out, and I was beginning to think seriously about how I could
return (in the deepest ways—because physically I was living in
Vancouver but I hadn't yet returned home in my writing) to the
background which was truly my own. Your novel both scared
and heartened me—the power and scope of it. I thought then, as
I think now (and I've read a hell of a lot more Can novels than I
had then, but haven't ever changed my mind about *The Mountain
and the Valley*)—I thought it was easily the most powerful
Canadian novel ever written, and one of the most powerful I'd
ever read from any country or culture. So for a long time, you
were a kind of myth or something, to me. For me now, to have in
some ways earned the right to be in the same class with a writer
like yourself—you must realize that that means a whole lot more
to me than any public image or publicity crap, which means
nothing to me at all.

I wish you wouldn't knock yourself. I mean it, and I think
maybe (perhaps) I have the right to say this to you, because I am
a person who took years and years and years before I could quit
knocking myself most of the time, both as a woman and as a
writer. I'm learning not to do it so much, I hope, now. I've written
the best I can—which is better than a lot of people and not nearly
as good as some, and that's okay, the way I see it. You're one of

our very best, and I just wish you could learn to value yourself even to half the extent that *we* value you—by *we*, I mean every person in this country who cares about Canadian novels; I mean writers and high-school kids and university students and housewives and anyone who reads and sees. Sinclair Ross, I think has had the same difficulty, and I would guess it is because both of you came to maturity as writers at a time and in a cultural climate which was rough and hard going. When I think of the neglect that you both suffered at a crucial time (I would guess) in your life, I get angry, but I guess there is no point getting angry at the past.

Re: the terror—I don't have the self-assurance which you think I have, Ernie. Life for me is a process of being terrified a lot of the time. It doesn't show very much "in public", but it sure as hell is there. Every time I start a book, I'm terrified. Also, and this may sound morbid (and maybe it is, altho I don't think so) I live every day with the knowledge of my own death. It's as though I'm still trying to get accustomed to the idea of mortality, although I've known that death was a fact of life ever since I was four years old, when my mother died. My childhood was full of deaths in the family. Another source of terror, perhaps the worst one, has been whether I can go on and write, or not. . . . Now I've reached the point when, for the first time in my life, I have ideal circumstances to write—a house which is paid for; my kids grown-up and on their own. And I think I won't ever write another novel. I just sense it, that's all. It's no tragedy, but it took me awhile to get used to that idea, too. I won't quit writing, but I won't, I think, enter another novel—not because I don't want to, but because it isn't there to be written. The ending of *The Diviners* pretty well sums up how I feel now, and I guess I worked out a lot of the inner terrors through that novel. What to do with the rest of one's life? I sometimes feel the Black Celt gripping my throat. But in fact, there are a lot of things I want to do with the rest of my life, and they're all things which concern and absorb me, and I don't think I'm going to find time hanging very heavy on my hands. However, the fact remains that it's not the same as a *novel*—that, to me, is the deepest involvement with life that is possible to me, to be compared only to the involvement I have felt with the lives of my children, and possibly the involvement I felt for the first ten years of my marriage. . . . So I may have to live without writing another novel—yeh, that's deprivation. But I can't and won't write a novel that isn't *there* to be written. There are a lot of good young writers in this country, Ernie, and I think we owe it to something (God, maybe, or maybe just ourselves) to do whatever we can for them—which is damn little, except in very practical ways like through the Writers' Union, or writing letters to the Can Council etc. They are our inheritors, as our children are. They become adults, the children do, and they take over and *that is as it should be.* I've said all this in *The Diviners.* It's an article of faith, but by God, Ernie, it isn't an *easy* faith. I'm fighting the whole damn way, mostly fighting my own terrors, my own fears of growing old. . . .

I think your comments about suicide are incredible. I mean, the fact that you say that you probably would not, because you're too damn curious to see what's coming next. I considered that course only twice in my life, and rejected it for exactly that reason, and Morag, in *The Diviners,* fleetingly considers it but rejects it for that reason, and Rachel, in *A Jest of God,* considers it much more seriously and finally rejects it because everyone else would be going on in somehow and she would be dead as mackerel, and wouldn't know. In one of the songs in *The Diviners,* Lazarus Tonnerre's son says about his father, "Lazarus, he kept his life, for life." It seems to me that we're stuck with it, and that is both tragic and triumphant. (Forgive me, Ernie, for talking about my books, the characters, etc., it's because I live there). Have you read Al Alvarez' book, *The Savage God?*[4] He is an English poet, and attempted suicide some years ago and lived. I found it fascinating, not from a voyeur point of view, but as the stance of someone who had been there and had still lived. He knew Sylvia Plath very well, and describes her situation and ultimate death. This really got to me. Because, in 1962, when I took off and went to England with my kids, I lived in a ghastly flat in Hampstead, separated from my husband, with no money and trying to write. That winter, I read in the Hampstead and Highgate Express about Sylvia Plath's death. She had been living in a ghastly flat in Hampstead, with 2 young children, separated from her husband, with no money, and trying to write. I had never met her, and at that time I had not even read any of her poetry or her novel *The Bell Jar.*[5] But I mourned her as though it had been myself who had died. I was luckier, that's all, and luckier just in the fact that my childhood had not damaged me as much as hers had done with her. I had been given some kind of on-going strength, from my stepmother (who was my mother's sister) and even from my much-hated grandfather. Until that moment, I didn't realize it. . . .

The end of life, Alvarez says, will probably be much longer and much nastier than suicide, but maybe we have to experience it.

And yes, I know what it may entail, and I get spooked by it every time I think of it, which is frequently. It will entail what happened to Hagar in *The Stone Angel*, a helplessness, a terrible anger. I hope I can meet it with pride—but I'm not sure at all I will be able to. Again, forgive my talking about the people in my books; they express what I feel, I guess, and seem to be so much a part of my life that I can't help talking about them as though they were here and now. You'll know what I mean.

Yeh, the humour-mask. It has been my mask, too, for many years, but never mind—it's real, too. . . . I wonder if it *is* a mask, tho? Maybe it is just survival humour. The old cliché about you either laugh or you cry—maybe you either laugh or you die, sometimes. Maybe it is a gift, like grace. . . .

Love. . . .

Lakefield, Ontario,
3 Oct 74

Dear Ernie—

. . . I want to let you know that I've just finished reading Bob Chambers' selection of *The Stories of Ernest Buckler*—Bob gave me a xerox copy. I'd never read any of your stories before, and it was like discovering buried treasure or something. Wow! They are *so good*, Ernie. So many things fascinated me about them— the ways in which some of them adumbrated themes in THE MOUNTAIN AND THE VALLEY and THE CRUELEST MONTH (or so it seemed to me); the way in which you catch the *exact* tone of the human voice, with a use of idiom that is never overdone or caricatured, so the reader has the feeling of actually *hearing* people speaking; the ways in which the stories communicate the sense of *place* so beautifully, so that the reader is enabled for awhile to enter, really to enter, your country, your place. Another thing— the way in which you can communicate and make comprehensible the sadness and even the tragedy of those hurtful silences between people who love each other, and the subtleties of father-son and brother-brother relationships, in which each must tread very carefully, but never, it seems, can tread quite carefully enough. I found these stories very moving indeed. I was reminded (as I have been with your other work as well) of something Mordecai Richler once said about his own writing and Montreal—"It was my time and my place, and I have set myself to get it exactly right". You've done that. I think it is terribly important that this collection should be published as soon as possible, so that it can be accessible to the young people in high schools and universities who are now studying your work. . . .

I know what you mean, I think, about not liking what one says when it's a crack about God. I guess God wouldn't mind so much, tho. If He or It or Whatever exists as a consciousness, He or It would probably just say "Never mind, Ern, often had the same thought Myself" or words to that effect. In a sense, what can one do, if there is a God, except feel sorry for Him? I hope the other planets aren't in such a mess as ours. Yet, on the other hand, looking out at the river from the window of my shack (I'm at the cottage at the moment, the last few days before I shut it for winter) and seeing the maples across the river—scarlet and *gold*, really gold—and the movement of the waters, causes a certain upsurge of the heart. It is such a goddamn beautiful country. I always think, like Hagar in *The Stone Angel*, "How I'll miss it." I won't, of course, at all, as I'm not a great believer in personal immortality and don't expect to be peering down from Cloud 13 and sighing over my lost land here below. But still. . . .

I, too, was more or less brought up on the St. James Version. There are parts which even to this day I cannot read aloud because they make me cry. The lines from Job—"When the morning stars sang together, and all the sons of man shouted for joy . . " And many others. The greatest poetry in the world. . . .

Please write again when you feel like it—I wish we had begun corresponding years ago. For me, it happens only with some few other writers—that I can feel really quite close to them, without ever having actually met them. But of course one meets another writer in the truest sense in the work anyway, I guess. Letters seem sort of an extension of that feeling.

God bless, and much love. . . .

3 Nov 74

Dear Ernie—

I got your letter just a little while before I was due to depart for

Ottawa for the Writers' Union of Canada conference. . . .

It was a great conference. It really was. There was such a great sense of tribalism, of belonging. Which totally gave the lie to the old myth that writers stab each other in the back and are totally un-practical people. Heavens, we are not un-practical—we have to think of how the next month's rent or mortgage payments are going to be made, and wall-to-wall swimming pools are not in our experience, I would think. We were all so goddamn reasonable and wanting to get some kind of general agreement on the things we are trying to do, such as Public Lending Rights, good contracts, etc. I found—I hope this will amuse you—that I am on the National Council as the representative from Ontario. Ontario! Me! Old prairie writer from way back. But I let my name stand and was elected for that council post, and I think that is fine. I do live here now, and our council has only one rep from Ontario—better it should be me than a writer who knows only Ontario, or so I think.

I'm enclosing Bill French's writeup of the conference, because you might like to see it. The whole thing about you and the first Honorary Member is in the last paragraph. Peggy Atwood made the motion, and I seconded it, and we both talked a bit about you and how much we all owed you, and I did say to the younger writers, "You're not writing out of colonial models any more, and the reason you aren't is because people like Buckler learned, by themselves, how to write out of what is truly ours, and you had better not forget, ever, how much you owe him." Peggy and I wrote the citation together, in case you might want to know. The entire conference had such a sense of brotherhood with you that it is impossible to describe. The signatures on the citation were done on the last day of the conference, and so some of us don't appear there, because some people had to leave before the final session. But there must have been about 69 writers there, Ernie, in the session that voted to make you our first Hon mem. Every one of these writers has read you and knows you through your work. I would guess that you probably don't even know that [y]ou and Jim Ross ("As For Me And My House"), are kind of similar. You don't seem to know how much we owe to you, not only a whole generation of Can writers, but the kids who you and Sinclair Ross are now telling, through those books, what it is to be themselves, here. I've talked to hundreds of them, Ernie, and I know.

Well, there it is, for what it's worth. And you *do* have me to love. And I *do* have you to love. And it is a tribe and a family,

Ernie, and we are not alone. We belong. In a community . . It stretches from Vancouver Island to Newfoundland. We know each other and we know one another's work.

God bless, dear man—

Lakefield, Ontario,
13 Nov 74

Dear Ernie—

. . . So far from being the doom-and-gloom documents that you seem to think they are, your letters are illuminated with such survival humour, and such grace (in both senses of the word, including the religious sense) that I am amazed and—well, grateful, I guess. I like your argumentative and ironic comments about God . . they correspond closely to my own feelings. In my own fiction, I guess God comes across as a being who is both jester and in pain, one of His own fools, perhaps. It was not lightly that I called one of my novels A JEST OF GOD. . . .
. . . Have just now had a phone call from an old friend, Marjory Whitelaw from Halifax. . . . she told me that she had heard recently on CBC radio a program about you . . . in which they mentioned this Writers' Union thing and also got out an old interview with you, and ran parts of it. Marjory mentioned one part which struck her the most, where you said that some contemporary writers were always talking about people who were falling down, but you felt you were living among people who were standing up. That was a good way to put it. I was talking, in my fiction, about survivors, long before Peggy Atwood said this was one main theme of Can fiction—and it *is* one main theme. And I guess what it means is living until you die. . . .

Lakefield, Ontario,
15 Dec 74

Dear Ernie—

. . . For someone who knows much more profoundly than I do,

32

what I mean when I say "The Black Celt" within, you write the most stubbornly witty letters I have ever read. Don't think I don't know how valuable this survival humour is, Ernie—I really *know*. And I appreciate you and value you so much for being able to do it. It also helps me, to read your letters and realize all over again what that kind of thing means. . . .

Love. . . .

Lakefield, Ontario,
23 Dec 74

Dear Ernie—

Congratulations on being given the Order of Canada! Honestly, I know you probably feel, as I did when I got it, that it is likely a whole load of b.s. But all the same, it is better than having our Orders given from England, in my opinion. Also, I think one has to assume that in our field, it really does mean something—well, we know we haven't contributed anything to the *economic* life of our country, and we haven't done any political wangling, and we have no friends at court *at all*, so maybe they really do think something of our work.

. . . And I do wear the little pin with the snowflake and the maple leaf—I kind of like it, to tell you the truth. So I guess I feel ambiguous. But I feel if Orders are being passed out, a) better they should be Canadian ones, and b) better that a few people in the arts should get them. . . .

Lakefield, Ontario,
15 Feb 75

Dear Ernie—

. . . Last week, I found myself on a panel at the Women's Art Association of Peterborough. "On a panel" sounds like an operating table, and that's about how it felt. The deal was this— I was not willing to be "guest speaker" . . . but because I sometimes feel I ought to do something locally, I'd agreed to have

33

a panel—not really a discussion, but 2 people asking me questions and myself hopefully saying something of uplift and cultural value. . . . I was told, beforehand, that some of the members (all of them, I later realized—no, let us say 89%) were really keen to hear just one thing—WHY HAD I USED ALL THOSE FOUR LETTER WORDS IN THE DIVINERS? Sure, I said, throw me that question: I'd like to field it. So they did. And Ernie, I gave what I thought was a masterful reply. I went on, calmly and at some length, to explain that the characters who used those so-called obscene words were people whose natural speech included them; if I hadn't put them in, it would have been a betrayal of the characters, who would certainly not have talked in the polite tones with which I was presently addressing the meeting. The United Church hall was packed—about 200 ladies. They sat and nodded their heads—I felt with relief that maybe the message had got through to them. Feeling a bit pleased with myself, I nervously fumbled for a cigarette, only to look down a second later and notice that the fringe on the tablecloth, right beside my hands, was merrily blazing away. I then heard my own voice announce in an agonized yelp over the microphone . . "MY GOD! I've just set fire to the tablecloth!" To do the ladies justice, about a third of them went into fits of laughter. A friend who had been present said to me later, "Never mind, Margaret, at least it was only a 3-letter word." "Yeh," I said, "but it was in the United Church Hall." Personally, I thought it was hilarious, in context. I may say I batted out the blaze with my bare hands and did not even get scorched—maybe The Great Spirit was chortling? I fancy He/She/It could do with a little light relief from time to time. . . .

Lakefield, Ontario,
26 Feb 75

Dear Ernie—

. . . I've just had a letter from Alan Young, of Acadia University, who tells me he's doing a book on you for M&S Canadian Writers Series.[7] That's good! . . .

Kind of odd to have people writing about one's work—do you feel that? It makes me feel (altho I'm certainly interested in what they have to say) that my books were written by somebody else. Book on my work coming out, with M&S this spring, too, by Clara Thomas,[8] and it is really very good indeed, or so I think. But it still seems a bit strange, like reviews only more so. Writing is a private work—when it is in the public eye, so to speak, one is glad but also a bit bewildered. At least that's my response. . . .

Am trying to clear the decks (i.e. to say NO to all invites to talk to High School classes etc etc), so I can begin writing a kids' book. . . .

Lakefield, Ontario,
20 April 75

Dear Ernie—

I put in my request to the *Globe & Mail* to review your book too late, alas; it had already been grabbed by Bill French, who is very responsive to your work, but who is, I can only guess, a city man. . . . Well, Ernie, I think all we can feel with reviewers is that they are journalists who get a bit jaded with their profession and who, well-meaning as they may be, and perceptive as they occasionally are, just do not know very damn much about fiction. Ernie, this isn't really a country matter, either—it's just that *writers* know how books are conjured up; reviewers so often do not know, at all. They make me angry, both on my own account and on behalf of other writers, but what the hell. If the review is somewhat favourable, then maybe someone will buy the book—I've come to that conclusion, sadly enough.

After having said all this, maybe my review will strike you as uninformed. I hope not. It was, at least, written with some attempt to connect and get inside the stories. Space, of course, is a very limiting factor in newspaper reviews. This will probably be the basis of my Intro for THE REBELLION OF YOUNG DAVID in the New Canadian Library, but there I'll be able to open out a bit more. I could, of course, write reams about your work, but won't, because novelists don't seem to do that kind of thing, I guess because they are too involved with their own work. Marian Engel, God bless her . . . did a review of Clara Thomas's book on me, and understood it, and said exactly that—the comments of journalists are often too superficial and too prejudiced; the critical works by academics are too often too jargon-filled; thank goodness a few academics still have the time to write about books, with a serious critical standard and yet without the academic jargon. . . .

Thanks, Ernie, and God bless, and much love. . . .

Lakefield, Ontario,
30 April 75

Dear Ernie—

. . . I wish I had sent you a copy of my review of THE REBELLION OF YOUNG DAVID, which will appear in the Montreal *Gazette*,[9] but I'll send you a copy when it is printed. . . . The stories are *good*, Ernie, *good*. (That sounds like, and is meant to sound like a line of young David's to his father, trying to get across the essential truth and having to *underline* it, because the other person finds it difficult to believe, Ernie. Goddamn it! Many of the stories made me cry—how much more can I say? They are so goddamn good; they wear so well.) . . .

Ernie, I have had an incredible week! . . . There is a letter from the Canada Council, telling me I have been awarded one of the Molson Prizes this year!!! . . . it means (gasp!) FIFTEEN THOUSAND BUCKS TAX FREE!!!!!!!!! . . . [Also] [l]etter by special courier, because of postal troubles. . . . It was telling me that THE DIVINERS had won the Governor-General's Award. . . . I really feel good about this, Ernie. I got it once before for A JEST OF GOD, but I never felt good about that (I did, but also I didn't), because it was generally said hereabouts that they gave it to me for that book because they thought later I should've had it 2 years before for THE STONE ANGEL. Well, you know, I guess, how I felt. One does not prefer any one of one's books; it's like saying, "Mrs. Laurence, which of your kids do you care about the most?" You have to say, "I care about them both, but for somewhat different reasons; I don't judge between them." So I didn't much like the thought that Rachel's book was not really the book which was being given the award. But this time, there is no way that they have not given it to me just for that one novel, and I am in some way terribly glad that it was THE DIVINERS that got it, not because I have a "favourite" novel, but because it may be my last, and I put a hell of a lot of my blood and guts into it. I did with them all, of course, but this one seemed to demand an awful lot of levelling with myself, etc. So I'm glad. And as far as all that bread is concerned for the Molson, my heavens, it will remove the pressure. Both my young want to go to university this coming academic year, and I hope they get in. They are both very responsible people, and do not expect me to support them totally or anything like that. . . . To see them through university, or whatever, Ernie, I'd work my ass off writing articles for *Weekend Magazine* or something. But it is nice now to know that I can write the articles I *want* to write, if I want to write them. I don't have to. I've written so goddamn many articles, of varying quality, mostly rather mediocre, throughout the years, to keep the roof over the head. Lovely, now, not to have to. . . .

Lakefield, Ontario,
18 Sept 75

Dear Ernie—

. . . I've been reading Bob Chambers' book (in galleys) on you and [Sinclair] Ross, and am going to review it for the Globe & Mail.[10] I think it's a pretty good book. He communicates his own enthusiasm for your work, and the book is mercifully free of academic jargon. He also says (and I agree—and I'm not even *asking* you if you agree, because that isn't something one should ever ask a writer) that the ending of THE MOUNTAIN AND THE VALLEY is *not* downbeat, doom & gloom, as some critics have maintained, but rather, at a much more profound level, an affirmation of life. To die—that is as inevitable as birth. But to have *seen*, even briefly—that is the truly important thing. . . .

Much love. . . .

ps. what has happened re: your sister?[11] Life is so goddamn difficult. The end-years should be easier, but I don't think they are ever easier. Strange to think that the last battles are always, or almost always, the hardest ones. Remember Browning (whom in general I love)? "Grow old along with me/The best is yet to be" . . even at 18, I knew that was untrue. (*Is* it Browning, or does memory fail?) "The last of life, for which the first was made . ."[12] Rubbish. The only comment on old age which I truly admire comes from the Anglo-Saxon poem, The Battle of Maldon . .

"Mind must be the firmer, heart more fierce,
Courage the greater, as our strength diminishes."

And even that isn't too accurate .. of course, it wasn't said about old age but about battles; same thing, though. It's not something anyone really achieves, I guess, but it seems to me a kind of goal. I had not read that poem when I wrote *The Stone Angel*, but it seems to epitomize Hagar—except the "mind" stanza, perhaps.

Lakefield, Ontario,
9 June 76

Dear Ernie—

... Now for my two incredible months of interesting but hectic labour. I had deadlines for four book reviews; I judged the Nova Scotia Writers' Guild Novel Contest . . . I worked in Toronto for a week and a half, with others on the committee, on the Writers' union standard contract; I attended the union conference the end of April in Ottawa; I worked on the Union Educational Project as a member of the advisory panel; I did final revisions on a manuscript of my own .. a book of essays to be published this fall and to be called HEART OF A STRANGER (the title is from Exodus); I tried to keep pace with the ghastly flow of business correspondence; I visited about half a dozen Canlit classes at Trent University and various high schools. . . .

I am now, thank God, at my cottage on the Otonabee river, about 20 miles south of Lakefield, and loving it. It's the same river I describe in THE DIVINERS. Just to be here restores my soul. . . .

I don't recall whether I wrote you anything about THE GREAT BOOK BANNING IN PETERBOROUGH COUNTY. However, I will briefly go through the whole thing. It was both comic and upsetting from my point of view, and I must say there were times when I couldn't help feeling somewhat depressed. In February, apparently a parent complained about the use of THE DIVINERS in the Grade 13 course in Lakefield High. The book was subsequently sent to a textbook review committee, who voted unanimously to restore it to the course and to make it possible for it to be taught in any other high school in the country. All this, you understand, was interspersed with much coverage in the local press, and many letters both pro and con the book. This kind of publicity I could live without. The anti-DIVINERS faction is largely composed of fundamentalists. I respect their religion, for them. I wish they'd respect mine. However, of course, they claim the novel is obscene, blasphemous, pornographic, etc. You name it. I am some sort of Jezebel in their eyes. Most of them, also, proudly stated that they had not read the book. It wouldn't have made any difference if they had read it—those of their number who had read it only noticed the so-called four-letter words and the sex scenes. They didn't notice the other 375 pp. Anyway, the School Board then had to vote on the book. In an open and very heated meeting (I was given a description of it by various friends as well as reading it in the *Examiner*) there were briefs presented pro and con. One woman said that Margaret Laurence's aim in life was to ruin the home and the family. How about that, Ernie? Matriarchal me! Another fundamentalist preacher said ML wrote "pornography for money". The Board voted 10 to 6 in favour of the book. Of the 6 against, only 2 had read it, by their own admission. Well—victory, anyway.

But the plot thickens. Then the fundamentalists decided to get up a petition against the novel. The Rev. Sam Buick opened the Dublin Street Pentecostal Church for one whole day so people could sign the petition of the Citizens For Decency. (!) He provided copies of THE DIVINERS, handily marked, and mimeographed sheets with page refs to all the 4 letter words and sex scenes. A sign in the church read: If Under 16 Do Not Sign Petition; If Under 18 Do Not Read Book. The book was considered by the Rev. Sam and cohorts to be unfit to teach in Grade 13, to 18-yr-olds, but it was quite okay for them to read the sex scenes totally out of context. Oh yes . . guess which edition they used? Yep. The American remaindered one, being sold by Coles for $2.99, on which I get no royalties! Adding insult to injury.

The next step was another School Board Meeting, also open and heated, at which the petition and also briefs pro and con, again, were presented to the Board. One guy got up to speak against the book, saying "I speak for a delegation of eight— myself, my wife, our five children, and God." I kid you not. No one had apparently ever told him of the sin of spiritual pride! Anyway, the Board voted as before . . 10 to 6 in favour of the book. Now it will be interesting to see what happens in the municipal elections in December, as the fundamentalists clearly plan to try to pack the School Board. If they do, the Grade 13 students will be studying the Bobbsey twins. How about all this, Ernie? If I'd made it all up, I couldn't have done better, eh? . . .

Lakefield, Ontario,
24 Nov 76

Dear Ernie—

. . . First, thanks for your incredibly oratorical and splendid defense of THE DIVINERS and comments on its opponents in this county! The problem, Ernie, is that as a political being (and yes, I'm that), I have to oppose the fundamentalists when they get into the political arena, which the School Board is definitely a part of, in my view, while, at the same time, as a fiction writer I have to try to understand their point of view, I mean really to try to make that leap of the imagination to get inside (to some extent) the minds and hearts of people like the Rev. Sam Buick of the Dublin Street Pentecostal Church. It is not easy, but in some way I feel it to be necessary. Maybe that whole thing, plus a whole lot of other things, is growing very very slowly and uncertainly into another novel—I don't know. We will see. But there is no way I could write about an Elmer Gantry. My feeling must be closer to what Joyce Cary did (and did so splendidly that can anyone again attempt it? The answer of course is Yes) in THE CAPTIVE AND THE FREE,[13] a novel which I don't think I dare re-read right now, although when I first read it (and it was his last—he literally kept himself alive until he had completed it) it seemed to me to be one of the most profound things I'd ever read. The man had *wisdom*, and he knew about spiritual pride and what is termed Christian humility (although it is by no means only Christian, just as spiritual pride in some way is defined by every culture in the world . . the Greeks of old called it *hubris*, of course). I guess two of the novelists in what we may term "contemporary literature" whom I have most admired and loved have been Joyce Cary and Patrick White. I recall so clearly when I first read Cary's THE HORSE'S MOUTH[14] and thinking . . Jesus, do I kill myself because I can never do it, or do I celebrate and give thanks that someone can? The latter course, naturally, is the only one open to novelists, thank God. I also came to the conclusion that we all do what we can wherever we happen to *be*, and maybe in the end it all relates. I believe so. Anyway, I'm thinking a lot these days about some characters—no, some *people*—who may, if God is good once again to me, develop enough for me to dare to write about them. I have to try to make a kind of space around myself, and turn down a lot of requests to do this and that, in order just to stay home and work, or even just to stay home and think. I'm sure you have felt that—you know there may be something there, perhaps a novel, and you don't yet *know* enough. Maybe one will find out, or maybe not. It's always a risk. Not only the practical thing—finding out the details, picking people's brains when it will be useful to one, but also the more difficult thing of being quiet and trying to listen. . . . In a profound sense, writers are perpetual amateurs. . . .

Much much love. . . .

Lakefield, Ontario,
27 June 77

Dear Ernie—

I have owed you a letter for months and months. . . . Truthfully, I seemed to have lost the entire spring, running around the country on various duty jaunts—Prairie Writers' Workshop in Saskatoon; visit to U of Guelph—seminars with students . . . Writers' Union annual conference in Toronto in May . . . out to Simon Fraser U in Vancouver, where I gave the convocation address plus a public lecture plus several seminars with students; out to Fredericton very briefly to be (wait for it!) installed as a Fellow of the Royal Society of Canada! God knows what that means. . . . Finally two weeks ago or around there arrived at my cottage *at last*, and for about a week simply sat in stunned and exhausted silence, looking at the river and the birds. . . .

A few small ideas may be coming to mind for new writing, but I won't ever do it unless I make a space for myself. I now have a form letter, in which I politely apologize for the fact that it is not a personal letter and go on to list 22 items which I can no longer do—e.g. give publishing advice; edit or read manuscripts; give seminars or interviews; give lectures or readings; etc etc etc. I was also driven to getting an unlisted phone, because so many people wanted me to do various things that I just can't do. . . .

Take care; God bless; and love. . . .

Dear Ernie—

... I note from your Aug letter that the book was just about to
come out. You hadn't told me much about it, but, as it happens,
I received a copy soon after it came out, on account of my being
(for my sins) now a member of McClelland & Stewart's Board of
Directors . . I don't think I'll last long, there, because I constantly
get so mad at the buggers, but let that pass. Anyway, I read
WHIRLIGIG[15] with great joy and laughter, of course recognizing
in many of the pages some of the damn-awful dilemmas of a
trivial and embarrassing or laughable nature that we all
experience. I loved it. I also felt both amused and angry when I
read some of the reviews . . well, some of them said, for heaven's
sake, here is a *serious writer* being flippant, and ye gods, like, it
ain't the same as a serious novel, is it, and what's this guy doing,
anyway? I laughed and was angry, Ernie, because *exactly* the same
thing happened to me when I published . . . HEART OF A
STRANGER, in 1976. That was a book of articles, some serious
and some (I thought) humorous. Reviewer after reviewer said
something like this—well, hm hm, Margaret Laurence has now
published this book of articles, and some of them seem like pretty
corny humour and well, chaps, it certainly isn't the same as a
serious novel, and why is she giving us this flippancy . . as
literature, it ain't as good as THE STONE ANGEL. Honestly, Ernie,
that is what they said. Who in hell ever pretended those articles
were to be ranked alongside serious fiction? Not me. Nor you.
AREN'T SERIOUS WRITERS PERMITTED A CHORTLE OR TWO, AN
IRONIC TWIST OF TWO, SOME LIGHT VERSE, SOME LAUGHTER
IN THE MIDST OF ALL OF LIFE? By me, Yes. By you, yes. By some
of the reviewers, No. The hell with them, Ernie. . . .
    ... I am surviving this winter . . we have tons and tons
of what they call in my village "the white stuff", ie snow. But my
soul, I'd rather be here than in Florida. Actually, I would have
made a rotten pioneer, but all of us Canadians somehow feel that
deep within our souls is the pioneer.
    ... I would like to write another novel, and maybe it will
be given. I'm still exploring, finding out about a lot of things I
need to know. If it is given, fine. If not, also fine. I feel sort of
calm about the future, although I'm not a calm person by nature.
Maybe I'm learning somewhat. We will see.
Very much love to you, and hope, and blessings. . . .

We'd been living in England for some time, and I can still remember the pleasure of hearing that flat Manitoba voice, formed about fifty miles from where my mother grew up. And she had an absolutely straight-ahead Canadian approach to things. God, it was a relief to talk with someone for whom you didn't have to explain everything, starting with the geography of Canada. And not to be watching your words, phrasing things in guarded ways for fear of breaking some peculiar British scholarly or social taboo.

Elm Cottage,
11 Oct 67

Dear Don and Anne:

... Sorry I haven't written sooner, but have been trying to resume my novel, and think I may be getting into it now, at last. Have the usual terrible doubts but this time must try not to look back, or like Lot's wife will be turned into a pillar of salt. Have finished my kooky children's book [*Jason's Quest*] and sent it off to Macmillan's, but somehow doubt it will be publishable. Did I tell you the grim details about it? The hero is a mole, and I was having so much trouble with the moles on my lawn that finally I had to call in a molecatcher, so now I feel like a murderer....

Don, I really don't know what to say re. your suggestion re: writer-in-residence [at Dalhousie University]. I don't think I am very well qualified for that sort of thing....

... I myself feel the need to go back and live in Canada, for 2 reasons—a) if I don't, I can't go on writing, because I shall have forgotten how the voices sound; b) I feel at this point in life a strong desire to lessen my own isolation and to take some part in the general aspect of Canadian writing—I've always avoided things like conferences, etc, but I feel now that in some peculiar way this is being a little irresponsible. Of course, until this point in my life, I had to work like blazes to get caught up on the writing I wanted to do, and to some extent this is still true, but now I've got this 1 novel to do, plus 3 short stories, and after that—what? Nothing much, or not yet. I do feel now that my own personal battle is there, not here, although I don't regret one minute of my time in England. . . .

Much love to you all. . . .

Elm Cottage,
21 October 67

Dear Camerons—

Sons of the hound, come here and get flesh!

Sorry. Have recently read John Prebble's *Culloden*,[1] which brought
back this most bloodthirsty of the Clan war-cries, that of the
Camerons! . . .
. . . I am in a very strange quandary. This morning I got a
letter from Dr. [Alan] Bevan, Head of Eng[lish]. Dept., Dalhousie,
in which he very charmingly asked if I would be interested in
applying for Killam Senior fellowship to be Writer-in-residence
at Dalhousie for a year. The terms are 12,000 dollars for the year,
tax free, with duties largely (I take it) what one wants to make of
them. This would be a worry, I must say. I would be relieved not
to have to do any regular teaching, although would *love* to have
informal-type classes on West African Lit., and would also love
to talk to students and younger writers and see what *they* think
about all those questions which have been bugging me for years—
how to penetrate even a little more deeply into the human
complex, in verbal terms, without becoming unreadable—and
the traditional narrative style for this point in history now seems
to me unreadable; something else has to be devised, even if in a
fragmentary way, and the only way I can see is through pictures
and voices—M. Macluhan [*sic*] would say "audio-visual" but I
reject those words because they are so theoretical and somehow
cold and unhuman. I have been beating my brains out about this
present novel, and all I can see (about 1 inch ahead of me, like in
a fog) is that the novel must be moving closer to the film, as a
means of catching the human dilemma. All this bugs me very
much, but it would be very interesting to see what people 20
years my junior see (I am sure they see more than I do in terms of
style; what they cannot see as I do is the way the pain feels after
20 years, and the uncertainty). In other words, I am really only
interested in the moment in this bloody novel which seems to
me to be quite impossible, and to be only an expression of what
I want to set down, and I can't think that I will ever be willing to

submit it to a publisher (damn all publishers). You think I'm not speaking seriously—wait; I am. This novel attempts to transform the ordinary, as previous ones have done, but never have I tried to transform anything quite *this* ordinary—and from that statement, you can see how much I care about the damn thing, because in some way that is the whole point. A critic in Toronto wrote a review of *A Jest of God* and said Rachel was someone you might sit next to on the streetcar and not notice, and so why write about her, because she wasn't interesting. Sorry, the novels aren't filled with kooky inhabitants of far-out boarding houses. The odd thing was that I met the gal who wrote that review, and she had to explain why she said that, etc etc, and I really could not reassure her because all I could find to say was "Rachel's pain is as real as Leonard Cohen's." End of conversation, I guess. Well, if I'd done it as it should have been done, maybe she'd have seen that. Anyway, this present one is probably not going to see the light of day and who cares? Not me. Really—I know this sounds phoney but it is absolutely God's truth; one gets in this position from time to time, when the externals cannot and must not matter. No literary set would take a bet on this one, I can tell you. But you know, Don, the people I know and have known are not those who clobber their mums with a pick-axe or rape tiny Lolitas. My territory isn't like that. We inflict pain in much more un-easy-to-see ways, and there is always the reverse side of the coin, ie we love our kids or at least we love-resent them with love sometimes coming out on the credit balance. . . .

Elmcot,
23 Oct 67

Dear Don—

. . . p.s. the only thing that really bothers me about this writer-in-residence bit (whether Dalhousie or anywhere) is that I cannot really feel I deserve any free cash at this point, having had a grant from the Canada Council, plus the money from the Gov. General's. I don't count the *Holiday* articles [written about a trip to Egypt],[2] as I worked for that money. Also, I think of the film, but there again, that was a business deal—I mean, someone was buying something they wanted. But it is the fellowship kind of thing which in some ways worries me—it doesn't seem that public money ought to be given to me at this point, as I have done terribly well out of this kind of thing in the past year. . . .

Elm Cottage,
3 Sept 68

Dear Don and Anne:

. . . Don, I honestly do think you are doing enormously well with your stories etc. Do not be discouraged that they haven't all been placed as yet. They will be. I know it sounds corny, but every writer loves to pass on these little tidbits of wisdom, and in my case I submitted stories to various magazines for several years before anything got accepted. . . .

THE FIRE-DWELLERS has been bought for serialization in the *Ladies Home Journal*[3]–did I tell you? For quite a lot of money. They will cut it to the bone and beyond, and it will be unrecognizable, but I don't much care. All I really care about is the hardcover edition—anything else is just a gift in financial terms and not important in any other terms, although it may be good publicity for the book—I hope so. . . .

Much love to you all. . . .

Elmcot,
20 Sept 68

Dear Camerons:

. . . I was very touched and grateful to read what Ernest Buckler had said about me.[4] As you no doubt know, I have long believed THE MOUNTAIN AND THE VALLEY to be probably the best . . . Can[adian] novel written so far. I've admired Buckler so much for a long time, and it means a hell of a lot to me that he felt that way about THE STONE ANGEL. I would love to meet him and talk with him. . . . It will, I hope, be possible next year.

. . . About next year—if all goes well, and I do take the job as writer-in-res at the U of T, then there will be time for trips to see friends. How much have I told you about this projected job? Can't remember. I have the feeling that the U of T is going to change its mind about wanting me, or else something else will stand in the way of my going, but this is really only superstition. . . .

. . . I want to write some short stories and I want to write them *now*. The Celtic gloom which always hovers is not hovering dangerously close at the moment. . . .

Delighted to hear that Fredericton is promising. Alden Nowlan is one of the best Can poets. I do agree heartily re: your reactions to *Duddy Kravitz*[5]—if it's not a good novel anywhere, then I don't know at all what a good novel is. Mordecai, as you know, is w-in-r at Sir George Williams this year. I wrote and asked him what a w-in-r did, and he replied that he didn't know any more than I did. I am hoping he can complete *St. Urbain's Horseman*[6] while there. . . .

Elmcot,
22 Nov 68

Dear Camerons:

. . . Re: Buckler—oh, Allah! I can feel what he means, re: taking the words of a person of one's tribe to oneself, and holding them, against all weathers. I could and have done the same with those words of his, re: me. Ironic, eh? The thing that one *must* accept— or must agree to learn—is that we are all very lonely, isolated, etc, etc, and you cannot be a writer without being that, but you are also a human being, who wants most terribly to make contact, to touch the people you care about, to comfort your kids. . . . We go through the valley of the shadow, but for me there are earthly contacts, and I thank God for them, however much I may not be able to be adequate to their needs. Well—I would love to meet Buckler; how little he needs to feel he would be terrified, but of course I know how he feels. He has probably been more isolated than I, even, and God knows I have been isolated enough. He wouldn't be really risking anything, to meet me—he's just a member of my tribe, whom I care about, and he cares about me, without our ever having met yet. . . . I think we could talk together, and for that reason I would like to meet him. The isolation which he has been courageous enough to live through, I couldn't have; I admire him for it and—what else? How terrible that there *are* people of one's own tribe, and one never really gets to talk to them—I guess that is the thing. But I've profited from being in England. I have learned something valuable. Want to know? No charge. Everyone who is a novelist has to cope with the bit about doing their work in private, and the loneliness strikes all of us, but the work can't be done without it, and if you cannot accept the loneliness, then you must give up the work. Buckler, I should think, is an enormously solitary person, and that is what he has to be, to do his work. I think I have to be, too, although perhaps less so.

. . . Let's face it, kid—we can't take off and go to that attic in Paris. If we did, we would hate it. Why? because [the family] wouldn't be there, and *they* matter. So what do we do? Do we compromise? I don't think so. I think we can remain true to our people, and still remain true to the god—we do not have as much time as some writers may have, but we have to make the best of the time we have. . . .

Elm Cottage,
20 Jan 69

Dear Camerons:

. . . First—many thanks for sending subscription to FIDDLEHEAD [literary magazine], a publication which I am ashamed to say I have never read. I look forward to it with enormous interest.

Second . . . congrats, Don, on all the writing and other work you've been doing. . . . Don't knock yourself out, will you? But you are right, to be getting it all done. I am sure you *do* need more experience in radio and TV, as you say, and the only way to get it is to do things. But don't press yourself forward too much, will you? I know these compulsive workers—am one myself. It has something to do with the old Presbyterian roots—one is only being virtuous when working. That is not only nonsense—it is damaging to the health. But I understand your feelings of haste—personally, at my back I have heard Time's winged chariot for about 15 years now, and am only just beginning to be able to relax a little and draw breath from time to time. One must look after one's health, though, and not drive the psyche too hard. It is difficult to cultivate patience—I still have to try really hard not to be impatient about everything I am doing. . . .

Dear Don—

A brief note, to thank you for sending your story and your review of Buckler's book [*Ox Bells and Fireflies*].[7] I liked the story—I could see the background out of which it came, and it interested me to realize all over again that it is true that all fiction is in a sense about the past, and how much more recent your past is than mine! The twist ending is good—it has a real punch, and the sense of sick emptiness the boy feels is rightly got across as the (perhaps first) real sense of compassion and sense of others' pain which he has known. Keep up the good work. I also liked the review. . . . the way you put in bits of Buckler's own voice. . . .

Am trying to learn how to relax and do nothing, after 14 years of going like a bomb. Nothing pressing to do at the moment, and I think fate means me to rest for awhile.

Elmcot,
12 May 69

Dear Don—

. . . I took David [Laurence] and a pal to Scotland during the Easter holidays and we had a marvellous time. . . . visited the battle-site of Culloden, and I told the boys all about the '45 [Rebellion]—any tour with me is a tour of history, absolutely inaccurate but dramatic as hell! . . .

. . . My novel [*The Fire-Dwellers*] has now come out, and so far I've only had 4 reviews from Canada. . . . I think now that this book in some publications is being reviewed as a kind of reflection of the war between the sexes—ie if a middle-aged housewife with 4 kids has any bolshy thoughts, some male reviewers just do not want to know. . . .

. . . I received Buckler's book—many thanks. I liked it very much although I thought that in places it made too much use of lists of things and impressions. . . .

Love to you all. . . .

Dear Don—

... I found your remarks reassuring re: THE FIRE-DWELLERS.
As you know, so far the Can reviews are either very pro or very
con. In this country it has so far had very few reviews, most quite
friendly but mainly missing the point. .... I must say the lack of
reviews here is quite terribly depressing to me. I realize this is
foolish, but I simply cannot help it. However, the feeling will
pass. ....

I thought COCKSURE was very uneven as a novel,[8] but
can't help being glad that Richler was given the GG. However, it
would have been better if he'd been given it for another book, I
think. ...

Did I tell you that my short story collection has been
accepted by Macmillan here? ... It is tentatively titled A BIRD IN
THE HOUSE—we are having our problems re: titles again, and
again I am writing passionate letters to agents and publishers,
explaining why my title is the right one. Macmillan would like a
title which conveys the impression that the stories are connected,
which indeed they are, but who can produce such a thing without
sacrificing everything a title should be? These are all the
Manawaka stories based on guess-who's childhood. I think
you've read some of them. ...

Dear Don—

... Reviews of THE FIRE-DWELLERS continue to be split down
the middle. How odd it should be reviewed so much (as it
apparently is being) as a part of the sex war. I never anticipated
that. Some male reviewers seem really to want to *kill* Stacey for
having those unorthodox and un-contented-cow thoughts. Well,
well. ...

There was a truth and generosity and gentleness in her portrayals of
those fictional women that let me see more deeply into my own family,

my own background—and especially my own mother and grandmother.

9 Westgrove Crescent,
27 Sept 69

Dear Camerons—

. . . Am learning fast here [Massey College, as writer-in-residence].
Was terribly stupid the first 2 weeks in that I committed myself
to speaking to about 6 different organizations, no fees of course.
What a nitwit. Now my answer will be No to all requests.
Speaking at a university is different—I'm going to Dalhousie in
the spring, and look forward to that. Also, will deliver a lecture
with material I really care about, namely how does one discover
the form and voice for a novel? . . . But women's clubs are OUT,
from now on. Otherwise I won't have time or energy to talk to
young writers, which is what I really want to do. . . . I did a TV
panel thing day before yesterday—one of a series, mostly about
sex, called Man At The Centre. . . . Was on with 2 psychologists
and 1 lady anthropologist, and the talk was mainly about personal
relationships in an urban situation—love in the concrete jungle,
as it were. Somewhat to my surprise, I quite enjoyed doing it
and found I was not nervous in the slightest. . . .

All sorts of fun and games here—univ opening with
student takeover of dinner at Hart House; Pres[ident Claude]
Bissell in all kinds of hot water; etc etc. I don't know enough to
have opinion which I care to express to anyone yet. And am
determined not to take sides—I know I ought to feel involved in
this problem, but I really don't. I almost feel like putting a sign
on my office door . . RE: STUDENT PROTESTS—SORRY, BUT I MOVE
TO A DIFFERENT DRUM. However, it is all fascinating and I am
glad to observe it—the nature of universities is certainly altering
radically, and maybe that is a very good thing. . . .

Elm Cottage,
6 Jan 71

Dear Don—

. . . Your projects, as usual, sound fascinating, hectic, and tremendously worthwhile. In many ways, what you are doing at the present moment seems more relevant than fiction, altho I admit I still believe the latter is worth doing. Who will read it, tho, when there isn't any planet? I know very well that basically one writes for one's contemporaries, but always before one was at least assuming the continuance of the human race even if not the continuance of any one culture.

The latest edition of *Mysterious East*[9] has just arrived with the Lit. Supplement. I think it is splendid.... [and] George Woodcock's assessment of the Criminal Code comes very close to being a kind of moral testament for our age. What an incredible man he is! Was glad to see my article on [Dave] Godfrey didn't seem too long, in context....[10] I also thought that in the publication proper, the articles on the FLQ gave me, for the first time, a better understanding of what actually happened re: Cross and Laporte, etc. And re: the War Measures Act, which seemed to me at the time to be highly dangerous, but I had not suspected how far-reaching would be the results.

Am still plodding away at this novel, which has not yet got off the ground, but maybe I'm beginning to see a few glimmers of light....

R.R.11. Peterborough, Ont.
8 Sept 72

Dear Don—

Well, old buddy, great minds—as they say—think alike. I have already read [Harold Horwood's] *White Eskimo*,[11] having asked him for a xerox copy, and have conned the *Globe & Mail* into letting me do a review of it, which they will . . . run on Sept 23rd, which will be the day after publication date. I think it is a splendid novel, and I say so in fairly strong terms. It will come as no surprise to you that I agree with his anti-colonial anti-missionary stance COMPLETELY, as I have been saying these same things about Africa for about 15 years. Also, as I say in my review, "In this age of non-hero and anti-hero, when nearly every novel is crammed with an assortment of bumblers, born to goof as the sparks fly upward, HH has done a daring thing. He has written a novel with a hero. What is more, he has made that hero believable and human, by no means infallible, but a man of worth and honour.

Worth and *honour* are not popular words in our mocking times, but let us not deceive ourselves—we have need of them." I go on to point out that most "Eskimo" books are pretty rotten. . . . I think you'll like the review, and I hope to heavens it convinces a few people that they should read the book.

Don—I AM FINISHED THE FIRST DRAFT OF MY NOVEL.

. . pause. Gasp! Whew! Zowie! Splat! Zonk! Argghh! Etc.

It is miles too long and will have to be cut a great deal. Later. Later. . . .

If I had to name two people who constituted the spirit of the Writers' Union in the early days—and I don't mean to downplay a lot of other people who cared about it very much and worked very hard, people like Graeme Gibson, Margaret Atwood, Harold Horwood, and others—the two real den-mothers were Margaret Laurence and Marian Engel. And Margaret, really, above all. At the union annual meetings she's still very much a presence; her name comes up again and again. It's quite striking what a big echo she has.

R.R. 11, Peterborough,
14 Sept 72

Dear Don—

. . . Have just read Denis Smith's *Bleeding Hearts, Bleeding Country*[12]—an awful title, but a fine book. . . . He does not go far enough, but that is to be expected. In yesterday's paper, I read that Trudeau says than even if Quebec elected a separatist government, the federal government would not allow separation to take place!! Shades of Biafra. Self-determinism is forgotten; any kind of human principles are forgotten; his federalism really leads him to say—I don't care what the people of Quebec want; this is what they're going to have, because *I say so*. This from a man who used to talk of participatory democracy. Power has corrupted. The terrible thing is that the majority of Canadians will agree with him, I fear. And now that the Waffle[13] is out of the NDP, what alternative is there. I don't think I could vote at all in this election, but that does no good, either. This country is in bad shape, Don. Which makes me want to come back permanently more than ever. It may be a mess, but I care about it in ways I don't think I could ever care about England. . . .

Dear Don—

. . . Saw yr article in *Sat Night*, re: the young man confined in
mental hospital,[14] and thought it was *good*, in every sense of the
word. Maybe that is finally yr role in life, Don, to fight the good
fight. Hardly anyone can do it effectively, in the kind of journalism
which is going to strike not only into people's minds but into
their guts as well. You can. I have some kind of feeling that you
still knock this gift which has been given to you; maybe you don't
anymore; I hope you don't, because it is rare and valuable. And
if you find that this sort of article is what you are doing, maybe
for God's sake (I speak advisedly) you could accept it and know
that it is valuable, and if you find that you aren't writing a novel
or whatever, don't worry about that. Everybody who has any
power of choice always does what they want to do the most, and
that usually is what they were meant to do anyway. If you really
need to write a novel, you will. If not, you won't and that is okay,
because you will be doing, as I may have suggested, the kind of
thing that hardly anyone can do well.

I am in a state of modified jubilation, having now finished
this novel. Hallelujah! But I have not yet done with it. I do know
that it will need more work, but as it has now gone through 3
drafts, and as I feel I really have not surfaced (until now) for
about 3 years, I know that it has to be out of my hands for the
moment. Jocelyn is typing a fair copy and will then . . . get me 3
xerox copies. . . . She gives me little comments along the way,
usually pretty perceptive. . . . Also, it is the last of what I might
call the Manawaka books, and everything is brought full circle
herein. This gives me an odd feeling, Don. I feel glad that I have
been able to complete what I (unknowingly) set my hand to, so
long ago. . . . Movin' on, Don, that's what I'm doing. It feels okay.
It feels frightening. It feels necessary and in some ways joyful.

My long-range forecast—I go to my shack end of May;
work on last revisions; in Sept 73 go to Western U [University of
Western Ontario] as w[riter]-in-r[esidence]; in Jan 74 go to Trent
U Peterborough as w-in-r and try to look for a nice old brick

54

house in P'borough. Return to Eng[land] Spring 74, sell Elmcot, and return permanently to the land of my fathers, namely Canada. That is the rough program, Don. It could all change in the doing, or I could have a heart attack or get run down by a bus. But that is where I am approximately headed, always knowing that, as with fiction, life can change at the flicker of an eyelash, so one's plans are always very tentative and flexible. . . .

Also want to go to Northern Manitoba, always provided that the bloody novel does not take up my whole summer. Feel a great need to go places and see people and do things, having been immersed in this novel for nearly 3 years. Wish it were really and truly done, but it isn't yet. However, the end is in sight, or so I hope. . . .

In a certain sense she may have emptied the deep well, the most important things she had to say about Manawaka—although I still suspect that the vein wasn't exhausted had the will and the desire been there to continue. The Manawaka material was so rich and so thick and there were still new characters turning up, new twists and turns in the material. That world seemed so full, and so alive, that I find it hard to believe it just died out on her.

Elm Cottage,
23 May 73

Dear Don—

Have just received CONVERSATIONS WITH CAN NOVELISTS,[15] and spent all day yesterday reading it. I think it is a splendid book, very very good indeed. I like the form you have given it, with the short Intro at the beginning of each interview, to set the tone, and the pics of writers, plus the Biog and Bibliog at the end. . . .

Both Knopf and Macmillan (London) have accepted my novel, THE DIVINERS. Haven't yet heard from M&S. Will have to do some final revisions. If I can't get them done before July 22, will have to do them at shack. Plus preparing a lecture for Univ of Sask, where I'm going for a day in Oct, plus trying to do a TV script (me? yes) an adaptation of part of novel, for CBC, which George Jonas more or less charmed me into agreeing to attempt. Never a dull moment. . . .

Dear Don—

... I'm doing nothing at the moment except unwinding after about 1 1/2 years of incredible pressure—did I say 1 1/2 years? I think I mean about 15 years! What a pleasure it is to be at the shack, just looking at the river and the birds and the wildflowers, and catching up on reading. I haven't even seen very many people . . just feel the need for total quiet at the moment. Hope to stay through Sept and most of Oct, but will commute once a week to Lakefield and to Trent U, where I'll work 1 day weekly as writer-in-res. . . .

Don, I've been corresponding lately with Ernie Buckler, and I am worried about him. . . . I don't know what his personal situation is, but he sounds just terribly depressed and lonely and alone. It breaks my heart to think of him like that. Also, I wish he wouldn't keep knocking himself and his own writing—that breaks my heart to read, too. He *must* know how he is valued in this country—maybe he doesn't really know. Do you happen to know anything about his situation at the present? And what, if anything, could any of us do?

Must go. I have 70 letters to reply to, having got far behind in correspondence . . am trying now to communicate once again with dear friends *first*, and then to answer all the others, which will no doubt be my winter project!. . .

It had not occurred to me until I was twenty-one that I could be a writer, because in order to be one you apparently had to be British and dead. For someone like Margaret to take me seriously as part of her circle, and indeed part of her tribe, made me stand a whole lot taller. It began to seem possible that I could actually be a writer myself, something I'd only really dreamed of. And beyond that was the emotional impact, almost the spiritual impact, which she had on me. I felt I'd been spending time with an extraordinarily large soul—capable of pettiness from time to time as well, but finally, a very large soul, and a great example.

Lakefield,
10 Dec 74

Dear Don—

This is the letter I always hoped I'd have to write to you. How is
that for an opening sentence? . . .

     I don't know if I owe you an apology or not. I think I do,
likely. I *did* think, as I didn't try much to conceal from you, in
past years, that your talents lay mainly in the field of freelance
journalism (I have now for several years been going around
saying Don Cameron is our best freelance journalist . . you want
to know what an article on *any* subject is all about? read Cameron.
And so on.) And please honour me enough (you do) to respect
my feelings about the field of journalism. I write articles for
Weekend, Don, from time to time, and probably they pay me
more than they pay you, but *I* know, and surely I hope *you* know,
that your articles are in fact better than mine. They are. In the
field of fiction, that's another story (no pun intended). I'm not a
good freelance journalist; I'm not a good literary critic or reviewer,
although I've done all those things reasonably well. To earn bread,
to keep the roof over the head. But my real work isn't there, as
you well know. This does not mean I knock that work. I don't.
What I am trying to say is that for a long time I have respected
you in terms of your work as a journalist, a critic, and yes, an
editor (in the interview book). But I guess until I read the story
in *The Atlantic Monthly*[16] (it has to go into some Can anthologies,
I would hope) I wasn't convinced of that other area of yourself,
namely fiction.

     Well, it's a good story. That is not a simple sentence, from
me. It is a *good* story. You get across, to me, the sense of that whole
crazy and tragic area; it's a very tough story, and I use *tough* in
the best possible way; it is also a story which conveys the area
and the individuals in their own voices—hell, I don't know them,
but you convince me. It's also very very funny, in the saddest
way possible—humour is so serious that it should only be given
into the hands of them who know tragedy. Do I make myself
plain? It's a good story, Don; you don't need me to tell you that.
It works at all levels—personal, idiomatic, the sense of the form
of the thing (which, honestly, is a lovely form—I care about form
in fiction; it matters.)

     Hey, man, you can do it! I'm not, by the way, trying to
persuade you to do it all the time, exclusively. That's up to you,

and you do the other so well and we need that, too. It's just that I now see you have a problem I didn't know you really had. *Which to do*? I never had that problem because I wasn't very gifted except in one area, which makes it simpler. Your decisions will probably be quite hard to make.

With much love and support for whatever you do. . . .

The censorship issue bewildered her, and angered her, and hurt her greatly. She was deeply offended at the suggestion that her work was immoral. She had been wrestling all her life, as hard as she could, with very complex and ambiguous moral issues—and here she was being brought to book by people who didn't have one per cent of her moral sense. It was like Elmer Gantry admonishing Oedipus. Those people had so colossally misread her that she had to recognize there was really no communication between them. They weren't talking the same language, they weren't living in the same world.

Lakefield,
28 June 79

Dear Don—

Thanks so much for your letter. First, business. Howard White of Harbour Publishing had already written to me, and I had replied saying by all means send me a copy of the manuscript [of Hubert Evan's novel *O Time In Your Flight*[17]], and that I would either give a Tender Message for the book jacket or would review the novel when it came out. I think now that reviewing it would be more useful, and I have asked Ken Adachi if I can review it for the [Toronto] Star, and he has agreed.[18] I've now received the manuscript but have not had time to read it as yet. However, whatever it is like, and my guess is that it will be pretty damn good, I still want to review it. The subject matter is so astounding, and Hubert himself is so astounding. I would guess he is one of our very few Grand Old Men. . . .

I am trying to get back to work—I have all kinds of severe doubts about what I am doing. Not a novel . . although I think ultimately I may be able to write another one. This time it is . . wait for it . . memoirs! So far the writing is dreadful, but I'm

58

finding this form very difficult, in a way more so than a novel. I'm only 18 years old thus far and about to enter college! Of course, I don't intend to spill every bean. . . .

She was conscious of examples like Sinclair Lewis, who didn't stop writing when they'd done their best work, and whose later work tended to devalue what they had already done. She was determined not to do that. She also believed that such writers probably didn't know when they were finished. If you're a basketball player it's very obvious when you're finished, but it's not so obvious if you're a writer. I think she consciously and deliberately closed the door far too early because of an exaggerated fear of dishonouring the books she'd already written.

Lakefield,
16 April 80

Dear Don—

I am enclosing a copy of one of my books for little kids, published last fall, namely SIX DARN COWS. . . . As you will see, it is in some ways A Moral Tale, but with, I hope, some sense of kids and parents loving and respecting one another. I enclose, also, a record, done for Promo purposes and not for sale. . . . It's me reading the story and Bob Bossin of The String Band playing the song and singing it at the end. Wait for it, friends! The tune is MINE! How about that? I am . . hem hem . . a COMPOSER. What happened was as follows. I agreed to try to write a little story for kids of 5 and 6, beginning to read, a read-it-yourself thing. I sweated blood over it, I kid you not. Lorimer is putting out a series of about 10 of these books, by different writers. They tested the damn things out in the schools. At one point [the editor of the series] kept phoning me up and saying they'd tried out my 2nd, 3rd, 4th, or whatever draft, and the kids said thus and so, and would I please go into one of the schools to hear what the kids were saying about this story. NOTHING DOING, I said. I can bear criticism from adult reviewers, but from those impeccably honest little kids . . ?! . . .
          . . . I am trying to get into another novel, and I have some ideas for stories and articles, and I am terrified out of my mind. However, despair is rightly termed one of the deadly sins, and I

am not feeling that. Frightened, yes. Despair, no. But it does not get easier as one gets older, I fear. I will be 54 this year. I have written, in all, 15 books, 7 books among them are adult fiction and the ones I care most about. From signs in the wind, one gathers that the next decade will not welcome books such as mine, but only the thriller style. If that is true, then I am up a creek without a paddle. . . . Publish or perish, as they have said so cynically in the academic world for many years. But what if you can't write to order, as indeed I cannot. Well, we will see. . . .

Her work came right out of the softest, deepest part of her, and it exposed her in a way that allowed her very few defences. Well, those attacks by the fundamentalists, and her celebrity status in Canada, and the whole change in her circumstances after she came back—I sometimes wonder whether those things created new defences, made her build a shell over that soft core out of which she wrote. And perhaps that shell became a bit of a prison, barring her from her own depths along with everyone else. Could she write another book like The Diviners *once she really knew what the result was going to be?*

Lakefield,
23 March 82

Dear Silver Don—

. . . I'm working very very very very slowly on what may in time turn out to be a novel. So many false starts, so many discouraging difficulties. But I find I'm not really depressed about it. If it comes, finally, then fine. If not, fine also, at this point. I'm not sure I really mean that! But I'm not broke or bored; life is full of interesting things; and I don't have to prove anything any more. Thing is, I think I still have some things I want to set down, but I am also very cognizant of how much the world has changed, although perhaps not in some essentials—thinking of my past fiction, some of the themes still seem extremely relevant, such as the terrible fear of nuclear war, which appears in *The Fire-Dwellers* as a constant thread although the book was published in 1969. I guess I know too much about the characters of this new thing, in a way, but have not yet found the right approach, although I've been trying at it for several years now. Mind you, when I consider that I ran full tilt for about 20 years or more, at my work, I'm not about to feel guilty if I don't want to do any more.

Sometimes I spend a whole day reading who-dun-its. Now there's decadence for you, says the old Presbyterian!! . . .

Much love to you all. . . .

Lakefield,
14 April 82

Dear Silver Donald—

. . . I have just written an Intro to Hubert Evans' collection of poems, a combination of ENDINGS and WHITTLINGS, which [Harbour Publishing] will publish in the spring. . . .[19] I am sweating blood over a convocation address I have to give May 6th, at Victoria University, U of T, to . . wait for it . . a class of graduating theological students from Emmanuel College, the United Church's theological coll[ege] there. They are giving me an Honorary Degree . . Doctor of Sacred Letters!! I take this as a vote of confidence re: the fundamentalist so-called Christians' many attacks on me, and believe me, I'm grateful. My address is all to do with the social gospel, and fighting vs the prospect of a nuclear war. It's be[en] v[ery] hard to write, naturally, as I feel so terribly strongly about these issues, and how to express with honesty and not too simply all these feelings? . . .

Love to you, Lulu, and all the kids. . . .

P.S.2. What a great experience to talk with Hubert on the phone the other day! He is nearly 90, and of course expects to be taken any time now to his ancestors, which he will. I said in my Intro what you'd said when you were a young man of about 36, about wanting when you grew up to be like Hubert. I said that at 56 I had the same feelings. I also . . save the day! . . quoted St. Paul re: Hubert . . . "I have fought a good fight; I have finished my course; I have kept the faith." And he has. He has.

61

MARIAN ENGEL

Lakefield, Ont.,
1 April 84

Dear Marian:

. . . The article on Bloomsbury folks is from the *N.Y. Review of
Books*,[1] and I really like the strong individual voice of the reviewer,
whose views of Bloomsbury tend to agree with my own, and
partly because I'm a Canadian who felt, years ago, somewhat
like a naive colonial girl in literary London, and came to resent
and then be amused by their attitudes . . . much later than
Bloomsbury but some of the same contempt for anything not
Brit was there in my time, although the upper-class Brit by that
time had all but vanished from the literary scene. It's
interesting . . . I've read Nigel Nicholson's book on his parents,
and a certain amount of the multitudinous material on the scene
of those days, and of course [Virginia Woolf's] books, although
none of [Vita Sackville-West's], and I feel, as I have always felt, a
profound sense of repulsion towards that group, not for their
sexual inclinations, heaven knows . . I couldn't care less . . but
for their amazing snobbism and hypocrisy, their malice and sheer
nastiness towards everyone in the world except their own little
clique. Their lack of generosity, their terror at standing up for
any principle, is mind-boggling. Poor Leonard Woolf must have
been heroic, although I guess his reasons were mixed also. I've
always . . well, for years, anyhow . . wondered what Virginia
would have done if there had been no one to look after her and
keep helping her in her periodic bouts of "madness". Maybe she
would have written better . . ? Those of us who have had to earn
our living and bring up our kids, virtually by ourselves, with a
lot of moral support from friends and colleagues, may well
ponder this. Personally, I think that a lot of women writers in
this country, whether with children or not, and whether with
mates or not, have been HEROIC. But one thing we have NOT
been is bloodless, and you know, Virginia's writing, much of
which I read long ago, never did strike a chord in my heart . . it
always seemed so cerebral, so bloodless. Which is not to say that
she didn't have magnificent gifts in terms of writing . . she did.

But she never chose to write about things closest to her own heart and spirit, and obviously I am not talking here about writing in any direct autobiographical way. I think a lot of Canadian women writers . . . quite frankly . . have been braver. The incredible snobbishness . . the almost unbelievable ignorance in that way . . of the Bloomsbury group . . . seems now to have been a very limiting thing in terms of their writing. I suppose it is an inability to know, really know, the reality of others. I read with suitable reverence, as was expected then when I was young, Virginia Woolf's books, and wondered why I didn't connect very much with them. Later, I saw why. They were written out of an exclusive spirit, not an inclusive one, and in some sense they were self-obsessed and unkind. We are not always kind, kid, nor should we be, but damn, we aren't exclusive!! And I believe that *caring* in the widest way does matter. And *principles* matter. This may be my Scots Presbyterian background . . if so, okay. Poor Radclyffe (sp?) Hall, thinking she might get some support, moral and vocal and financial, from those upper-class twits. Her novel was really a pretty awful one, in literary terms, but she fought her fight without the support she should surely have had. Of course, what bothers me most and always has, is that those were the people who thought they had a natural right to all the goodies of this world, and who thought they had a right not only to rule England but to be the supportive colonial force that ruled the Empire. I suppose I detest them both in a human sense and in a political sense. They thought they were superior in every way, and they did not *care* at all or feel any sense of responsibility. Creeps. . . .

Lakefield, Ont.,
18 May 84

Dear Marian—

. . . I find myself writing odd things, not a novel, more like things about my ancestral families, especially the women. History has been written, and lines of descent traced, through the male lines. More and more I want to speak about women (always have, of course, in my fiction, but now I want to get closer to my own experience . . not necessarily directly autobiog, but close, I guess). We will see. What stuns me, looking at my own family, is how pitifully little I know about the women, even my grand-

mothers . . . and how much about the men. Lost histories . .
perhaps we must invent them in order to rediscover them. . . .

Dear Marian—

. . . Had three days in Montreal last week. . . . Lovely, but a bit
hectic. Had dinner at a super restaurant, Les Filles du Roi, in the
old city, right beside the Sailors' Church. Can you imagine what
it must have been like for les filles du Roi? Some hulk saying,
"I'll take that one", or worrying that no one would! Ugh! Some,
I understand, took orders and became nun/teachers . . . can't
blame them. Our lives have been difficult, but at least we had
some true choices. So many of us, women writers, have chosen
to be married, at least for a time, and to have our kids and do our
work. I often think of us as heroines.

Much love. . . .

Lakefield, Ont.,
17 Sept 84

Dear Marian—

It was so good to talk with you on the phone yesterday. Your
voice sounded so strong. How alike women writers are, or so it
seems to me. Your practical arrangements with your study, and
plumbing therein, seemed so sensible. But then, we *are* sensible,
amidst everything else, aren't we? I think Jane Austen would
have loved us, but I suspect she might have been a bit in awe of
us, as well she might, we who have coped with having and
rearing our children, writing our books, earning our livings, and
not hiding the manuscripts under the desk blotter when the vicar
came to tea. Wild Emily, of the Brontës, wouldn't have understood
our practicality, as she had so little of it. Charlotte Brontë would
have understood, and yet I relate in some area of my heart more
to Emily than I do to Charlotte, although Charlotte was not only

more like I am, but also the better writer.

I didn't talk to you about two wonderful things that will happen this year .. the publication of Sylvia Fraser's novel, BERLIN SOLSTICE, and Tiff Findley's novel, NOT WANTED ON THE VOYAGE.[2] Both, in my view, quite brilliant. I rejoice.

God bless, dear friend and colleague. . . .

Lakefield, Ont.,
17 Nov 84

Dear Marian:

. . . on Thursday, Clara Thomas and I went to a performance of a 4-woman show called "Love and Work Enough", by a professional group Theatre Direct. It is about early pioneering women in Ontario, and the young women have done all the research, the putting together, the music, the choreography, etc etc, as well as the performance. It is superb! They have done other performances as well, and specialize in taking their plays to high schools. The entire group of Theatre Direct includes, of course, business and publicity managers, but it is still a small and to my mind very exciting venture. They got the title for this show from Clara's biography of Anna Jameson, "Love and Work Enough" . . . Anna's words, but of course the young women would never have found them had it not been for Clara's book, and they give graceful tribute to Clara in their program, which is nice and also right. York U got the show through the York Women's Centre, as part of a celebration of Person's Day. You know, Marian, that for the first three years of my life I wasn't a person. Naturally, I was not aware of this interesting fact, and doubt that my mother, my step-mother, and my aunts (not to mention my grandmothers) ever felt they were not persons, but in 1929 Canadian women got the official status of persons for the first time. Anyhow, the show was just so moving and also so funny . . . I literally laughed and wept the whole way through.

. . . I went out with a dear friend, last week, and bought myself a new cassette tape-recorder/radio. . . . I can record my voice if I want to, very simply, and I sometimes do this to send tape/letters to Hubert Evans, who is blind. . . . And oh joy, I can play all my old tapes. . . . I have marvellous tapes of old records, including tapes made from old 78's . . . Spanish Civil War songs,

65

songs sung by Woody Guthrie, Billie Holiday, Paul Robeson, West African highlife . . . as well as songs by young friends, over the years. . . . This little machine is quite easy to operate, and I really like her. I call my electric typewriter Pearl Cavewoman, as I think I told you (my family name being Margaret Wemyss . . Margaret meaning "a pearl" and Wemyss "a cave dweller"). I named my new little charmer Laurel Whortleberry, the plant badge of the Laurences (a sept of the clan MacLaren) being laurel, and the plant badge of the Wemyss family (a sept of the clan MacDuff) being whortleberry (whatever the hell whortleberry is!). I suppose I try to humanize machines, and perhaps, as with fictional attempts to do this with animals (of which I am as guilty as anyone else, in *Jason's Quest*), it is called "anthropomorphic". So what, I say. Laurel Whortleberry is just great.

God bless, and much love. . . .

Lakefield, Ont.,
12 Jan 85

Dear Marian—

. . . Jane Austen, the more I read her and think about her, was such a subtle and strong feminist! *In them days!* But those days, apparently so far back, are not so very different from our own. Is this not always the way? I think so. Strong women did always have the difficulties that Austen presents, and people like you and I have lived through that, too. With, I may say, totable [*sic*] success. We pass on a whole lot of things to the children, both female and male, or so I hope and pray and know. . . .

Much much love. . . .

P.S. Canadian-type crisis . . my furnace was off for 6 hours one day this week; it turned out that it had run out of fuel. I and a friend paced the floor, freezing. These mini-crises make us Canadians feel we are PIONEERS.

Lakefield,
4 April 75

Dear Hubert Evans—

Don Cameron has just written to me to say he had visited you. He gave me your address, and I thought I'd like to drop you a line to tell you how much I enjoyed MIST ON THE RIVER. . . .[1] I know [it] is gaining a whole new audience among young people—I was, in fact, told about the novel by a young friend who had been working in northern B.C. on archeological work and who found the novel extremely helpful in terms of attempting to form some kind of relationships with the local native people. It's a fine novel, full of the kind of insights we need to know about.

I'm sending you a couple of my books, in case you'd like them.

With all best wishes. . . .

Lakefield,
14 Nov 75

Dear Hubert:

I was delighted to talk with you on the phone the other day, and I would really love to have a copy of your book of poems [*Endings*[2]] when it comes out. . . .

I'm trying to get back to writing—I want to do a children's book, if I can, and may also try to get together a collection of essays, a few of the articles which I've written over the years. I've been doing so much travelling around recently that I haven't got any real work done. I'm going to stop, for awhile, going out to high schools and universities, etc—I feel I'm in danger of turning into a performer. I really just want to stay home and work and read. . . .

All the best. . . .

Lakefield,
28 Sept 76

Dear Hubert:

Thanks so much for sending me your book of poems. I love
them—and I mean that sincerely. You catch so many feelings and
experiences *just right*. I have a new book of essays [*Heart of a
Stranger*] (articles, really, many of them published throughout
the years here and there) which has just come out, and I'll send
you a copy when I get them. . . .
　　　. . . I'm out at the cottage now, looking at the river and
the trees which are turning colour. Yesterday streams of Canada
geese flew over—those beautiful eerie voices in the sky.
　　　I think you are marvellous to be clearing land and planting
trees. I think it is right to go on planting trees as long as one
can—it is a kind of act of faith, it seems to me. Keep up that and
the writing, Old Journeyman!

Affectionately. . . .

Lakefield,
17 Feb 77

Dear Hubert:

It seems a long time since I've written to you, and I hope you
will forgive the silence. I really loved the poems you sent me in
your last letter. They *speak* to me. I had news of you, a bit, a short
time ago, when an old friend of mine . . . went out to see you and
you were listening to the tape of THE DIVINERS. . . . Thanks. I
mean it.
　　　Amid all the difficulties of life, Hubert, there are some
things which are really joyful, and thank God I have experienced
them and continue to do so. I and my adult kids and their
respective mates went to England for Christmas, and I was lucky
enough to go to the Albert Hall for a carol service given by the
Royal Choral Society. It was fantastic. The Choral Society sang
the lesser-known carols, with great beauty, and the audience was
invited to stand and sing the well-known carols. Hark the Herald
Angels Sing. The First Noel. Once in Royal David's City. It Came

Upon a Midnight Clear. And so on. And that whole mighty audience, *thousands*, including me, rose and we sang our hearts out. It was magnificent. I could not see the printed words through my tears, but that was okay—I knew the words anyway. To me, the remembrance of Christmas in childhood, plus the sense of worship . . . in the midst of all the awfulness of our world, Hubert, I still believe that there is hope. I was thinking, that evening, of the hymn Old Hundred . . *All people that on earth do dwell/sing to the Lord with joyful voice* . .

I guess that sometimes I must connect in my heart not with all the problems of the world (although one cannot ever not connect with them) but with some of the simple/complex things, such as you write about, and when I see snow here, white, and look at the winter river, and recall how it will be, too, in the spring and summer . . then I think I thank God that it has been given to me to see these things. Of course, everything is very difficult and complicated, but maybe we do after all (as I think you have done) have to look closely at the details of our earth and give praise for what we have. . . .

Lakefield,
7 June 78

Dear Hubert:

I was thinking of you the other day, and thinking it was time I wrote to you, when lo and behold, the next day your book of poems [*Endings*] arrived. Thanks very much for sending it to me. I like the poems a lot. I like their sense of place and of harmony with the land and sea, and their sheer wisdom in this lunatic world. I also like the drawings, especially the ones of the forest.

After a very busy and tiring spring, at last I'm out at my summer cottage. I've only been here 3 days, but already I'm beginning to feel a bit renewed. The first few days, each summer, all I do is sit and look at the river and the trees, and begin to feel the winter's tensions easing up. A few weeks ago we had a heat wave, after a very cold and late spring, but now the weather is fine. The mosquitoes, alas, are flourishing.

I want to try, if possible, to get started on another novel. It is very difficult—I don't know if it is my own reluctance to take on another long haul, or simply the fact that I don't yet know enough about the characters. Both probably. . . .

Lakefield,
30 Oct 79

Dear Old Journeyman:

A copy of O TIME IN YOUR FLIGHT[3] reached me from Cannon-
books a week ago. I would have written sooner but I had to spend
all of last week in Toronto (known to me as the vile Metropolis)
on various business things. Hubert. . . . I am glad [Harbour
Publishing] decided to do it as a paperback, because that cuts
the price and it will sell better. But it is an *elegant* paperback, and
the presence of a dust jacket makes it almost like a hardbound
edition. I love the jacket picture, and . . . those delicate line
drawings of objects of the period are just right for the book.

My review came out in the [Toronto] *Star* last Saturday. . . .
I am going to give the book to dear friends and to my kids for
Christmas. . . . This book has *got* to be read by a whole lot of
people! But fear not—it will be. . . .

With love. . . .

Lakefield,
4 July 80

Dear Hubert:

Thanks so much for your letter . . . and for the tape, which I have
now played three times and enjoyed more each time. Gosh, it
was good to hear your voice! . . . Your voice is exactly the same
voice that I can *hear* in your letters and in your prose and poetry.
You do not have a "public persona", thank heavens. I don't think
I do, either.

Well, I have to admit that I was one (among MANY) of the
people who thought you must be an honorary Life member of
the Writers' Union. All of us, even the young sprouts of writers
who don't know this, owe you an awful lot, in terms of what you
have written and how you have persevered and been true to your
own principles and faith. . . . I honour and love you for it. . . .

I'm struggling hard, feeling good about my life, unhappy
about the world situation. It seems hard for me to find enough
time to get back really strongly into this new novel, but it will

come. I have just recently sold my cottage. It has been wonderful for 10 years, and I wrote most of THE DIVINERS there, but I think it has served its blessed purpose. I find it a bit of a hassle to have 2 places, and in 6 years I have come to love this village very much and to feel a part of this small community, so I don't need to get away. Also, the cottage was so much bound up in my mind with the writing of THE DIVINERS that I found I couldn't really write there any longer. This doesn't mean that if I manage to write another novel I'll have to sell up here in Lakefield! The cottage itself wasn't part of the novel, but that particular view of the Otonabee river really *was*, and that is the first time ever that the view I looked at, each time I raised my eyes from what I was writing, came into the writing naturally and as if meant to be. I think, too, I am trying to simplify my life in order to concentrate as much as I can on what is ahead, I hope.

I am sending you a tape of my convocation address in June at York University in Toronto. . . . Before, any convocation speech I ever gave was bound up with need for teaching more Canlit in our schools and universities, blah blah etc. Of course I still believe all that. But this time I felt I had to tell these kids how I myself was feeling right now, about the world, about life itself. . . . I suppose that is one reason I feel so much connection with you and your writing, because we are both, in our different ways, Christian radicals. Would you agree? To me, it seems that good works without faith isn't enough, as we all stand so much in need of grace. But "faith" without "good works" . . ie a sense of social responsibility and the belief that the world around us *is* our responsibility, seems to me to be . . if not an empty faith, then at least a faith lacking in some kind of human dimension, the recognition of the reality of others and of others' pain. Well, in about 2 weeks I'll be 54, Hubert. I hear you muttering "A mere tad". But I feel I've been awfully fortunate in my life, and have learned a lot from quite a lot of wise people, including you. I still have much to do . . as Robert Frost said, "and miles to go before I sleep." But however much of it I am given to do, I know (and this is so important) that the inheritors are there, my own real kids among them, and in a profound sense, *all* those young people are my children, and yours, and all of ours, in this strange but surviving tribe of ours, the story-tellers.

God bless you—

Dear Hubert:

... I haven't seen Kate Hamilton for a long time. ... her grandfather, Arthur Phelps, taught me at United College. He was a genius. He was one of the most inspiring, humorous, dedicated teachers this country has ever had.[4] When I was in 2nd year (it was my first year at college—Grade 12 in Manitoba then counted as 1st year), I very shyly but very determinedly approached Phelps and asked him how a person got to be a member of the English Club, which met monthly at his home. He invited me to come along. Hubert, I *did not know* at that time that hardly anyone had ever asked . . I guess you were supposed to wait until invited. But this girl from Neepawa knew she *had* to belong—my thirst for talking about literature with other people who were as passionate as I was on the subject was just boundless, I suppose. It was only a few years ago, some 33 years later, that I met someone who had belonged to [the] English Club at that time, and he told me that Phelps had told the senior students that there was a 2nd year student coming along . . and *they had better be nice to her*! Oh Hubert, I wish I had known before Arthur Phelps died— I would have liked to thank him. ...

Dear Hubert:

... Silver Don sent me a xerox of yr letter to him. ... You had asked him to do that. I'm really grateful for it. You say too many kind things about me, old Journeyman, though—it's from *you* I have learned a lot, and in a way what I seem to have learned from you, Hubert, and I hope I truly will learn it, in my own way, is a sense of grace. Yes. I think that's partly what I have indeed been writing about, all these years. A sense of the gift of God's grace, the sense of something *given*, not because deserved, of course, but because just given. That is how I have felt about my writing. Naturally, that does not mean mystical stuff and no work! God does not pick up the biro and write the words! But as

I grow older, Hubert, says the young one of nearly 56 now, I come to feel more and more a sense of true gift and grace, as far as my work is concerned. It *is*, however, my own responsibility, as a human being with a free will, to do with that as I can and as I choose. I think I've chosen to try to do whatever that gift of grace has made me think and write. But one is so far from *certain*, now. I think, Hubert, if I may say so, and maybe I have said so before, I cannot recall—at this point in your life, without at all ceasing from true work until you depart, it could be said of you (natch you will never say it of yourself), in the words of St. Paul, those mighty words . . "I have fought a good fight. I have finished my course. I have kept the faith." Perhaps, at the end of all our individual lives, as writers, as diviners, that is what we would hope for. . . .

As I grow older, which I seem to do daily (surprise surprise), it seems to me that I have to look at myself as a kind of very unorthodox Christian, but a Christian all the same. The social gospel is what seems to matter to me more and more. Why should any person say, as the fundamentalist born-again (?) Christians do, that saving *one's own* soul, by proclaiming Jesus as yr spiritual saviour, is ALL that is necessary in this life? Hubert, I am astounded and downcast by those guys, I tell you straight. This seems to me a totally blinkered view of a gospel that I feel very greatly drawn to, and responsible to. Given the fact (as I have to think of it, and probably so do you, as a Quaker who has connections and caring with the Unitarian church) that the Gospels were written in history, by people (men, not women, alack), some several hundreds of years after the man of Nazareth died, and that we have to look at those books as written by people in their historical time, as indeed we have to look at the Old Testament in the same way, it seems to me that what still comes across, throughout those thousands of years of history, is a message by a young Jew who was educated probably by the Essenes, and whose new doctrine was simply another commandment . . "Thou shalt love thy neighbour as thyself." Our Lord's Prayer, I think, says a lot of this, too, and it is a difficult prayer because some of its terms are (although said lightly, too often) very hard, very searching. Indeed, almost all of them. "Give us this day our daily bread". Does that mean what it says, as *I think*? or does it mean, give us twenty million bucks so we can lord it over the lesser breeds without our law? "Forgive us our trespasses, as we forgive the trespass against us". Do we really acknowledge what our trespasses have been, I sometimes ask, and do we really know how bloody hard it is to forgive those who have really hurt us? That is a difficult command, but a right one. It is appropriate to the human condition, in which we are honoured to find ourselves, that we should have these moral problems, or so it seems to me. Am I too much my ancestral Presbyterian ancestors? Oh shoot, I don't think so.

I'm writing—I think—a novel, or, as it may turn out, some stories. I no longer feel I have to run at full speed, re: my writing. I have to let it be. I do, however, feel that as a citizen in this damn awful world, I have to make a lot of statements about the state of the world. Which is awful. Hubert, you will be either pleased or touched, or both, to know that I belong to so many good causes you couldn't shake a stick at them all. This is no credit to me. It is just that I believe in so many things and feel we have to proclaim them, and work for them and (metaphorically speaking) fight for them. The one great problem in our world is, as I see it, the ignorance and lack of imagination of our so-called leaders about nuclear war. I feel it is *unthinkable*, totally, and must be seen to be unthinkable. With every breath, I have to proclaim my feeling about this unspeakable *evil* . . . the fact that some people (namely Reagan and his cohorts) feel that nuclear war is thinkable—how do they really imagine it will or would be, Hubert? Two thirds of the world's people killed, slaughtered? I have to say that I feel, as a long-time pacifist, that those people are very evil and do not know that what happens in any kind of a war, never mind a nuclear one, is that MANY PEOPLE DIE HORRIBLY BEFORE THEIR TIME.

Hubert, I worry. I set myself to fight all these things, in any verbal and non-violent way that I can. Non-violent is the key word. I understand all the terrible revolutions that have gone on in Africa and in South America, etc, and I understand, believe you me, the main difficulty of a liberal conscience such as mine. The main difficulty is—if you are faced with a fascist, authoritarian, relentless regime, how do you answer? Nicaragua is faced with a people's republic, having overcome, militarily, a right-wing oppressive (and Amer-backed) regime. America is determined to overcome that independent country, while at the same time giving many arms to [El] Salvador, in which a right-wing govt is killing lots of people every day, including outside church people, and Argentina, where the right-wing govt is every day making more and more people "disappear", i.e. be murdered. These are the terrible and fascist governments of S. Amer, but there is also the situation in Poland, where the so-called "left-

wing" govt is repressing a genuine trade union movement towards true union bargaining.

I feel, dear old friend, that I do not care whether the
repression and the terror and the horrible stuff is coming from
what is called the "left" or the "right". What I care about is that
awful things are happening, and I think we must speak out
against man's inhumanity to man, wherever it happens.

Hubert, I want so very much to tell some more people's
stories. Well, I think I will, or I will try. What seems to matter to
me, more than anything, is the individual stories of individual
human persons.

Because . . if you can't see and know one person, you can't
see or know humankind. Or so it seems to me.

God bless you, and for pete's sake, let's recall how much
the humour gives us grace. (I don't know who "pete" is . . maybe
St. Peter, at the Gates of heaven). . . .

Lakefield,
15 Feb 83

Dear Hubert:

. . . MOSTLY COAST PEOPLE[5] is just fine—I ordered and have
received an extra dozen copies which I am busily giving away to
friends who I know will understand what you are saying in the
poems. Thanks very much for the signed copy, which I will
cherish. Also, many thanks for your letter, which was very
touching indeed. When you say you wish you had done better
in your life, I want to cry out—and do cry out!—Hubert, you've
done so much and done it so well!!! Of course, we always think
that we could have done better, and I guess if we didn't think
that, we would be complacent and self-satisfied, so we're
lumbered with the feeling we should have done more. But I
wonder if you know how much you have given, in terms of
wisdom and a greater understanding of what really matters, to
one person, namely me? And to countless others. Also, talking
that day on the phone, the day of the Hubert Evans Celebration,
I was so struck with the affection and true admiration towards
you expressed by your son and daughter. Gee, Hubert, I have
always known, as you have known, that we must live as well as
write. One of the best things . . probably *the* best . . in my life is

75

the fact that I have a communicating and warm relationship with both my kids. . . . I consider myself to be blessed in that. . . .

I'm busy as always, and am doing a lot of work with the peace groups but I feel I *must*. Am getting into a new routine with my own writing . . blocking out 2 hours in the morning instead of trying to get in 4 or 5 hours on weekdays, which is unrealistic.

As always, with love and gratitude. . . .

The writing was superb because it delivered the honesty of Margaret Laurence. She came onto things from a woman's point of view that women, in my experience, had never dealt with successfully before. Things about sexuality. Things about being a woman in other ways that other people approach from a ranting point of view, or that other people approach such a subtle way that you might miss it if you weren't reading it for that reason. There are moments in Virginia Woolf like that. There are wonderful statements about being a woman in Virginia Woolf that you get because that's what she's doing. But the rest of her work is suffused with it. And you might not get it because you get caught up in the rest of what she's doing and she, in some ways, perhaps undermines the feminist aspect of what she's about by . . . clouding it, cloaking it, I don't know. . . . But Margaret, when she came to the subject of being a woman inside her writing . . . you didn't feel someone was shouting at you, but you sure as hell knew what she was saying. And that's the difference. It was this forceful grabbing you, and having her way with your mind without leaving it damaged but merely improved and opened.

Elm Cottage,
26 Oct 70

Dear Tiff—

. . . I thought THE LAST OF THE CRAZY PEOPLE[1] was an extraordinary piece of fiction . . the whole thing totally comprehensible, in the end, and the actions of everyone so thoroughly looked into, perceived, but with some kind of respect for them all, some—well, *delicacy*; does that sound odd? None could have acted otherwise; none were judged. I thought that as a novel it succeeded quite remarkably well. I thought THE BUTTERFLY PLAGUE[2] was closer to the younger generation's myth-legend-fiction than probably I can be; as a study in nightmares and dream/reality it is fascinating, disturbing. Probably its main difficulty (in terms of connecting with readers) is that it falls between two (supposed) categories . . . it isn't quite the dream/myth/legend fiction of the young, because the people in it are individuals, with faces and personalities; yet it is also not the novel of strong individual character/narrator which is typified by a great deal of contemporary N. Amer fiction (mine included). It is, I think, in the mainstream of a certain kind of European fiction of the past 30 or 50 years .. which maybe began with Kafka, and has gone on, through a kind of allegory/folk-tale form (actually, I have just read Jerzy Kosinski's STEPS,[3] and it seemed to me that this novel was so much rooted in Europe and way back in folk tale, where the characters have roles but no faces). Being v. much N. Amer, you have to bring individuality into your novel, and this makes it a kind of hybrid .. which, Tiff, is fine. There *must* be room in this world for lots of different kinds of novels. I thought THE BUTTERFLY PLAGUE connected pre-war Europe with Hollywood, in a bizarre and peculiar way, and I think it worked.

Motto for the day: SCREW ALL REVIEWERS. They never seem to know, or only a few. Hells bells, I just got a batch of reviews about a kids' book I wrote [*Jason's Quest*]. Reviews from Canada. All took the book seriously, A POTENTIAL CANDIDATE FOR A CHILDREN'S CLASSIC, said one. BRILLIANT NOVELIST FLOUNDERS IN JUVENILE FIELD, said another, enquiring why the allegory, etc. Heavenly days, and I wrote the christly thing only for fun. Let us be calm. . . .

God bless. . . .

Here was the first, in my experience, successful depiction [of sexual matters] that had ever been written by a woman. The one kind of writer that most people believed would be incapable of writing about sex successfully. And it wasn't that there wasn't the necessary lyrical distance between reality and the written . . . that is what art is about. Margaret had that in spades. This isn't mundane achievement. It's really the depiction of mundanity.

Elm Cottage,
30 Dec 72

Dear Tiff—

. . . Glad the Writers' Union is getting off the ground—I'm 100% in favour, as no doubt Graeme [Gibson] and Peggy [Atwood] told you. She is, I think, brilliant as a writer, and I also love her as a person. Guess she does sometimes take some getting to know—it just happened that she and I have so much in common in many areas that we hit it off okay from the start. Maybe it helped that we met for the first time in the ladies' john of Govt House in Ottawa! Such a bizarre first meeting could only be a good omen!

Finished first draft of my novel last summer and am now typing first draft—it is much too long and am trying to cut and re-shape as I go along, but it is still hugely long, alas. I've stopped worrying about this. If it is long, it's long, and that's that. I have astounded myself recently by composing 3 songs for it—in the persona of a Manitoba Métis of about my age! Don't faint! Actually, this guy (Jules "Skinner" Tonnerre) is part of the Métis family which I've now known in fiction for 4 generations, so I feel I know them all pretty well. They appear in all my Canadian writing (except, I think, *A Jest of God*) . . . I really need 2 more songs (1 more by Jules and 1 by his daughter, who is also the daughter of the novel's protagonist, Morag Gunn) but I dunno if they will be given to me. Also unsure of writing in the idiom of a generation younger than myself, altho christ knows I've heard thousands of the kids' songs from young Canadians visiting here, not only from records. . . .

Much love to you and Bill. . . .

By the time you hit the early 1970s, when Margaret came back to Canada from England, and became a physical presence to us here, as well as everything else, it was like turning around and suddenly realizing, the room is full of people—I'm not in here alone. But the symbolic moment—and it is far more than symbolic, it is the moment—[is] when the Writers' Union was being formed. . . . You're talking about a moment when clarification was happening. All the crystals stopped being diffuse and started to gather and have a shape.

We had in our midst, by the mid-1970s, Margaret Laurence, Pierre Berton, W.O. Mitchell, the Callaghans, and the MacLennans. We had in the world of poetry the Webbs and the Avisons and the Laytons and the Purdys. There was Alice Munro. There was Mordecai Richler. There was Leonard Cohen. There was Marie-Claire Blais and Gabrielle Roy. And they were all there in that moment. And the top of the heap and the person everyone chose [for] a symbolic chairman who would say it for everybody was Margaret. It was unanimous. You couldn't possibly think of anybody else.

Lakefield, Ont.,
1 May 75

Dear Tiff—

... I got a letter from Andy Schroeder this morning, and he mentions the same tribal feeling. I think it's terribly important, and I think the Union has made all of us very much aware of it. And I agree—it's not a competitive profession. Which is why we are able to be generous to one another—the best reviews these days, of novels, are written by other novelists, who don't feel they have to prove their critical acumen (sp?) by ripping a book to shreds. Personally, if I hate a book, I won't review it. I do, however, think that critics are necessary to point out really bad books, and to maintain some kind of public standards. But it's not our role to rip each other apart, and you notice how damn few writers *do* damage one another in this way. I think one of the most important things about the Union, truly, has been that the sense of tribehood among us has really extended coast-to-coast, for the first time, I think.

Anyway, Tiff, when Adele Wiseman and I were both young and working on our first novels, we used to communicate by letter all the time. She was in Italy, and lived in a house owned by 2 old Italian ladies, who, when Adele was discouraged, used to say to her .. "Corragio! [*sic*] Avanti!" It became our rallying cry to one another.

So, dearest Tiff—Courage! Forward! (and you *will*)....

Lakefield, Ont.,
5 Nov 81

Dear Tiff—

Thanks so much for sending me the (2nd) copy of FAMOUS LAST WORDS.[4] It's a splendid novel! First, your handling of your chosen form is elegantly done—the "present" (ie 1945) interweaves with the past like a kind of counterpoint, never detracting from Mauberley's story, but, rather, commenting on it, questioning it, and bringing up the serious moral issues involved in it. Your use of so-called "real" people as fictional characters is done with great skill and authenticity .. all those vapid, shallow, frivolous, scheming, sinister characters in their various stances towards one another and towards life in general. Your fictional speculations re: the Windsors are fascinating, and the Duke himself comes across very much as he must have been, poor sod. Wallis is another kettle of fish entirely—a truly sinister woman, finally, who could comfortably contemplate being queen at whatever price.

Of course it is the character of Mauberley himself who is the most compelling. This character (like so much of the book) seems to me to serve as a dreadful warning to us all. An intelligent, talented character who is personally ambitious and with a large streak of weakness and moral blindness in him, can be used, as Mauberley is used, by the forces of true evil. Naturally, we all hope we don't have *any* streaks of weakness or moral blindness in us, but everyone does, in some way or other and as Mauberley unfolds his story it becomes horrifyingly clear that he is being sucked into the Nazis' sphere *almost without realizing it* for a long time. Writers are especially vulnerable to being "used" in a variety of ways, as we all know. I have lent my name and given money to more good causes than you could shake a stick at, and I always try to be extremely careful to ascertain the exact nature of the cause, but this process has taught me how careful we must be. This does *not* of course mean supporting *no* causes . . that would be moral blindness indeed. Mauberley's story shows, in fact, that someone who takes no definite moral stance is guilty of a conspiracy of silence. In bearing witness to his times, he also at the end is bearing witness to his own complicity with the fascists. He failed to *care* enough about others, he failed to realize the true *reality* of others, and that is fatal for a writer and for his relationship to life itself. Engrossed in his own petty concerns, he had no feelings towards the sufferings going on in the war, in the death camps, everywhere except those tiny sheltered falsely glittering spots where he himself was. Of course, as he had no real concept of goodness, he also had no real concept of the reality of evil, that cruelty towards others which has no recognition of the others' humanity, their human-ness. The counterpoint of the arguments engaged in by Quinn and Freyberg are done with marvellous complexity. Of course there is something to be said for both stances. Quinn is by far the most sympathetic character, and yet and yet. . . . I know myself the dangers of the small-l liberal approach. I have been aware of them for over 35 years. We are too easily satisfied; we tend to have impulses towards forgiving and forgetting . . . but some things are unforgivable and if one forgets, they are there, waiting to emerge. In this way, I have considerable sympathy with Freyberg's last appearance, when he kicks Quinn.

Anyway, Tiff, it's a complex and powerful book, and I thank you for it. I'm honoured to be one of those to whom it is dedicated. . . .

Because she was a giant. . . . Margaret was so earth-bound. I loved dancing with her. I love the image of that; the dance on the earth is the image of Margaret rising from the ground where she was so firmly planted. When she walked, it was her flat-footed prairie walk. "I'm going there," said that walk. Or "I'm sitting here". . . . She was like that glorious painting of Gertrude Stein by Picasso. The impact was that it altered every Canadian writer's attitude to what they were doing. Not utterly defined, and not defined alone, by Margaret Laurence, but clarified by Margaret Laurence's presence.

Lakefield,
8 Jan 82

Dear Tiff—

Further to our phone discussion, I now write this letter. . . .

You have doubts about FAMOUS LAST WORDS. You think I have doubts about it. Quite right. You have attempted to grapple with prime matters, good and evil, and probably you have not entirely succeeded. Does anyone? As I said to you on the phone, even Milton didn't entirely succeed. The important thing is the grappling. If I could take issue (which I could) with some things in FAMOUS LAST WORDS, that is to your honour. You raise issues which *demand* to be talked about, not hidden, not ignored. And you do it via people who are living fictional characters as well as people who were so-called "real" people, and that is some accomplishment, believe me.

. . . I think it is a fantastic effort to cope with prime matters, and if I would take issue with some of it, it is because I myself have to try to cope with Good and Evil in my own life and in my writing. These things are not simple, as you know. But to try to grapple with the most important issues, plus trying to create human individuals on the printed page—this is the real role of a novelist. You have seen this terrible and awfully responsible role and have taken it upon yourself, as few have. Do we really succeed? I guess not. But we keep on trying. You are among the few who *see* what we have to try *for*.

With love and hope and (believe me) love
for your work. . . .

If you say the word "stylist" you immediately think, well, style is decoration or style is radical . . . a radical way of presenting material. But the stylistic achievements of someone like Margaret Laurence I don't think are acknowledged enough because, by God, did that woman ever work. She worked terribly terribly hard to achieve articulation that was as precise as the voice inside her. . . . She really did work hard at the precision and that is style—to capture the voice exactly.

Lakefield,
15 Jan 82

Dearest Tiff—

. . . I am grappling with this novel (?) of mine like Jacob with the Angel of the Lord. I wonder how many false starts would put me into the Guinness Book of Records. Maybe *this* time I'll progress beyond Chapter One. Reason you couldn't reach me— a) turned phone off on the Saturday; b) Sun I was on phone nearly all day; c) Mon–Wed—I was in Ottawa. Back now to switching phone off in work hours but phone is always on between 9 AM & 10 AM, & after 3 pm until about 7 pm (usually on in evenings, too, but if I'm exhausted I switch it off and retire.)

Much love, dear brother—

Lakefield,
9 Nov 83

Dearest Tiff—

I do hope you will understand—I'm not going to be able to go into T.O. [Toronto] for the premiere [of *The Wars*⁵] tomorrow. The reason is that for months and months I have been into T.O. once a week for various good causes in which I believe, or business of one kind or another. . . . So if I went . . . tomorrow for the film and reception, that would be indeed 4 days out of my week, which alas still has only 7 days. Plus a National Film Board crew will be here on Saturday . . . to interview me for a film they are doing on Women and Peace. I couldn't say No to that—I care too much about the whole peace movement and the dire (and getting more dire) threat of nuclear war. . . . I have just written a fund-raising letter for Project Ploughshares (inter-church peace and disarmament organization) and another for Artspace in P'borough, and on Nov 21 I'm going to T.O. to take part in a fund-raising dinner for Lynn McDonald, NDP federal member for Broadview-Greenwood, because I think it's very important that she gets in again at the next fed election. This is only a *fraction* of my activities, my dear! So I just feel I can't go to the film. I DO want to see it, *naturally*, and will, as soon as it reaches P'borough on general release. . . . You know, one might say that I should not be doing all this stuff . . I should just stay home and write. But I conceive of my role in life to be not only that of writer, but also citizen, parent, friend, etc. I know you will agree. It's just that sometimes there isn't enough time for everything. . . .

Her vision was really immense. She told us the whole of a world. The only other writer I can honestly say I believe has done that in this country is Alice Munro.

Lakefield,
25 Nov 83

Dear good Tiff and Bill—

. . . Your schedule, Tiff, sounds just gruelling . . . all those readings; the PR stuff for the film, and on and on. Gosh, I don't know how you do it. Well, I do know. We do what we have to do, and somehow, miraculously, we get through it. . . . and then people say to us "My goodness, aren't you lucky that you're never nervous!" When you said in your letter, Tiff, that you could feel my hands trembling, I was so moved. Yes, yes, they do, and my knees knock and I shake all over with fear when I have to do a public speech or reading, etc. Lucky for me, I have learned how to cope. I have to have a lectern that is strong and upon which I can lean . . . even a hand on *something* will restore me. I deliver as many talks and so on, sitting down, as is humanly possible. I don't suppose I'll ever get over that kind of nervousness. One just learns to cope, that's all. I always think, however, that I am blessed in one way—I can absolutely rely on my voice, which never shakes. Thanks God, Sir or Madam! But your *understanding* of the fact that these goddam public appearances ain't easy for me—I can't tell you what that meant to me. It just meant so very very much. Also, your understanding that I'm not sitting here in my village, on my butt, doing nothing, but am in fact doing things that I feel I must, things to which I feel a deep sense of commitment. It was really so heartening to hear from you, Tiff, in that regard. Because I'm so involved with things outside the literary community, I sometimes have the fairly desolate feeling that many of my fellow writers don't know I'm active at all. Thanks dear friends.

I'm so glad the film premiere went well. Don't thank me for the contrib[ution] to Parkinson's Foundation. As I told you, I put up Jim [Sinclair] Ross's name for the Order of Can, and we will just have to put it up again . . we will mount a campaign in 1984, I hope.[6] He doesn't want money, as I told you. He would be grateful for some recognition. Of course, he already had a lot of recognition in his own country, but he finds it hard to know that, really know it. Very very sad. A very brave man and a great writer.

. . . I'm writing very different stuff now. Seems absurd, but one writes what is given. I'm writing a few songs, with no musical training. How embarrassing, in a way. . . . I've got a swell voice in church, to belt out the old and noble hymns, with the organ and the congregation. A different matter when singing alone, with the old tobacco voice! However, we will see. There are so many things I want to do, and am doing, but not enough time, as you rightly say. What I'm hoping to find one of these days is a young woman who plays guitar and who might not intimidate me and who might agree to listen for awhile and maybe. . . .

Much love to you both. . . .

P.S. Am enclosing a copy of OLD WOMEN'S SONG.[7] Folk songs, I guess, are composed by folks who aren't very knowledgeable or sophisticated. The tune isn't bad, either. Or so I think. . . .

She was a very spiritual woman. And I'm not going to deny that's a connection we have. Her spiritual world was far more formalized than mine is. There was a focus that had to do with the church, in other words, and with religion, and I don't have that. But the spiritual sense of things was shared.

Lakefield,
14 Aug 84

Dear Tiff—

. . . I enclose the Tender Message [dust jacket blurb] I've done for NOT WANTED ON THE VOYAGE. . . .[8] It's a splendid novel, Tiff! I would like to write something longer about it one day, although not a review when it comes out . . . something more considered and perhaps that may come to pass. I loved it. I loved your sense of the phoney quality of so much "organized" religion, especially the literal-minded, and your sense of outrage at the cruelties that have been done in the name of a god, religious or secular, throughout the ages. I loved Mrs. Noyes and I loved Mottyl . . . brave, brave and loving. There is so much in the novel that one is almost at a loss to do a T[ender].M[essage]. . . . I did 5 drafts, I need hardly say. In my experience, however, a long T.M. is virtually useless. What one wants to do in a few words is to say . . "hey, read this!" I read it non-stop and it took me 2 days and I am a fast reader. It is, quite simply, a wonderful novel. I know now why you call your writing-house Arkwright. There are playwrights and shipwrights and from time to time arkwrights. You probably called it that in hope and with considerable misgivings. You've done it! It's a fine novel. . . .

Lakefield,
13 Sept 84

Dearest Tiff—

. . . I don't know if you've seen my article on censorship in Sept

Toronto Life. I enclose a copy.[9]

I have just listened to you on CBC, the phone-in program on censorship. . . . I think you are *heroic!* Some of the callers were incoherent but well-meaning; some were incoherent and awful; some were quite intelligent and very supportive of *our* general views. There are lots of rednecks out there, though—& lots of them really hate us. You were *great.* Isn't it strange how many people said *"of course* I'm against censorship" & then went on to support *every* form of censorship! It must have been *so* difficult to respond to those phone-ins. As you will see from my article, I'm in agreement with everything you said. . . .

. . . I'm working like crazy on an article for a feminist journal "Canadian Woman Studies"—the theme of this upcoming issue is "Women in the Future"—gulp! So far, 6 drafts! . . .[10]

Life is hectic, as always.

Love. . . .

P.S. . . . Remember Isherwood's book "I Am A Camera"?[11] I should write one titled "I Am A Stress Situation". . . .

The psychological effect of that whole [censorship] episode, both those episodes [1976 and 1985] on Margaret Laurence was devastating. . . . It was evil-minded. It was an evil-minded thing to do to a great spiritual creature, let alone a great spiritual piece of work [The Diviners].

8 Sept 86

Dear Tiff:

Got your letter today. . . . I am keeping up my Journal, and I have typed about 35 pp of 2nd draft of memoirs, which I am determined to get done. I am, of course, still in hospital but hope to be home sometime this week. . . .

I am really determined to get these memoirs into 2nd draft, after which Jocelyn can do further editing until they are in submittable shape. Turns out I have cancer of kidney and one lung, too far advanced for treatment except palliative. Prognosis is about 6 months, although they can't say definitely, one way or another, of course. . . .

No sympathy, please. I do know that my friends' thoughts, and indeed many people's, are with me, and I am grateful, believe me. I am so lucky that my children are adults and that I have lived to do the lifework that was given to me to do. The best anyone can do would be to write from time to time altho I may not reply, as saving energy for memoirs.

Please, dear Tiff, when I depart, tell the writing community that I DO NOT WANT A MEMORIAL FUND ESTABLISHED IN MY NAME!!!!!!! In the heat of the moment, this is done, and then there is a very real difficulty to maintain and deal with same. If people feel moved monetarily, when the time comes, please make my wishes known, at that time. Tell them to give a donation to one of the following: Project Ploughshares; Energy Probe; the Marian Engel Award Fund. I will tell my kids this as well. I feel not too bad at all, which is kind of odd. I wish to heavens I could go home, tho. . . .

Don't worry. I am getting excellent care. I am not sinking into the slough of despond, nor do I intend to. Odd, you know, from being here, where there are so very many old women, chronic care patients, I can now see (as possibly I didn't quite, or not entirely, before) that I did get it right in THE STONE ANGEL. . . .

I read her work initially without thinking much of questions of gender at all. It didn't occur to me there was anything different about her work from any of the other great writers that I've ever read, like Virginia Woolf or Conrad or Faulkner. . . . It's just that in retrospect I look back and I see this strange web of women characters and there hadn't been that many strong women writers in Canada, in fiction—Martha Ostenso, Gabrielle Roy. . . . And as a man I just identified with Margaret as a wonderful writer. But for young women looking at her . . . marginalized or disenfranchised or having lost their language, she must have had an even greater impact.

Elm Cottage,
26 Jan 73

Dear Gary—

. . . Got your letter yesterday and have sent a note to Michael Macklem [Oberon Press] saying it is quite okay to use quote on dustjacket. Thanks much for sending *rivers inlet*,[1] some of which I think I have read, but have only just glanced at it, on account of I am in a state of terrible concentration over this novel, which I have just 2 days ago got into typescript, from the 28 large scribblers full of something, which took me 1 1/2 years to write. The 2nd draft has been much cut and rewritten from the 1st, but still have a lot of work to do on it and do not think I can leave it at all, even for a day, until it is done. Have seen no one—won't have any friends left probably. . . .

Sorry for this brief communication, but am just about at end of psychic energy, re: novel, and am just having to hold self together in order to get it done.

God bless—

ps. it's a crazy damn novel—I've even written 4 songs for it!

We got talking about her work and I asked her if she would do me a favour and read me her favourite passage from The Diviners, *and it*

turned out that it was also my favourite passage. And she read it in the
broadest Scots accent you can imagine. Piper Gunn's Lament. And I
just sat there. I think both of us were blubbering by the end of her reading.
The whole conversation, all evening after that, for four or five hours,
was conducted in the broad Scots. . . . We went through the novel out
into some other kind of terrain in which we had an enjoyable and much
lighter, sillier time of it.

Lakefield, Ont.
4 Feb 85

Dear Gary—

. . . It [*The Terracotta Army*] is a splendid book . . a poem. It is, in
some ways, like MASTER OF THE HORSE.[2] Maybe your true talent
is to connect with some of those ancestral people and give them
to us. Gary, it really is so good. . . . the poem-cycle for the China
figures is a NOBLE one. You have done some wonderful stuff,
but in my view, Gary, the MASTER OF THE HORSE and the CHINA
poems are your best. I am stunned and awed and this is so good.

God bless you and yours,

In the end, I ended up saying to her exactly what she'd said to me over
the years: "Look, you talk about me being distracted. You've got to learn
to say no. You've got to get on with the work that will be most important,
and that is your fiction." I think she was getting to be of two minds by
then. I think she realized that perhaps she'd done her major work and
that time and health considerations would, perhaps, prevent her from
doing any other major work. . . . But she still had the sense of anxiety
about it. . . . Like a ballerina. You know, "My body tells me I will not be
a good dancer and I do not want to go into decline. So I will get on and
help other people apprentice." That would have been fine, but I don't
think she felt terribly easy about that. That was more or less the direction
she was taking. It was a rich period for us to have her doing that, I
think. I just know of so many people that she was supportive of.

Elm Cottage,
3 Nov 72

Dear Graeme—

. . . Thanks much for yr letter, and I am glad you both [Margaret Atwood] will be in Van on UNION BUSINESS. Hope all goes well. Glad to hear that Rob[ertson] Davies is in favour—I expected he would be.

. . . Began work on novel again three days ago. It is, to be frank, a MESS. The basic material is there, all right, but what I had forgotten was that I worked out the (ultimately involved) form by a kind of do-it-and-see-what-happens way, so that the first quarter of the draft is in strange shapes, if indeed any shape at all. All this is fine, really—just confirms my already-strong feeling that A Lot of Work remains to be done. I reckon I need: a cook-housekeeper, a daily woman twice a week for cleaning, and a gardener, all loyal unpaid slaves. However, in their absence, I try to juggle all these things with a minimum of time and effort, and to keep at the novel mostly. Also, I would like a secretary to cope with all my business letters. The only writers I've ever heard of who had all these various helpmates were invariably members of the Eng upper classes. We soldier on, cussing somewhat.

All well here, really. Odd, though. I love this place, but in my head I now live in Canada, I suppose—keep wishing I were there, not here. It will come to pass, and not too long in the future.

Love to you both. . . .

ps. have to write a review of Peggy's novel [*Surfacing*] for *Quarry*[1] . . wish now I had done it before leaving Can—not that it is a chore, but simply because I should have written it when I first read the novel, instead of after reading it twice. Am now in doubt that I can in any way do justice to the novel, in a review. That is *some* novel.

ps. Graeme, it doesn't sound facile to me when you say you were glad to meet me this summer. It's just that wordsmiths expect too much out of words while at the same time realizing only too

91

clearly the words' limitations. I know what you mean, all right. I feel the same, as I have about every member of my tribe whom I value and care about.

When you take a look at her books, in some strange way, instead of getting the first full book out like so many people, the one most easily identified with, she did it totally the other way round. She did the African novels, and she moved back and closed these things off, closed off alternatives. I'm not saying intentionally. I'm not even saying this is right, but [it's] almost as if she starts in Africa and comes back into writing The Diviners, *writing that becomes more and more personal, and when she gets there, what's she going to do? She felt herself that with* The Diviners *she was writing her last book, which was also a self-fulfilling prophecy.*

Elmcot,
10 Nov 72

Dear Graeme—

. . . Novel going ahead great guns—have got 80 pp typed in last 1 1/2 weeks, and altho this will still need rewriting, at least some rewriting has been done in process. I begin to feel that maybe perhaps just possibly I might have a novel here. Am very happy and working very hard and not seeing anyone—seems like a good life, at the moment. Have also worked out a Foolproof Plan for running this huge castle single-handed—I clean ONE THIRD of it every week, for one half day. That is all. It isn't all clean at the same time, but my Presbyterian Conscience is placated sufficiently and I am spending most of my time where I want to spend it, on novel. This sense of well-being may not last—my next letter may be all Black Celt, but for now, things are looking up. . . .

Elm Cottage,
23 May 73

Dear Graeme—

. . . Glad to know Writers' Union is coming along. Would just love to attend conference 15th June, but no way. But you have my 100% support, I need hardly say, and I anxiously await news of how things are shaping up. Also tell me how I pay my dues and get my union card. I do hope ultimately to be able to do a fair amount of slog-type* work for the Union, once I'm settled in P'borough.

. . . I'm excited about the thought of moving back permanently—I think I'll settle in Lakefield, altho not, probably, in CP Traill's house there! . . .

Love to you and Peggy. . . .

*or even non-slog-type work—I never think I'm any good in organizations, and this is *not* a female-inferiority thing, but rather the unwillingness to learn about negotiations etc. except where these affect my own personal work and relations with publishers and agents, in which case I am a pretty good business woman. But we'll see. Anyway, I'm willing to do whatever appears that I can do for the Writers' Union, especially in between books—I guess that condition holds for us all.

I don't think she instilled that sense [of tribe], but she certainly embodied it. And I think from the very beginning there was a strong sense in the union that it was right and proper we were doing this [forming the union]. . . . She was the first titular chairwoman, before we had our founding meeting. We needed someone to go through that and she did that quite happily. She wouldn't do it again, nor would she do it when it involved a lot of public postulating and negotiating, because she hated that. She literally would tremble. But she was quite happy to be symbolic, and I think she wanted to be symbolic.

R.R. 11,
Peterborough, Ont.,
29 Aug 72

Oh Harold—!!

Full marks to you, for your Moose Collection! I was talking to
Clara Thomas on the phone today, as I had sent her, too, a
collection of my Moose garnerings, and she said quite rightly
that the way in which one could judge whether or not a book
was truly Canadian was whether or not one could put the word
moose in there, in a crucial place. *Moose To The Laundromat* is
absolutely fine; as is *Never Cry Moose* and *Death Goes Better With
Moose*, and *The Ecstasy of Rita Moose*, and *The Moose and The Valley*,
and *Moose At The Close*, and *The Moose That Ends The Night*. Oh
wow. This is, however, a game which can only be played by those
who *know*. Last wkend, Edith Fowke (great folk-song person;
distinguished folklorist, etc, and a great member of the old Left)
was here with her husband . . . I read them my Moose list—well,
Harold, all I can say is that there was a deadly silence. She knows
everything about Can and other folk-songs, but about books she
don't know. So my clever hilarity fell on deaf ears. It was then I
realized that [Eli Mandel's] game is only suitable for Our Tribe,
brother.

Oh heavens . . *Sunshine Sketches Of A Little Moose* is really
fine!

In re: *Place D'Moose*, how about (God bless Scott Symons)
Civic Moose? And thinking of Scott with love and gratitude, how
about *Heritage: A Romantic Look At Early Canadian Moose*?

I thought of *Who Has Seen The Moose*, after I wrote you.
Also, *Jake And The Moose*.

Harold, it is absolutely Essential that we compile a
Dictionary of Canadian Moose. Probably Eli has it patented. How
about *The Rich Moose; The Moose And The Lamp; The Double Moose;
Sarah Moose*? And did I, in my letter, say *St. Urbain's Moose; The
Incomparable Moose; Son Of A Smaller Moose*?

It can get to be an addiction. . . .

Best. . . .

R.R. 11,
Peterborough, Ont.,
17 Sept 72

Dear Harold—

... Please don't feel compelled to answer this letter right away, Harold—I'm afraid that one drawback of having me as a correspondent is that when I receive a letter from a true member of my tribe, I often feel I want to sit down right away and reply— it's like talking to them. I sometimes think of my typewriter, in this area, as my radio transmitter, through which I'm sending out messages to people of my own kind, and receiving messages back. I recall writing to Al Purdy just after Martin Luther King was murdered, saying something like "Are you still there?", because it felt like chaos and night were descending. He knew what I meant. I guess that letters, to me, are a kind of sustenance, a way of being together with friends whom I can't see all that often, for geographical reasons. Anyway, don't let me impose on you in this way, will you? I would guess you probably feel much the same about letters as I do, tho. . . .

Have been reading *The Foxes of Beachy Cove*,[1] which is fascinating. It must take a hell of a lot of patience to watch wild creatures like that. . . .

My energy is at absolute rock-bottom level, after finishing the first draft [of *The Diviners*]. I was still kind of hyper last weekend, but the letdown came after I came back here, and this week I have done very little except reading and river-watching. . . .

Love, and God bless. . . .

When I read [A Jest of God], *because the schoolteachers were all so vividly portrayed there, and the various types of schools and the various people, I asked Margaret if she had ever taught school. She said, "Oh no. Those were things that I remembered from my own childhood, teachers that I had when I was nine years old." I said, "Well, you certainly drew on them very vividly," and she said, "Oh, I have a novelist's memory."*

Elm Cottage,
14 Nov 72

Dear Harold—

... I would love to go to Beachy Cove next summer, and if you
are there, certainly will. The summer may be pretty relaxed for
me, if I can get this goddamn novel finished and typed out.

Yeh, I agree re: Al [Purdy], I need hardly say. I think
Peggy's [Margaret Atwood's] poetry is extremely terrific, but it
is more cerebral than I can always take. With Al's stuff, you
somehow get the whole man. . . .

I have been working pretty hard on the novel, and have
got about 85 pp of typescript done. Am cutting out a lot of the
crap as I go along, but probably much rewriting will remain to
be done. I sometimes feel very happy, and have faith that there
really *is* a novel there. Other times, doubt gloom uncertainty etc.
I am interested in this character in the novel, Harold, but I am
not at all sure that many other people will be. This is not false
modesty, I need hardly say. But she is a middle-aged female writer
(not me, but related in many ways of course) and I am only too
aware that I'm on dangerous ground. Actually, I now see, her
being a writer is really only a means of getting at the ways in
which our ancestors stalk through our lives, the ways we make
myths of our parental figures and even of our own lives, the ways
in which we see ourselves turning into ancestors and myths. But
as I don't explain any of this, will anyone see it? I sometimes
think not. No fault of the reader—I don't mean that. But simply—
is it clear enough? Who knows? Not me, at this point. But I'm
happy when I'm working on it, so for the moment maybe that's
enough. . . .

Elm Cottage,
9 Feb 73

Dear Harold—

HURRAH, HALLELUJAH AND MAZELTOV! My novel is finished!

Well, maybe not entirely finished. I have done the typescript
which was really the second draft, as I rewrote and cut vastly

while doing it. I then thought I would put it all away for about a month, but of course did no such thing. Got it out the following day and began re-hashing it, this is now the third time through. I have now done everything I feel I can do for the moment, and my daughter is typing it for me in fair copy. I know that it needs more work, but cannot see what to do at the moment, or else I just don't feel strong enough. I think I need an editor to see it, and to say what I probably already know—that the parts set in the present time are too long, and various other flaws which I will not bore you with. Anyway, the worst (or best, I guess) time is over. If the English publishers (and, save the day, even the Amer publishers) turn it down, I will not be one whit surprised. If the Can publishers turn it down, I won't kill myself, either. It had to be written, and parts of it *do* come across and other parts don't come across so well, and that is the way it has always been and always will be. I could write two very intelligent reviews of this novel—one totally damning it and the other totally favour-able, and both would be valid. Ambiguity is everywhere. . . .

Anyway, Harold, I am terribly happy and also terribly nervous about this novel. I suggested to Joc that maybe she could type it blindfold, so as not to read it, but she did not, funnily enough, think that would be such a good idea. I'm ecstatic at the thought that the bloody thing is down on paper, and that I've actually written 4 songs, which I desperately wanted to do but never thought I could until much encouraged by Ian Cameron [who composed music for the songs] to have a go. And yet—migod, what if it does not speak to anyone but myself? Don't comfort me with kind words—you know as well as I do that one just does NOT KNOW at this point. We will see. . . .

I have writ 22 letters in last 2 days, many of them to odd people who write me about various things, but some to dear friends, which are the letters I really want to write.

Morale is high, but I feel a bit let down, too. This will be the last Manawaka fiction, as all the threads are tied in this novel, or the wheel comes full circle, or something. I feel a kind of emptiness, as I shall miss those people quite a lot. They have lived in my head for so long. . . .

*I remember her saying, "I've got this book finished [The Diviners].
I've got all the real revisions done that I need to do on it." This was long
before it was ready for publication. And she said, "Now all I've got to
do is go through it and cut out all the bullshit." Those were her exact*

words, which meant that all the extraneous stuff had to go. I don't know what she did with her extraneous stuff. I know what happens to some people's. It winds up in the archives.

Lakefield,
27 June 74

Dear Harold—

... Wasn't it great about Rudy getting the Gov Gen's for BIG BEAR!!!![2] It's a novel which is in a class by itself. Have just recently read Ray Smith's LORD NELSON TAVERN and Clarke Blaise's A NORTH AMERICAN EDUCATION,[3] both of which knocked me out. Migawd, Harold, there are some good young writers in this land! What, of course, makes me wild with rage is that so many of them are not published outside Canada—what is the matter with Eng and Amer publishers, that they can't see? Of course, it is true here as well . . Leo Simpson's THE PEACOCK PAPERS,[4] being so damn under-reviewed that it made me sick—a brilliant satirical work. Sometimes I think many reviewers suffer from one simple thing—they can't read. Have had some pretty stupid reviews of my novel, which came on as favourable but were just goddamn blind. . . .

Love to you and Corky and your large family. . . .

She had complete contempt for some successful Canadian writers who weren't creating the Canadian bibliography, if you know what I mean, but were doing pop stuff. But she had a strong feeling that the people who were trying to write not only serious fiction, but serious books of any kind, were all co-operating in the effort to create a literature for Canada.

Lakefield,
22 July 74

Dear Harold—

Thanks much for your letter. I am enclosing ... a copy of my statement re: you, to the Canada Council—hope it's okay. They *must* give you the grant!! You must've got less $$$ from the Council than damn near any other Can writer, and the things you want to finish just have to get done—of course, they will get done, grant or no grant, but it certainly would expedite their completion and also make life a little less anxious for you. Can't see that the Council can possibly refuse you.[5]

Glad you liked THE DIVINERS. A few people's opinions really matter to me, and you're one of the few. . . .

Re: the Union—I just couldn't take on the job of President, Harold, for the chief reason that all the stress situations in the past year apparently added considerably to my developing diabetes—stress, not surprisingly, adds to anything that goes wrong with the body. I don't mean I have to live like a hermit, but for a year or so I am going to have to try to cut down on the Heavy Stress situations, or I may find myself in serious trouble. Comes of going like a bomb for too many years, too much pressure. . . . So I'm going to have to work for the Union mainly in behind-scenes ways, if possible. Nope, I never have been as strong as I appear to be, either physically or mentally—comes of having a "carrying" voice and a build like a Russian peasant woman; people think you are tougher than you really are. Marian [Engel] really has done a terrific job, and of course it is NOT a job that anyone should have to do more than a year at a time. Graeme [Gibson] would be very good, I think. I wonder who else? Someone from another part of the country, perhaps, but that does give rise to practical difficulties. Also, who isn't at the moment writing a book? I'll be at the conference in the fall, of course. We'll have to give serious thought. I don't feel I've done as much for the Union this past year as I should have, but the Pres job I don't think I could handle, and I think also I must concentrate on Health Program for a bit. . . .

Lakefield,
5 Sept 78

Dear Harold—

A thousand thanks for book and T-shirt! I will proudly display the foxes of Beachy Cove across my ample bosom. I usually wear a T-shirt under my plaid shirt . . and, as with a prized black T-Shirt with TRUTHSAYER in white, which my daughter gave me, so with Foxes I will from time to time dramatically open plaid shirt and say "Whatd'ya think of that?" It is a refeened middle-age form of flashing, harmless and unembarrassing to all.

Of course I want to read BARTLETT.[6] In fact, you have just saved me the price of the book, as I was about to order it. . . . I happen to be more interested in explorers than you might think. There are, of course, many kinds of explorers; as I am one of the inner kind, I have somehow a great interest in and admiration for the outer kind (who sometimes . . maybe always in some ways . . turn out to be inner as well).

It's been a strange summer for me. Doing, as usual, a lot of v. serious reading (eg. THE CANADIAN LEFT by Norman Penner; THE VERTICAL MOSAIC by John Porter; DANIEL MARTIN by John Fowles; Tim Buck's memoirs; JUNG AND THE STORY OF OUR TIME by Laurens Van der Post; etc etc)[7] in between some thinking . . a lot of thinking . . and note-making about what comes next for me. I hoped it would be something short, simple and not very complex. Such is not the case. I feel choked up with all that I want to try to get down, and yet I now feel that I will find the courage at least to attempt it, not that the book that finally emerges is ever as complex or extensive as that which exists unwritten in the mind. An odd thing about all my self-chosen reading for 2 summers now (as contrasted with the fact that being on the board of judges for the G.G.'s for 2 years, I have to read all the Eng-Can novels . . the best of which I would have chosen to read anyhow) is that it is apparently quite eclectic but not really— I'm led into reading things I need to know about.

Much love to you. . . .

P.S. re: reading . . I've also been doing some gloriously frivolous binge reading . . my occasional treats like salted peanuts . . Rex Stout's who-dun-its! I have a friend who owns all of Stout's novels, and he is doling them out to me, three at a time, enough to feed my addiction but not to take over my life!

Her principal characters were always people with whom she had a great deal of sympathy. She liked them. This [attempt to write a novel after The Diviners] *was the first time that she tried to do one of those modern books about antiheroes in which, instead of liking the people you're writing about, you dislike them [i.e. fundamentalists]. . . . She was too sympathetic to people generally to be able to treat unsympathetic characters in a major way. I think this was one of her problems.*

Lakefield,
31 Dec 78

Dear Harold—

The last day of the old year seems an appropriate time to be writing to wish you all the best for 1979 and to thank you very much for BEYOND THE ROAD.[8] I found the book fascinating, both the photographs and the text . . what you wrote and what the various people said. Your part of the text puts what they say in the right context, I think, and their voices . . one can actually hear them! I loved the photographs, and agree with you about them. I don't find them *at all* stiff . . ye gods, reviewers!! In fact, although my own small town was very different from Newfoundland outports, those pictures in some ways reminded me of my childhood . . that is exactly the way people do (or should I say, *did*) sit in their kitchens, their parlours, their familiar places. Shy, in a sense, and yet enormously proud. You know, prairie farmers and their families, in my childhood and adolescence, the 30's and 40's, had something of those same qualities. Now, of course, most of the farmhouses stand empty . . the farmers leave their machinery in the barns, but they live in town and commute these days. On my last visit to Manitoba, this past October, as on a previous visit three years ago, I found this fact very sad, although naturally I can understand why they would prefer to live in town. I never lived on a farm but I had plenty of friends who did, and I visited them. My first boyfriend (I was 14) was a farm lad, and I used to go out to his place. It was no damn joke in winter, living in that kind of isolation. And yet . . a quality of life is missing now, a connection with the land that was there when people lived with it, occupied it. A lot of your and Taylor's book struck echoes in my mind. I found it a very moving book. . . .

All okay here. I am writing again, thank God. But it is a strange thing I'm trying to do, and I'm experiencing the usual awful doubts. I realized last summer that I had not one book but two, simmering in my mind. A novel that isn't ready yet to be written, and . . I tell you more or less in confidence . . a kind of memoir, a kind of discursive story of my life, not perhaps as it actually happened but as perceived by me. I do not intend to

101

spill every bean, I need hardly say. But there are a lot of interesting stories I'd like to share, and some strong views as well. I don't even know if I will want it published. We'll see. But it feels good to be working again. My main problem is business letters . . Harold, they get me down! The innumerable well-intentioned requests for this and that. Even if one says No, it still takes time. I hate not answering, but I think I am about to be reduced to that way out. I could spend all my time being my own secretary.

Elm Cottage,
26 Jan 72

Dear Myrna—

... You ask how I manage to do everything all at once—well, I don't, really. I seem to work in fits and starts. I really have a one-track mind, so if I have to think a lot about the plumbing or something, I just don't write. And when I do write, the meals deteriorate sharply. Then after a chapter or so, I spend about a week catching up on correspondence. It's a crazy way to live, I guess, but the only way that works for me. . . .

    This novel is killing me. It is going to be far too long, and I have terrible doubts about it at all times except when actually writing. This is usual, of course, but never have I had to endure such a lengthy period of writing the first draft. I have millions of miles to go yet, and sometimes my spirit flags considerably. However, I can't go back—that is obvious. . . .

Love to you both. . . .

Elm Cottage,
18 Feb 73

Dearest Myrna & Bill—

Thanks for your good letter, Myrna, and sorry I have not replied sooner. The reason is that I have been working Full Steam Ahead on novel, and—wait for it—IT IS NOW FINISHED! HURRAH!! HALLELUJAH! Modified jubilation, actually, as I know it will need some further revision. . . . It's a strange kind of novel, and I fear that if it is ever published some reviewers are gonna say I am picking on topical themes such as The State of Women, etc. Well, I'm *not* picking on topical themes—I'm dealing with themes close to my own psyche and heart, that is all. And one main theme is *fiction*—the way we make fiction from our own pasts and the way we make legends from our parents and ancestors, and are

103

ourselves in the process of becoming legends and myths; that sort of thing. History as fiction; fiction as history. Ambiguity is everywhere. But I have this strong sense of a continuum—even in the midst of our contemporary chaos. I get the sense of *flow*, of the past always being both the present and future, of one generation departing and another generation arising, which is a good not a bad thing, of life being like my beloved river which flows both ways. . . .

Myrna, I've been following your articles in *Sat Night* with enormous interest, and I think they are really excellent. When the last *Maclean's* arrived, with yr article,[1] I was really pleased— the article was v. good indeed, and it is such a good thing to have broken into another magazine, which was what I was profoundly hoping would happen. I hope yr classes[2] are okay, more or less— yeh, I can see that that sort of class could arouse some hostility, but let's face it, unless you are preaching to the converted (which is not necessary) you will always have to meet that uncertainty of response, and I think that for many women, their refuge has been (as M. Atwood says in another sense in *Survival*[3]) in the denial of themselves as victims. "I'm okay—I love housekeeping; I love little black cocktail dresses, and darning sox, and being a little helpmate to my man"—well, if they really *do*, okay, but it's often a cover-up. And when things begin to come out, it can be Pandora's Box for awhile, I think. So much pent up for so long. Whoompf! Explosions. But all necessary. I did so much agree with yr article in *Maclean's*—such a danger, in moving from one lifestyle to another, in repeating *all* the traps, not seeing that they may have different trappings but they're the same old traps. Down with traps for anyone, m[ale] or f[emale]. . . .

Lakefield,
2 Jan 78

Dear Myrna—

I have just read ALL OF BABA'S CHILDREN,[4] and wanted to let you know that I found the book fascinating, impressive, well-written. Congratulations! It confirmed some of my own memories of aspects of the Ukrainian community in my home town and later in N. Wpg, and added very greatly to my pretty scant knowledge of the background and history in the prairies of the

Ukrainian people. I read it straight through in a day, and couldn't put it down. I wish Hurtig had included an index, as the work is both a popular (ie readable by a wide audience) history and a scholarly one. I suspect it'll be around for a long time. . . .

. . . I'm trying to feel my way into a novel . . . doing odd eclectic reading etc; so far "feel" is the operative word . . I don't seem to be seeing all that clearly, but am fairly optimistically groping my way. . . .

ROBERT KROETSCH

Both she and I begin from geography in a certain way, and I'm not sure young writers would share that feeling, but we really felt life was a literal place in the world, on the Prairies. We'd work out of that place, and I think we would both feel that the story was the way to map it, and we both felt that some of the stories we inherited were incorrect or lies . . . or we might both feel we were under incredible pressure to remain silent. We were almost taught silence in our generation, as writers on the Prairies, a kind of wrestling with that silence, which I think went on until the end of life. . . . To resist the silence, in resisting it through story.

Lakefield,
25 Nov 76

Dear Bob—

First, hurrah hurrah hurrah about THE WORDS OF MY ROARING and STUDHORSE MAN[1] coming out in PaperJacks!! Believe me, that will be good news to a lot of students and teachers in Canlit courses—I don't know how many people have told me they wanted to put the books on courses and couldn't obtain them. Of course they should be kept in print permanently.

Re: Sask Summer School—oh hell, Bob, I hate to turn it down . . I know it would be fun and interesting. But I seem to get myself into all kinds of things during the fall/winter, and I just feel I have to keep the summer for myself. I'm beginning to think quite a lot about another novel which may possibly be forming in the head, and I just want to leave myself the space for it to grow if it is meant to be. So reluctantly, I have to say no thanks, but thanks a lot.

Alas, I can't make it to Manitoba in March. I've already made previous commitments at that time. Gee—sometimes I feel like a human yo-yo. One has to try to keep clear spaces, but it isn't easy.

Re: book banning—THE DIVINERS is now back on the Grade 13 course here. School Board finally voted in favour of it, thank goodness. But the opposition hasn't given up. And municipal elections for school trustees are in December. We shall see. . . .

All the best. . . .

I remember gauging my own sense of the west against hers because I was intending to write about the west. She and I are almost exactly the same age, but she was way ahead of me in getting started. And I sensed that her Manitoba was a much tamer place, a much more tamed place, than my Alberta. . . . I was very much taken by her work. Just utterly taken.

She was very wary about speaking to others about how she thought about writing. I had the feeling she read as a writer reads . . . that sense of "how did this writer do it?" And she thought about these things. I think she consciously elected to stay on the ground. She stayed on it as a writer. I got that feeling talking to her one day, that she simply wasn't interested in the kind of reckless behaviour I was willing to engage in as a writer. But she knew about it. She knew about it. . . .

[The censorship struggle] was incredibly important. I think we're still benefiting from her willingness to do that. One of the many ironies involved is that because she had occupied that middle ground [in her writing], her fighting said more than if a more experimental writer did the fighting. Because she could, in a certain way, speak from both sides of the border. [But] I think it hurt her imagination finally.

By working with the Manawaka material, she avoided the problem of having to begin from zero. . . . After The Diviners *she was back at zero in a certain way, and I think that's pretty terrifying for a lot of writers. . . . You know, there is a sense in* The Diviners *of completion even for all its openness, and so that's pretty terrifying for a writer to read. Or it is for me—[her] having exhausted literature as she was conceiving it.*

The Diviners *honours the oral against the written. It finally says the oral is right.*

One of the models operating is the notion of the isolated artist. . . . but she was trying very hard to be the writer in the world. I think we came to respect that a great deal, because she was saying, "You don't create art by retreating from the world. Go out there and get messed up." So that was one of the things about the model. She was willing to really suffer that attention between one's impulse to be isolated or else the model that says be isolated and, on the other hand, that notion that the writer is in the world and has an obligation to be in the world.

It's very hard to educate the audience. There are a couple of ways. One is, you build instructions into the book, and I'd say Margaret Laurence did that a little bit. I think she tends to build the act of reading into the book. . . . The reader who reads is being educated about reading. But the other way is to put your life on the line and go out there and show people, talk to people, really be visible, kind of hands on. . . . She was concerned with our communal efforts to tell a story. She doesn't believe that one person has the story. It's a group activity, not only among a group of writers but a group of readers. . . . I have no trouble at all calling her postmodernist. People who say she's at the end of an era are just mistaken.

I think in the late sixties I'd seldom met a person who was on her scale of talent, plus both the old-fashioned rectitude and all those Presbyterian virtues and the apparent non-importance of ego. I never got to know Margaret all that well, but I got to know her more, and it would be sentimentality to say that ego played no part in her life. But in the chief and obvious ways, it did not play an important part in her life. I knew some generous and warm people who were good writers at that point. I'd never met such a concentration of those things in one person before.

Elm Cottage,
10 May 73

Dear Dennis—

... By all means add my name to the list for the letter [to the Canada Council] for Scott Symons, together with my heartfelt support. Although I haven't read *Helmet of Flesh*,[1] I have some idea of its scope and material, as Scott discussed it last summer when he visited me, and I felt then a great hope for the novel and for his ability to convey it well. . . .

    . . . please tell Scott that I send him my sincere love and faith and hope.

All the best. . . .

Elm Cottage,
23 May 73

Dear Dennis—

I hope and trust you got my letter re: Scott Symons. . . . if seeing Scott, as no doubt you are, please give him my love, and I mean it, as writer, as friend, as human being. He will understand, I hope and know. He was once of great help and reassurance to me, when I much needed help and reassurance, and used to come over to my office at Massey [College] the year I was there and talk with me, and that was a help, more than I can say. . . .

*I think a lot of writers, certainly half a generation or a full generation
younger than herself, found with* The Stone Angel *especially, and with*
A Bird in the House *and the others too, here was somebody who finally
gave us a version of the realist tradition fully in and of this country
that you didn't have to feel apologetic for, you didn't have to make excuses
for, you didn't have to say, "Well, they were still trying to catch up."
And given that realism has been the dominant mode in the Anglo world,
at least in the last century or two, 150 years say, to have something
that sums up and defines that quality . . . it becomes a starting place for
people who work naturally within the realist mode and for people who
naturally find they want to work against it, find other ways of operating.
So I think she became as much of an ancestor in a certain way for people
who wouldn't have written realist if their lives depended on it.*

Lakefield,
3 April 75

Dear Dennis—

Have heard you may be here [Trent University] next year as
w-in-r—do hope so! You would be just great. I don't think I want,
next year, to take on the w-in-r job, even part-time—have done it
for two years, and I think that is enough. Also, I feel strongly
that if a university is to have a w-in-r, then there should be a
prose writer and then a poet, but of course, as I have suggested
to people here, with you they would get both—i.e. a poet plus a
very talented editor of prose. Anyhow hope you decide to take it
on.
        Dennis, in your connection with Macmillan's, do you
know anything about a collection of short stories [*Spit Delaney's
Island*[2]] by a young writer named Jack Hodgins? He apparently
sent his stories to Mac's months ago, and hasn't heard. . . . Dennis,
I've read about 4 of this young man's stories, in JCF [*Journal of
Canadian Fiction*] and *Can Fiction*, and he is really very very good
indeed. I hate to think of him being buffeted from pillar to post
re: publishers. If you know about him, at all, could you perhaps
shove someone's elbow at Mac's, and if they're not interested,
get them at least to return his manuscript to him? Gee—how

incredible that this sort of thing takes place, but it does, it does. . . .

Love. . . .

She was the most loved writer in English Canada for a decade or so, about fifteen years from the mid-1960s to 1980. There were people who found that she spoke for them. I remember my parents saying, "God do you know Margaret Laurence?" These were people who'd have roots in small towns, who were intelligent, who were no longer constrained within small-town Puritan Canada. . . . and who also had enough breadth and cultivation that "I think that I shall never see/A poem as lovely as a tree" didn't exhaust the artistic qualities of how words could be. I think they found, reading Margaret, that decency and passion could come together in writing and not be mediocre writing, and be rooted where they lived.

Lakefield,
21 June 75

Dear Dennis—

Thanks a whole lot for your letter. To know that THE DIVINERS connected with you means a very great deal to me.

Incidentally, in the past month I've given 3 convocation addresses . . at Brandon, Queen's, and Western, and last November I gave the same address at Carleton. It was a straight pitch for Canlit being taught not only in our universities and high schools, but in our primary schools as well, and I ended up quoting the last verse of your poem about Wm Lyon Mackenzie ["1838"]. Always have to psyche myself up for that talk, because "Mackenzie, come again!" makes me cry, but you can't do so if addressing a convocation. . . .

I'm exhausted after all this to-and-fro stuff, and am a person who should spend her life at home (and has), doing her own work. Am off to the shack early next week. . . .

Much love. . . .

Elm Cottage,
2 Jan 66

Dear Mr. Levine:

Thanks very much for your letter of December 23rd. I have written to John Braddock and sent him a short story which was read on CBC Wednesday Night—I don't know if he would be interested in a story which has been broadcast but not published. Anyway, thanks for telling me about *The Atlantic Advocate*.

I wonder if you might be interested in the enclosed story ["A Bird in the House"], for *Canadian Winter's Tales*?[1] It was published by *The Atlantic Monthly* last year. . . .

. . . I'm afraid this is really the only story available at the moment. I don't seem to be writing many short stories recently. . . .

Sincerely. . . .

She wasn't being smart. She wasn't being sophisticated with any kinds of tricks in the writing. It seemed to me a very earthy kind of approach. . . . There were no preliminaries, there were no kid gloves . . . it was just a genuine immediacy . . . a very human one.

Elm Cottage,
16 May 66

Dear Norman—

I'm very glad you like "A Bird in the House", and I don't mind your making comments about altering a part of it. I think your suggestion is very sensible, and I think that the paragraph in question could end "Perhaps it would not have been possible anyway." You're quite right about not beating the reader over the head with explanations. I often seem to have this difficulty of not knowing whether I'm being too obvious or not obvious enough.

I wonder if it would be possible for us to meet sometime? . . .

By the way, *The Atlantic Advocate* did take a story of mine,[2] so many thanks for suggesting that I submit one to them. . . .

She's a bit like a Russian writer. I'm thinking about the good Russian writers of the nineteenth century. That is, aware of family, of the relationships within the family, aware of the undertow that's there all the time, and of the place where they came from.

Massey College,
11 Nov 69

Dear Norman—

. . . I am indeed having a busy time—really too busy, in a sense, for the limitations of my energy and psyche. However, I'm enjoying it, tho I find myself sometimes nearly dropping with fatigue. I'm not surprised you didn't get any of your own writing done—I'm not either. I'm doing a few articles for the Vancouver *Sun*, that's all. Plus having written some 2 lectures and about 6 talks. But no more bloody talks—I refuse everything these days. Have taken on all I can cope with.

. . . I'm so glad yr new novel[3] is coming out in July. I'm returning to England in the spring, but have actually bought a cottage in Otonabee Township, 76 feet on the Otonabee River, so as the real estate ads say, I now OWN A PIECE OF CANADA. In the future, we'll see. . . .

I think Margaret came from a background and the times [in which] she was writing where, if you were a male writer, the woman would look after your life so you could write. I remember talking to Alice Munro as recently as the middle 1980s. She said, "Oh, before I can sit down and write, I've got to do the shopping, I've got to make the beds, I've got to do all those things." Well, I never had to do anything like that. I think I may have cleared out the fireplaces in Cornwall, but the meals were ready, and I had coffee and biscuits brought up. A woman was expected to be the domestic in the house. And [Margaret] did that and then she had to find time to write. . . . She told a lot of women readers what it

113

was like, how trapped they were in a situation that was common to all of them. I don't see her influencing other women writers, but readers.

Elm Cottage,
2 April 71

Dear Norman—

It was really good to talk with you and Margaret [Levine] because I felt I had met you before, altho hadn't.

Don't know what to say about FROM A SEASIDE TOWN, because I felt the quality of its pain communicated very directly with me. Also, in an odd way, the ability to survive against all odds, which is I guess what all writers do or try to do. Plus the guilt thing, which is very familiar to me—one would so much like to write without any inconvenience to anyone else but alas not possible. The book seemed to relate a lot to the book I am trying to write to come to terms with myself, and haven't yet. . . .

Love to you both. . . .

HUGH MacLENNAN

Massey College,
16 Feb 1970

Dear Hugh—

It was lovely to see you again and to have a chance to talk, even if briefly. I appreciated very much the fact that you attended my talk, and my qualms at seeing you there lasted only a moment. I really wanted to tell you that day, that I feel very deeply that I owe you a debt of gratitude as a novelist. It was really only through your novels, and those of Ethel Wilson, and Sinclair Ross, and very few others, that I came to an understanding of the simple fact that novels could be written *here*, out of one's own background, and that in fact this was the only true soil for me to write out of. I would think all novelists of my generation, and those younger than I, must feel the same toward you. I was too shy to talk about this, the day I was at McGill, so I felt I wanted to write to you, because people really don't know what our feelings are unless we say, but there are some things that I find easier to write than to speak.

Sincerely. . . .

Lakefield,
29 Jan 79

Dear Hugh—

I apologize for not having replied sooner to your very nice and heart-warming letter. . . . My quiet country life is more like a three-ring circus than anything. I enjoy it, though. . . .

First, let me say how very much I enjoyed your book of essays.[1] I loved the ones about your days at university in England! Re: the matrist (permissive) and patrist (authoritarian) view of history, I totally disagree, I have to say—seems like once again women get blamed when things go wrong, and I am darn sure it isn't women who have wished so many wars upon the world.

115

Maybe I misunderstood your views. But I agreed passionately with almost everything else you had to say in the book—my heavens, if only the government had paid heed to what you said about bilingualism 20 years ago, we might now have a largely bilingual nation. Twenty years is just about all it would take, starting with kids in kindergarten and going up through high school and university. One really *despairs* of governments—do they not have any common sense at all, I ask myself. Of course, with education being in provincial hands, it would be a very sore issue. I am especially aware of this, having grown up in Manitoba—and to the everlasting shame of the educational system, it was not until many years later that I finally understood what the Manitoba School Question had been all about, namely depriving francophone Manitobans of their right to their language in state-supported schools, in the provincial parliament, and in the courts. One of my own great-grandfathers was very briefly premier of Manitoba when the Norquay government fell in about 1889, and I dare not think what his stance would have been—not pro-French, you can be sure.[2] Anyway, thank you for those essays—witty, profound, wise.

This is turning into a real letter, to my surprise. I really like writing letters to people I like and admire and value. Alas, most of my letter-writing energies go into answering boring business letters, or writing to schools etc to say I can't go and do a reading or whatever it is they want me to do. I am trying to stay home and do my proper work, and it isn't easy. As Alice Munro once said to me, "We get daily opportunities to do good." If we accepted them all, or even half of them, we would be nervous wrecks—and broke, too.

I'm enclosing some stuff that I think will interest you—the pamphlet that the Writers' Union got together for the Book and Periodical Development Council, on censorship, plus 2 articles from *Books In Canada* in case you didn't see them. In the first article, a journalist, Paul Stuewe, interviews a couple of the Pentecostals in Huron County (where my novel THE DIVINERS has recently been banned from high school courses).[3] What made me so enraged about this article was that Mr. Stuewe at no point ever hinted that what these guys were saying about me and my books might be a little off course, in fact dead wrong! One of the Pentecostals . . . actually blames me for the existence of V.D. in Huron County! . . . Timothy Findley (have you read his splendid novel, THE WARS, that got the Gov-Gen's last year?) has written a fine rebuttal.[4] Anyway, I have found all these ignorant attacks very hurtful indeed, but feeling hurt isn't going to achieve one damn thing. Now I am prepared to give battle, in whatever way I can—I believe there is no use in our directly confronting these guys; we have to go after the uncommitted majority. "Renaissance Canada" (to them, the word Renaissance doesn't mean what it means to you and me . . it means Born-Again Christian) has taken, not surprisingly, for its main method the old trick of trying to make it appear that if you are *for* motherhood, God and the right, then you must be *for* them, and *against* everything they are against. We must, of course, never fight on their terms—they would not afford us that freedom of expression that we must steadfastly afford them. All this goes without saying. But I have been having some discussions, both in terms of personal meetings, and through letters, with some of the United Church ministers I know (you would probably not be surprised to learn that I went to college with quite a few people who became United Church ministers) and who are very concerned, as I am, about this growing reactionary force within the Christian church, as elsewhere. Hugh, like you, I also believe in God and that is what scares me. But it also gives me hope. What scares me is that I do believe man has been given free will, and I think we have, as a race (all of mankind) not used it well. What gives me hope, I suppose, is the possibility of grace. But as to salvation by faith alone . . which is what the born-agains believe in, there is no way that I can find that anything except off-putting. The belief in the doctrine of good works is too deeply implanted in someone of my background, ethnic and religious. I have always felt—(and I think this would hold true of your writing as well; hell, *of course* it would; partly I *learned* it from your writing!)—that the real themes in my writing were both political and religious, and the two were in no way mutually exclusive. Well, I think we have to fight the would-be oppressors, but we also have to know that the enemy is real, suffers pain, knows joy and discouragement— this is a difficult thing, more difficult than I ever realized until a few years ago, although it's a part of my faith, held for years. I would like some day to deal with some of this in a novel, but although I've been thinking of it for over a year, it's too close; I can't do it yet. Maybe it will not ever be given to me to explore that region; I can only wait and try to understand, as a novelist, the very people whom I am battling in my role as citizen. I agree so profoundly with you about the engaged writer. Which, as we both know so well, does not mean writing in any didactic sense *at all*, but simply writing of human individuals within their society, as we feel it. I think that I have carried on at this length because so much of what you said in those essays spoke to me, at this time in my life. The other book that has spoken most to me in the last few years, out of this situation of mine, has been Frank Scott's ESSAYS ON THE CONSTITUTION,[5] also a collection of essays written over a long period of time, a noble book if ever I read one. . . .

Thanks again for your letter, and God bless—

Lakefield,
4 June 80

Dear Hugh—

It is with tremendous hesitation and embarrassment that I write this letter. I will come to the point immediately. I would like to apply for the three-year Canada Council Arts grant, which is given once a year and means $17,000 per year for three years. I would like to ask you if you might consider writing a letter of reference for me to the Council. If you agree, I will send you the form for such a reference. But please, please, *do* think about this— I will NOT be offended if you feel you cannot write such a letter. In fact, I am just terribly reluctant to apply at all. I feel the grants ought to be given to writers younger than I am, or more needy, and yet I feel I am going to be able to write another novel and I am damn worried about my income. I have made about 4 false starts on a new novel, but I do feel the people are *there*, and indeed have been there in my mind for some two or three years, and are demanding to be expressed. I would like, if possible, to be able for the next three years to work on this novel without having to do articles, reviews, etc.

I did have a Council grant in 1970, for $7000, which was then their top grant for Senior Arts Awards. Ironically, the next year they doubled it, while *that* year the federal government decided that writers had to pay income tax on grants. However, that money did enable me to come to Canada to my cottage for the next 3 summers, where most of my novel THE DIVINERS was written, so it was a great boon to me. At that time, I was, as you probably know, living in England, and moved back home permanently in 1973. After that, I felt I should never apply to the Canada Council for a grant again, and I was confident I would

118

not have to do so. For the next five years, I thought I was more or less home free. Some of my books had gone into the New Canadian Library paperback editions, and in due course all of my so-called "Manawaka" fiction went into the Seal paperback edition. For those five years, if you can believe it, my income was just about as much as a full professor of English—I thought, wow! And that really *was* something, Hugh, as you know. However, last year my income dropped by almost exactly 50%, a nasty shock that told me I had been living in a fool's paradise— taking my time in getting into another novel (really, taking my time because for a long while I did not *have* another novel to write), going out to dozens of high schools and university classes in Canlit, mostly unpaid, spreading the good word. Well, ho ho. The recent and escalating crisis in publishing has hit us all. Most of my books are now, of course, out of print in the hardcover editions. The NCL doesn't seem to be doing much, possibly because (in my case, anyway) the same titles are available in a much cheaper Seal edition. But Seal is a partner of Bantam Books, NY, and I suspect that when my sales drop even a little, those books will go out of print.

Anyway, if you feel you could write a letter of reference, I will be most grateful. If not, please don't worry. My Scot's pride makes it difficult for me to ask people for letters of reference— no doubt you understand that only too well. . . .

All the very best. . . .

Lakefield,
18 June 80

Dear Hugh—

. . . I am very grateful to you for agreeing to write a letter to the Council on my behalf. Yes, it certainly is an ironic kind of world— we work as well as we possibly can, and after some years people appear to want our work, but we're certainly never going to be secure financially on that basis. Well, I guess it is an honour and a privilege to have been able in this life to do work that one really loved doing. How many people can say that?

The great news is that you have another novel coming out!! As for England and America, I fear that the former, in

119

publishing terms, is so financially strapped that they may not be interested much any more in any except Brit writers, and the latter is increasingly going into the spy–oil–spill–adventure–doom fantasy bit, quick sales and the hell with anything else. But as I know, and as you know even more than I do, serious writing has always been an endangered species and yet has kept on, and will. My generation, of course, was very fortunate in that writers like yourself had paved the way—had, indeed, broken ground with novels that were *not* the colonialist novel of our country's past—I think of you, and Buckler, and Ross, and Callaghan, and others, as our true literary pioneers, because you wrote—really, for the first time ever—out of the Canadian experience.

Anyway, thanks a million, and I look forward to the novel. Things are bad all over, but WE WILL SURVIVE. . . .

Lakefield,
4 July 80

Dear Hugh—

. . . The things you say about THE DIVINERS mean a great deal to me. That novel certainly took a lot out of me. The reactions to it were (and still are) very interesting—people either loved it or hated it. It is still receiving angry denunciations from fundamentalists and other very conservative people. Well, as you once told me in a letter, that kind of thing has been going on a long time, and you experienced it yourself 25 years ago.

The publishing industry is indeed in dire trouble. It just seems unbelievable that a N.Y. publisher hasn't taken your new novel. And yet they all seem (and so do Can publishers) to be going in more and more for the quick-buck sales and novels that deal with Arab oil princes, beautiful blond spies, oil tankers being wrecked, and so on. I don't say I'm totally against pop fiction—I like reading good whodunits. But when serious fiction is being rejected, it looks very scary indeed. When and if I complete another novel, I really don't think I'd expect my English publisher to take it, and the chances with my Amer publisher would also be very uncertain. I have a little kids' book coming out this fall [*The Christmas Birthday Story*], produced by Knopf (it will appear in Canada with M&S's imprint) with beautiful full-colour

illustrations by the Toronto artist Helen Lucas. We have recently
learned that this may be one of the last kids' books put out by
Knopf with a wide colour range in the pictures.

Again, many thanks and God bless.

Love. . . .

Dear Hugh—

I have recently finished reading VOICES IN TIME,[6] and I wanted
to write and tell you how much I admired and was deeply moved
by the novel. It seems to me to be one of the very finest things
you've ever written, and that is saying a great deal. It reads to
me like the culmination of many years as a novelist, many years
of observation and of caring. It is in a profound sense a *wise* book.

The form of the novel perfectly suits what it is saying, as
does the title (a marvellous one, with many echoes). The voices,
playing in counterpoint, as it were, illuminate one another. It is a
complex form, about which one is tempted to use the word
"orchestration", because that is how it seems to me, like a noble
work of music.

The sense of *outrage* at mankind's misunderstandings of
one another, man's inhumanity to man, the complex nature of
good and evil, the terrible dangers of simplistic thinking, of
arrogance, and yet the sense of redemption possible through
individual love and loyalty . . loyalty and love towards persons
not causes—all these seem to me to be communicated with such
authenticity, such passion.

The characters of John Wellfleet, Conrad Dehmel, Hanna,
Esther, Timothy, will continue to inhabit my mental country. They
are wonderfully portrayed, all of them, and the others as well
(Conrad's parents, Stephanie), for in this novel I feel there are no
"minor" characters.

You have, incredibly, managed to portray the sweep and
terror of history, and to do it both in terms of a kind of overview
and in terms of human individuals, real people who suffer and
love and are pawns and who *try*, according to their own
backgrounds and beliefs and inner necessities. Comparisons

really are odious, but the novel I want to compare it to, in a sense, because with that novel I had the same sense of history and human individuals, is Pasternak's *Dr. Zhivago*. Also—do not laugh; this is a valid comparison—*War and Peace*.

You have given this land and indeed far more than this land a great gift in this novel, Hugh. More and more people will recognize it as time goes on. Of course, time, for humankind, may not go on, or not as we have known it. In that case, we pray that not everything of us will be lost. Even if it should be, it was worth the doing, and more.

Thank you, from my heart. . . .

Lakefield,
12 April 81

Dear Hugh—

I got your note yesterday—very many thanks. I'm glad you heard the program on Ethel Wilson [died 22 Dec. 1980]; I missed it, but I was very glad I'd been able to pay tribute to her for the program. She was a great lady, and I do not use those words lightly, as you know.

I'm sorry for the long lapse of time between my receiving your previous letter and your phone call, and my response. It was wonderful to talk with you on the phone. In terms of our writing, and life-views, I think we have a great deal in common. It helps such a lot to talk with and to get a letter from someone who really is of one's tribe, so to speak.

I did get the [Canada Council] Arts Award, which means $18,000, and I want to thank you so much for being one of my referees. The Council has (sensibly, I think) stopped the 3-year grant. I hope this one will be the last I shall ever apply for.

I am trying to keep regular working hours, and I turn my phone off from 9 a.m. to 2 p.m., weekdays, and I have a sign on my door that says I'm working at those hours and please will people call later! It is agony, as well you know, getting into a novel. This one has been growing in my mind for some 4 years. It will be dreadfully slow work. So far, I've been able to write for 2 to 3 hours most days (the rest of the time being spent in thought, sometimes in awful self-doubt, etc). I am not going to re-read what I've written thus far until I'm much further on, or else I know I'll just rip it all up. Of course it is garbage so far, but I feel I must not look back, lest like Lot's wife I be turned into a pillar of salt. Or Jello. However, I think the characters are there, somewhere, if only I can find them and do some kind of justice to them.

I read the page proofs of Elspeth Cameron's biography of you.[7] I think it is a fine piece of work. I offered to read it, and have written a paragraph on it for the publishers to use in publicity, or whatever. I hope you don't mind. I was interested to read about your experience with some of the T.O. critics. I, too, have suffered at [their] hands. . . . Yet on the few occasions when I meet them they greet me like a long-lost buddy. Curious.

God bless you. . . .

Lakefield,
11 May 84

Dear Hugh—

CONGRATULATIONS . . . CONGRATULATIONS . . . CONGRATULATIONS!!

I was so delighted to learn that you had received the Royal Bank Award.[8] Very greatly deserved. It is marvellous to see that sometimes justice is done. Frankly, after Northrop Frye got it a few years ago, I thought (with you very clearly in mind) . . "oh hell, they won't give it to another writer for about the next 25 years." Of course I was glad that Frye had received it, but I did feel that you as our *undoubtedly* senior novelist in terms of achievement, should get it. I'm just so glad.

Things are well with me. I have found I was not meant to write the novel that I laboured on mightily for some years. That's okay. I'm taking other directions. One cannot force it, as who should know better than you . . . one has to go where the writing leads. I find myself more obsessed (if that is the right word) with my own personal (and hence everyone's) ancestors and with the survival of our earth. . . .

Somebody phoned me the other day to say that P.E.N. headquarters was being moved from Montreal to Toronto. I can't actually see that that is necessary, but let it pass. Apparently Margaret Atwood has agreed to be President, and they wanted me to be Vice-Pres. I do support the work of P.E.N., especially in trying to get imprisoned writers freed, but I had to say I couldn't be V-P. I serve on quite a few boards that I think are good causes, and cannot spread myself too thin or I wouldn't be effective in any area. But this T.O. thing worries me a bit. I live in Ontario, but to me Toronto isn't the centre of my world. Maybe I'm wrong to be concerned . . I don't know.

Anyway, best wishes to you, and again . . HURRAH! . . .

Lakefield,
6 March 75

Dear Joyce—

I haven't yet read LOVERS AND STRANGERS, but I'm writing now because I want to get PRESENTLY TOMORROW[1] back to you, as it seems to be your only copy and I worry about having anyone's only copy of anything! Especially a *novel*.

Written in a wasteland, indeed. I can hardly believe that it was called scandalous in 1946, but of course I can believe it quite well. Suggesting that our blameless womanhood might even *think* about sex, at 17 or 18! Well, thank God the climate has changed somewhat, although in Lakefield and Peterborough, apparently (as no doubt elsewhere in the land) some people strongly object to my use of a few 4-letter words. Amazing. Well, I think you were really brave to write PRESENTLY TOMORROW in such a cultural climate. You know, the way I read the book, the character for whom I felt the most sympathy was Flip, who I thought was not only intelligent but also sensible and so much less shut-in than any of the others. It's kind of an ironic comment on society at that time (and probably now, too) that through making love with Flip, Craig is actually led to overcome some of his longtime hangups and comes to a better understanding of himself; he is, in other words, helped by the encounter. But Flip, of course, ends up hurting her friends through the encounter, and being described as "not quite normal". Of course, in many areas of life now, the wheel has come full circle, and Flip would be the *only* one whose point of view could be understood by some people now, whereas the volatile Carol, and Ann, who early knows her own particular dedication, and even the religion-oriented Tammy, all have equal claim to the validity of their points of view. Thanks for letting me read it. . . .

Lakefield,
6 May 75

Dear Joyce—

The other day I was browsing in a second-hand furniture shop in the village. They also handle 2nd-hand books, and to my delight I found your first novel [*Presently Tomorrow*]. Actually, that's a lie—Al Purdy and Euritheh [Purdy] were here, and it was Al who found your novel. I then virtually tore it out of his hands, saying "Joyce has only got one copy and it's not in too hot shape and she loaned it to me, and I am certain she'd like a copy in good shape!" Purdy, who is a hard man to beat down when on the quest for Can books, allowed as how he *did* have a copy (altho not signed by you—I have taken the liberty of giving him your address; he has the largest collection of signed Can books in the country and ultimately will turn up or send his copy to you for signing, I am certain). So here it is—I was so delighted that it turned up, and in Lakefield, and in almost mint condition.

Haven't yet read LOVERS AND STRANGERS because my life has been unbelievably hectic and I seem only to read newspapers of late. Have ordered A PRIVATE PLACE.[2]

Love. . . .

Lakefield,
16 March 76

Dear Joyce—

I must apologize for not having written sooner to thank you for sending the NCL of THE ROAD PAST ALTAMONT. . . .[3]

I thought your Intro to Gabrielle Roy's book was absolutely splendid, and quite unique as such Intros go. I've never seen before an Intro by the person who did the translation and who hence stands in a particularly intimate relationship to the novel, with insights into it that such closeness would give. I mentioned this when I wrote to Gabrielle Roy, and in her reply, she says "Yes, indeed, Joyce's introduction to *The Road Past Altamont* is an exquisite and strong piece of work, and as you so rightly say, unique." She wrote such a lovely letter back to me— I shall write again to her soon. . . .

Lakefield,
12 April 77

Dear Joyce—

... I am really so pleased at the thought of the story SO MANY
HAVE DIED being expanded into a novel.[4] That old lady simply
steps off the printed page and into one's life. I, too, have known
women of that generation who were "career" women—one of
my beloved aunts, now 87, was one of them—a very distinguished nurse and the first head of the Public Health Nursing
Division in Saskatchewan. Also, all the other themes which the
story suggests—I can *feel* them combining into a really splendid
novel! It seems such a right thing to be doing. Especially now. . . .

JOHN METCALF

Elm Cottage,
5 August 70

Dear John—

Many many thanks, both for your letter and for your book. . . .
how very generous of you to have written in that way, to
communicate the feeling you had about my stories; your
comments meant more to me than you probably realize.

Re: THE LADY WHO SOLD FURNITURE[1]—John, it's a fine
collection, I had read only 2 of the stories previously, but felt the
same about all the stories, including the title piece, as I do about
most of your writing—mainly that it is a joy to read someone
who writes in a subdued and subtle way, without loud screeches
of style, and who communicates in this manner such a lot without
actually saying it. The character of Jeanne, contrasted (without
comment—hurrah) with the drab sadistic school situation was
just absolutely right, and she comes across so very well—dunno
how you managed it in so few words. Also, one feels for her and
with her, but (for myself, anyway) one also feels Peter's unspoken
sense of both pity and horror about the messes she creates—even
while knowing they are only physical messes, not the spiritual
damage the school does. It's a beautiful piece of work, John. I
loved it. With the others, I thought with many of them as I have
about some of your other stories (the ones in N[ew] Can[adian]
Wr[iting]), that you manage to catch the voices of children as no
one else I know can with the single exception of Alice Munro—
ie there is a veracity about the speech, and it communicates the
child-person, totally without condescension or phoniness or
sentimentality. I'd read the one about the boy and the old man
before ["Keys and Watercress"], and think it is one of the most
subtly terrifying tales I've encountered. Anyway, I just wanted
to let you know how much I got from them all. . . . The book
should be published in both Amer and Eng; the problem being a
book of short stories. Novels, yes; stories, no—that is the general
cry of publishers. I think they're wrong, but they don't think
so. . . .

With all best wishes. . . .

128

She's really the turning point, it seems to me, between a kind of fairly old-fashioned realism and the beginning of something which more or less after she finished writing accelerated very very rapidly. . . . As time went on and more and more things were written, her books were left stranded and more historical. I don't mean historical novels, but it seemed to leave her in a place in history rather quickly.

Elm Cottage,
26 Oct 70

Dear John—

How goes the battle, and have there been more reviews of your book? I can't believe it won't have more—what in hell is the matter with the bloody reviewers? Actually, I know what is the matter with many of them—they are nit brains. Yes, I did finally see [that] review of A BIRD IN THE HOUSE. . . . What an idiotic review . . talk about damning with faint praise. And what is "feminine" humour? It is like [another critic] saying of Alice Munro, "feminine talent" . . . that really gets me down. It is so often said about women writers (me included), and however you look at it, it's a putdown. A kind of echo of Milton's "He for God only; she for God in him" . . silly bastard! However, John, we must face the fact that if there's one thing which some reviewers detest more than a man who's written a good book, it's a woman who's written *anything*.

The reviews of my children's book, JASON'S QUEST, from Canada, have been unbelievable. Just because I've written serious novels, the reviewers take the kids' book seriously, ferreting out allegories and saying this is a crumby thing to do in a kids' book or else (in some cases) a marvellous thing to do. . . . One reviewer said he believed this was my attempt at contributing my views to the generation-gap situation. Really, I ask you. It is only a simple tale of a mole, 2 cats and an owl who go on the classic quest. . . .

Am trying to get going on a new novel and am scared as hell. Feel I will never get it done; won't be able to handle the material; will die just as I'm coming to grips with it or else will wait to die until I've been working unsuccessfully on it for 2 years, thus leaving my children penniless. Etc etc. All kinds of gruesome fantasies along these lines. But at least I know I have to write it, however it may turn out. It doesn't get easier with the years . . it gets more difficult—not the actual writing, the beginning of the thing; getting enough courage to begin. Wish you would pen a few lines of encouragement some time when you've got a moment . . like, "Quit bitching and start working" or some such thing. . . .

ps. god, what a mess [October Crisis] Canada is in. I hope you are okay. I worry about my friends in Montreal.

Elm Cottage,
2 Nov 71

Dear John—

I was so glad to hear from you. . . . I'm delighted your novel is so nearly finished. I wish I could say the same. I worked like hell all summer in my shack, and it was really a lovely time. Got the equivalent of about 200 typescript pages done, and am ONLY A QUARTER THROUGH THE MATERIAL. Obviously, I will have to cut it down drastically if it is ever finished. I don't *want* to write a long novel, but it is proving very stubborn. Have not got back to work since returning to England, as I've been writing some articles for bread . . one of them for Maclean's My Canada series[2] . . hope it isn't too schmaltzy. I hope to get back to the novel in about a month's time. Also, have had the usual flood of Canadian visitors, lovely to see them all but not good for the writing.

Good news about Alice Munro's novel [*Lives of Girls and Women*[3]]. Do you think you could do me an enormous favour and ask McGraw-Hill to send me a copy of it. . . . I really would love to see it. . . .

Elm Cottage,
29 Nov 71

Dear John—

Many thanks for sending Alice Munro's book to me. I've nearly finished reading it, and think it is just splendid, like all her writing. She really is so damn good. So many facets of her town strike a chord with me, not unnaturally. . . .

I'm glad you want to use To Set Our House In Order in your new anthology [*The Narrative Voice*[4]].

I'm so glad your novel is nearly done. Whatever the length, I think one always feels absolutely drained afterwards.

At last I've got back to work on my novel, after doing 8 short articles for various Canadian publications. Hope they are all accepted. Most done by request, but you never know. It's good to get back to the novel, altho frightening in a way because the bloody thing is so long. However, maybe I can cut it by half when I've got a first draft. . . .

Love. . . .

Elm Cottage,
9 Mar 72

Dear John—

Brief Communication. THE NARRATIVE VOICE arrived yesterday, and because I had ten million other things to do and was paralysed by how much I had to do, I just sat down and spent afternoon reading book. It is very good, I think, and I hope it will get across to students etc. Well, to kids generally. You've done a good job of putting it all together. I like especially (apart from the selection of stories, which is fine) the variety in the layout— the pics of writers, the various bits written by us all. I think that is interesting. At least, I found it so—hope kids do, too. . . .

R.R. 11,
Peterborough,
20 Aug 72

Dear John—

Thanks much for your letter. I have just finished reading Going Down Slow[5] and have been mulling over possibilities of a review—John, I really would like to do a review, but the problem which presents itself is that I am getting a bit panic-stricken re: finishing my novel, as the summer seems to be streaking swiftly towards its end and I still have two long chapters to go. I don't think I can make the mental shift into review writing at this time, and I am really sorry. However, what I have done is this—I have written to . . . M&S, giving . . . a tender message re: Going Down Slow, and suggesting might use in advertising. . . .

. . . kind of like a capsule review, I suppose, but if they will use it in adverts, it might be just as useful as a review which would appear in only one paper. What I wanted to get across, mainly, was that you do take swipes at David as well as everyone else—he is a very sympathetic character, although self-dramatizing and in places arrogant, and in the end I found myself feeling very sorry for the poor guy while also having a quiet admiration for the unspeakable M. Gagnon and his poisonous alcohol. I think this is a point which may be missed by some critics, who, in nationalistic way, will snarl—If you don't like it here, Limey, go back where you came from. Thus totally missing the point, of course. If this does happen with some of the reviews, console yourself by remembering that the Montreal Jewish community for many years (maybe even yet) considered Richler an anti-Semite! My one big complaint with novel is that I would have liked to see it longer—to have extended the timespan a bit. But this is not very reasonable, and anyway, there will be a novel to follow, I hope. . . .

As a writer she was closing a tradition in Canadian writing . . . and maybe another twenty-five years will change this perception again entirely, but to me now, looking back, she really seemed more the summing up and closing off of a tradition of writers like Sinclair Ross and maybe W.O. Mitchell, maybe even someone like Edward McCourt.

Elm Cottage,
26 Jan 73

Dear John—

. . . Re: novel—I have, I think, got absolutely out of my head in my middle age. The novel is now in 2nd draft, i.e. I have finished the typescript from the 28 scribblers of bezaz, and this was finished only two days ago, so tomorrow we are all (Elmcot Commune, my kids and various Can friends) going to open a bottle of champagne. However. It still needs a lot of work, general cutting of corny bits and putting things into reasonable shape and so on. My daughter, God bless her, has offered to do final typescript for me—I will pay her, of course, but what a burden it would take from my shoulders, to have her type it accurately in triplicate, instead of me doing it. BUT—oh John. Wow. Zonk. Kapow. Etcetera. Goddamn novel is in present typescript 527 pp, *and* I have written 4 songs for it, *and*—what I really want is to convince publishers that there should be: this novel, with maps, portraits, songs, music for songs, records of songs being sung, and all that. I may have gone berserk, John, but I DO NOT THINK SO. I feel great. Jack McClelland, when I tell him, will probably feel lousy, but let us not think of that for the moment.

I am obsessed and cannot seem to do anything else at the moment. Only with greatest difficulty do I make meals, do laundry, and write essential letters. This is known as The Last Stand. Pray for me.

Elm Cottage,
23 May 73

Dear John—

Sorry to be so long in replying to your letter. First, of course I'm behind the Writers' Union of Canada 100%, and will get in touch with you, Graeme, Peggy Atwood, etc when I return. Can only wish everyone well, at this point, but hope to be pretty active in organization when I return. Got a letter from Graeme a few days ago, saying [initial] conference now mid-June—wish I could be there, but no way. Will be thinking of you all, and lighting a few mental candles that all goes well. . . .

I wouldn't call all the young writers that I deal with "my tribe" because I find that slightly sentimental. . . . But I certainly learned from her and feel that older writers have to take care of younger writers and have to bring them along and help them and do all kinds of things for them, because that's the only way in which we will build and continue a possible literary tradition in this country. . . . That's something I got directly from Margaret.

Lakefield,
28 March 75

Dearest John—

Woe and alack.
    But also, yipee-ki-yay!
    With that kind of introduction, obviously you know that something is going on with me, eh? What is going on, John, is that (a) I have decided I will try to pull together a collection of some of my travel essays, writ over many years, some unpublished and see what happens . . e.g. I once wrote a 35-pp essay on the Mad Mullah of Somaliland, as he was termed by the colonialists, who held out vs the Brits for 20 years, did you know, and who was a ruthless guy but also a fine poet . . this has never been published, and sometimes now I think, why not?; (b) I have begun writing a kids' book [*Six Darn Cows*?] . . well who knows how it may turn out, but I want to have a crack at it, and it's beginning to entice me more and more. . . .
    Most of April will be a bit free for me, and I hope to get into the typing of those old essays and articles then . . who knows, John? I have written some 40 articles throughout the years, for bread of course, but there are no more than 10 or 12 which would be worth reprinting. Some of them, I now think, do have a kind of odd historical interest, e.g. the 2 articles I wrote on Egypt in 1967 just before the Israeli War, when I and my kids had been in Egypt for 2 months, me doing articles for, if you will believe it, Holiday Mag. Articles never published, of course. Who needed tourism in Egypt after that? So I think I'll see what transpires—they've all been sitting there in my files, for some years.
    After that, I do want to just go out to the shack and lock the door and work for awhile, eh? Who would ever have thought that working would be difficult, after one's kids are grown and away from home? But it is. . . .
    Re: Jack Hodgins—to whom we both talked that nite in Van[couver at Writers' Union Conference]. . . . I think that Hodgins' stories are first-rate and very valuable. John, we only do this for those we believe in, those who we sense from the first

134

look at their work are members of our tribe. It's a bloody world, as we all know, but I guess I feel it is the responsibility of those of us who are now published, and whose word may count for something, that we try to do what we can for those of the tribe who are our inheritors. Corny, I suppose. But one does not try to do anything like that except for the few people in whose work one does believe. John, the number of times I've really gone to bat have been remarkably few. But, as I think you know, for writers I really do care about, we just have to try very hard in the face of a cold world. One only does it if one is totally convinced. I *am* convinced about this guy's writing. So enough of that.

Vancouver was good, eh? I got a letter from An[dreas] Schroeder, saying how much he felt it was a good thing to have council meetings in the far-flung lands of this country, and how much he was beginning to regain a family. I take that as a good omen. . . .

Lakefield,
23 June 76

Dear John—

God knows when I'm going to get back to work. All these darned fundamentalists gunning for me verbally has gotten to me a bit. I did a short report on the latest for the [Writers' Union] Newsletter. Just heard the other day that they (the Pentecostals) have stirred up their brethren in Dufferin County, where the book is now under fire. They have, of course, a readymade and obedient organization. It isn't just this one novel which will get it in the neck if they have their way. . . .

Lakefield,
21 July 77

Dear John—

Thanks so much for your letter, and for sending the Can Fiction Mag. Actually, I'd already seen it and thought your section[6] was exceedingly good. I especially liked the blend of real pain with

135

that wry straight-faced humour you're so good at! What do you mean .. you're not sure that the earlier sections of the story are fitting for a lady's eyes? You are, you remember, addressing the Jezebel of Lakefield (at least, in the eyes of the local Pentecostals I'm that!). I look forward to seeing the book.

I'm delighted to learn that you're into another novel. That's just great! I'm not actually writing, but I'm doing a lot of thinking and sort of freewheeling reading—stuff that I think is going to fit in somewhere although I'm not sure how or where. It all may become a novel—pray for me. I mean it. I had an incredibly rushed spring .. I always seem to miss the spring, travelling hither and yon on duty assignments. Out to Simon Fraser U, then to Fredericton, and so on and on. Got back home end of first week June, totally exhausted. Not depressed, just at low psychic ebb. Since then I've been out at the cottage and now feel much restored. . . . Also, now having achieved more than half a century (I was 51 this week), I seem to have the crazy notion that there is time for everything. I don't seem to feel Time's winged chariot at my back as much as I once did, re: my work, anyway. I've decided, however, to turn down all future commitments re: readings, talks, seminars etc etc etc. I've paid my dues in that respect, I think, and am thoroughly sick of *talking* about writing. So we'll see.

John, have you left the union for good? I do feel badly about this, and can't help believing there has been some misunderstanding which might perhaps be put right. Of course, no organization is perfect, nor is it going to act in total agreement, as a body, with every individual member's views. But I do wish you'd reconsider. The union owes you so much, and we need you. And yes, I do sometimes feel that too many writers are doing readings, but on the other hand, this does spread canlit a bit further afield, and also is a source of some income for members who need it. Anyway—let me know what you think. . . .

I didn't learn from her emotional possibilities about writing. And I certainly didn't learn anything technical from her. But I think you could say that in many ways she shaped the way my life has developed, because I've been editing and anthologizing and getting younger writers published, and I would say that was very largely the influence of Margaret. I've never forgotten her kindness, either, and the care she would take with younger writers and the time with unknown people. . . . Her impact was just huge.

Dear John—

... First, thanks so much for THE GIRL IN GINGHAM .. did you say it would be part of the forthcoming book [*The Teeth of My Father*]? It is a terrific story .. moving, and, in the end, absolutely chilling. Sometimes looking at the New Statesman's classified ads, I have wondered about the people who put ads in, looking for companionship .. how dreadfully sad, and one does wonder if *ever* it works out, done that way. A fine story. ...

[Re:] CANADA WRITES, a compilation of union members. ... If we seem to you to be touting the cause of Canlit, it is only because for so long Canadians undervalued anything being done here. For years our writing was totally ignored at home unless it had the London or NY seal of approval. We were simply colonialized and didn't know it. What has happened here in the past 15 years is comparable to the upsurge of writing in Africa ... people began to value themselves and their own heritage, their own perceptions, their own land. If this pendulum now is in danger of swinging too far (and I think that this is always a possibility to be guarded against), then please try to understand that we as a people have been undermined for so long by imperialist doctrine.

Of course we must uphold standards of quality. But let us not fall prey to the error that only the British or the Americans in our universities have any right to be telling us what we should be reading. Each culture must try to develop its own voices, and this is what we are doing. Of course, you are right .. glancing through CANADA WRITES one is immediately aware that some writers have a higher literary standard than others, but on the other hand, we're not presenting it in terms of qualitative judgements. ...

You ask me if it does not worry me that my lightest word is considered Literature? I don't think this has happened? Au contraire .. what worries me is that I'm not supposed to have light words, or so some critics seem to think. When my essays HEART OF A STRANGER came out last year, some reviewers said that some of it was pretty light stuff and not to be compared with a serious novel. Re: the possibility of writing an awful novel which would then not be distinguished from my best work ... I think it would be distinguished from my best work, all right;

what would worry me is that it might just possibly get published, if it were only going to be published in Canada, on the strength of my previous work, instead of being properly turned down. In this way, I would feel, alas, that I would get a more objective view from my editor in New York or London. Naturally this worries me and depresses me from time to time. A Canadian publisher might quite conceivably accept an awful novel from me just because they would think it would sell whatever it was like. This might throw me back on my own ultimate judgement of the work more than any writer should be. I don't know. . . .

CLAIRE MOWAT

Lakefield,
26 May 84

Dear Claire—

... I have just this moment read your Mermaid Inn column in
the *Globe*.[1]
JOIN THE CLUB!
I reproach myself mightily, as a matter of fact, for not
having written to you at the time to tell you how much I enjoyed
THE OUTPORT PEOPLE.[2] I thought it gave a wonderful picture of
those people and of your own relationships with them ... so
tentative at first, so warm later, and yet in a sense always
(inevitably) as an outsider. It is a very good book.
I am not in the least surprised at the English publishers'
views, the bastards. All my books were published in hardcover
in England, by Macmillan, owing largely to the editors there at
the time. They are all out of print there now, despite a brief
renewal of a few of them in paperback for a time. My Eng agent
is now trying to get a few of them back into print in paperback. ...
But the old order has changed, and not necessarily for the better,
at my agent's and publisher's places. ... I keep getting letters
from people in Brit universities (not an overwhelming volume, I
may say, but still ..) saying they want to teach one or another of
my books but can't get them as they are out of print. THE STONE
ANGEL was on the "Contemporary Novel in English" course last
year at all the universities in France, at the *aggregation* level
(required for those taking teacher-training, as I imperfectly
understand it). ... they had finally to get paperback copies from
Canada, as none were available from the standard English sources
they normally get books from. But so what? Big deal. The Brits
couldn't care less. Who is this wild colonial lady? Ho hum.
Canada? Where's that? If I sound bitter, it's only because *I am*.
When my books first appeared in England, most of the reviews
neglected to mention that they were set in Canada and that I was
a Canadian writer. I kid you not. When A JEST OF GOD came out
in 1966, one of the Brit reviewers, obviously thinking himself
very well-informed, referred to the character of Nick Kazlik as
"a new Canadian" ... not realizing that it was Nick's grand-

139

parents who had originally come to Canada. During the 11 years I lived in Eng, I became more and more disillusioned about the British attitude towards Canada in every area. The literary world of England thinks of Canada as insufferably dull, although none of those people bother to inform themselves about us or our land. I decided long ago that it is they who are in the backwater of history and we do not need them anymore. Our books are of more interest, these days, to the Americans, the French, the Italians, the Russians, the Japanese, etc etc etc, than they are to the English. One exception—Canadian books *are* of interest in Scotland, but then, they're not the Sassenachs! I sound horribly prejudiced, and I am. But with reason. Our own universities have suffered from the dimwittedness of English profs who came over, getting instant tenure, in the 50's and 60's, and we're stuck with the blighters until they die or retire. I myself have met many Eng professors in our universities who say "Well, we don't really want Can writing taught because there really isn't any" . . . and one says "What have you read?" and the answer is, "Oh, nothing, of course, because there isn't any worth reading." A tiny episode that happened some years ago . . . a friend, whose husband then taught in the English Literature Department at McGill U, was at a cocktail party and spoke with the wife of a newly acquired staff member of the same dept. The Brit lady said, confidently, "I have now met everyone who counts in the English department." My friend said, "Oh, then, I expect you know Hugh MacLennan." The well-informed lady said, "Who's Hugh MacLennan?"

The novel in England has deteriorated over the past 20 years, in my view. They're still writing domestic comedies. They haven't a damn thing to say (and yes, of course there are honourable exceptions). So forget them, kiddo. Our strength is *at home*, with our own people, and in that wider world of other countries and other languages. Money to doughnuts Farley [Mowat] would bear me out in this assessment.

Love to you both. . . .

She had some of the wisdom that the tribal elders, the women tribal elders [of] the Iroquois tribes had. These were the repositories of wisdom and compassion. And it didn't matter what the age was; usually they were older women . . . but they didn't have to be deep in their dotage. She always [had] that about her, almost a reincarnation . . . born too late in the wrong place when wisdom and compassion—women—were no longer respected and admired by the tribe at large. . . .

I'll tell you what kind of writer she was. She was my kind of writer. She was a storyteller first, foremost, and absolutely. Everything else is a matter of skills, acquired skills, acquired with great labour, some of them, but honed to perfection. She was a storyteller in the grand tradition, and the story she was telling was the story of my country, my people, so the combination to me was irresistible. I think she's the greatest writer we've ever had.

—Farley Mowat

We talked when I went to her house [in Vancouver]. I remember talking about kids, housework, writing, all those things you talked about as soon as you met another woman who was trying to write. And there was immediate rapport that way because everybody had the same problems. I remember her telling me she ironed all her husband's shirts. And I said, "You musn't do that. You must find some other way." I have the impression of someone who was trying terribly hard to do everything. She was trying to be a good housewife, and mother, and she was trying very hard to write. She was very serious about her writing, but she was also very serious about the whole thing that the culture demanded of us at that time. And so was I. So we became very friendly almost immediately, but not close friends in the sense that we tried to see more of each other a lot, because I think we were both desperate for time.

Lakefield,
29 Jan 81

Dear Alice:

Welcome home from Australia! It sounds hot and trying. If you have 10 readers there, that is 10 more than I have. However, I suspect Canadians have much in common with Australians in terms of writing.

I probably over-reacted (as I am wont to do) to the piece in the Eng mag. . . .[1] I was so mad that I sent my copy to Jocelyn and told her to throw it in the garbage when she had read it. Stupid. . . . But is there no sense anymore of apprenticeship, of having to go through that period of one's professional life, or is it all instant success these days? (Gee, do I ever sound like the kind of comment I used to *hate* in my younger years . . it was better in *my* time, and of course it *wasn't*.) You ask what the rest of us looked like in the pics. . . . Well, Susan Musgrave and Myrna Kostash looked great. . . . Yours and Gabrielle Roy's were about one third that size. (Yours was very nice, actually . . a good pic, and Gabrielle's was, I think, that marvellous and famous one of her, but in space terms, you both really weren't in it.) Jane Rule's was long and very narrow . . about 5 inches long and 1 inch deep, which made her, perforce, look about 10 feet tall. Mine a not very good one, rather resembled the size of a postage stamp. What the hell. It is mean-minded of me to be cross about all this, but I *am*. Simply because most Brits know absolutely nothing about our writing, and from this article they get a totally false impression. I sent my letter to the Editor of the mag, who wrote me back a sort of frosty courteous letter saying they couldn't cover *all* Can writers. . . . Let it pass. I'm glad you refused to be interviewed as the OLD GUARD among Can women writers. Ye Gods!

All is more or less well here. I've made 5 false starts on a novel, and I'm damned if I'm going to begin again until I'm more sure of the territory. But I'm not in despair.

Love. . . .

When [the censorship issue] started, I thought it was a huge joke. And I wrote her a funny letter about it because I thought it was so funny. But she and I, who were both verging on—at least into—middle age, were both rather cautious writers who had difficulty with some scenes, and suddenly we were thought of as being dirty. I thought this was hilarious. It gave me a new lease on life, like being thought a scarlet woman.

She was a more serious person than I was, in the sense of her life in the world. I'm serious about my work, but she was serious about both things. I guess she was very surprised that people could read her books and think they were dirty, that they could be so misread. It didn't surprise me, but it did surprise her. . . . She was deeply wounded. . . . But she grew up in a small town. She should have known there's lots of ill will.

The Wingham Advanced Times *wrote a blistering editorial criticizing me, calling me a "warped personality". It didn't surprise me or hurt me because you know what you can expect if you try to do anything that comes out of your real self. If you've grown up in this kind of community you should know that you're not going to be rewarded for doing something honest or real.*

Lakefield,
26 March 81

Dear Alice:

... The novel that maybe I will be able to write has been brewing in my mind for some 4 years, but only this week have I got myself into the New Regime—lucky me, to be able to do it—working from 9 a.m. to 2 p.m. weekdays. Actually, I think I am trying to do a ridiculous thing that probably NO ONE else will be interested in. That's okay, I'm interested in it. First, we tell the story to ourselves, to find out what happens next and what goes on there. Or so I feel. It has taken me YEARS to get to this starting point once again, the starting point one always has to get to, where nothing matters except the story and the people in it. I have found this harder to do, as you know, as the years go on. But I'm turning my phone off from 9 a.m. to 2 p.m., and the sign on my door says: Work Hours—9 a.m. to 2 p.m. Please call later. So we'll see. I have had many years of being terrified to begin anything new because of all the commentaries pro and con, re: my writing. One has to forget and ignore them all. Pray for me, kid. I need it. But I feel better just recently about all this than I have in years. ...

I didn't know what made her become [a] public person. Whether it was that people got hold of her and she couldn't refuse or if it was her own Presbyterian heritage, which was very strong, about what is one's obligation in the world. ... When she came back to Canada she came more deeply into herself, into what she was bound to do. She was, in a way, the kind of person who might have become a social force, even a political force, if she hadn't become a writer, because her concern was so deep. ... One of the problems about being a writer in Canada is that the literature's still new enough to want stars, and to try to make them out of people. She felt such an easy sense of obligation. She felt obliged to work hard for the Writers' Union. She felt obliged to do all kinds of things as soon as she came back to Canada. She could be touched by causes like Canadian literature, not just by causes like censorship, nuclear war, and so on, but by Canadian culture and things like this that would absorb so much of her energy.

And you know, it's easier for everyone who comes after. It's easier for me than for her because she was the beginning of everything. ... [Her] visibility was for everybody, and it would have been very, very hard for her to see the consequences of every action. ...

But it becomes harder and harder to keep yourself together if you are playing the required role.

I remember a wonderful night I spent at her place at the cabin she had on the [Otonabee] River. I remember we had dinner . . . and then we put on some records and we drank a lot of scotch. She had Scottish music. Oh, she had pipers and she also had early songs, folk songs. We got up and danced, we both danced, and we had a wonderful time. We were both wearing long dresses, the kind you wore then, and we danced around the cabin for hours to this music . . . and we improvised words, too. That is the greatest memory I have of her. Yeah, that was a wonderful night.

FRANK PACI

She was the voice in Canadian literature that said, "You're doing okay. Keep going. Keep going."

Lakefield,
6 June 78

Dear Frank:

I was really delighted to receive a copy of *The Italians*.[1] I've just finished reading it, and want to tell you that I think it is a splendid novel. In the years since I last saw you, your writing has come a hell of a long way. . . . The novel is such a compassionate and moving account of your family—it's got the real true feel of authentic and it's loving without ever being sentimental. The prose is quiet, clean (in the sense of being spare and pared-down, not ornate) and enormously effective. You are writing here with a sure touch, of things you know from the inside. I think you've done a fine job on all the characters, and I'm especially impressed with the portrait of Lorianna, not because she is more alive than the others, but because she is a woman, and you seem to have got her feelings and responses down just right.

I'd really like to hear from you, if you ever have a moment to write a note. I recall so vividly that in 1970 when I was writer-in-residence at the U of T, you were the only young writer I met that year who actually completed the manuscript of a novel during the academic year! I remember saying, "Hey, that's marvellous! You finished it!" and you said gloomily, "What's so marvellous? I'm six essays behind!"

I like the dedication to the book, and I hope your parents feel really good about the novel. I think it is a marvellous picture of the lives of two generations. . . .

All best wishes, and congratulations. . . .

146

Lakefield,
11 March 79

Dear Frank—

A brief note. I have just seen the recent BOOKS IN CANADA, and I note that THE ITALIANS is on the short list for BOOKS IN CANADA First Novel Award, to be announced next month. This is really good news. Also, whether it wins or not, I just want you to know that I have read all the other novels on the short list, and in my view your novel is the best of that group—and at least two of the other novels impressed me quite a lot.[2] So—take heart! be not discouraged.

All the best. . . .

Lakefield,
11 Feb 81

Dear Frank—

Don't lose heart, please! It won't take you another 10 years to get another book out, and teaching high school isn't going to affect your writing adversely. I might just as well say that about 20 (in all) years of raising kids affected my writing adversely. It didn't. The writing isn't fragile—it will survive. And Frank—I think I was wrong in my advice to you. I really don't see now how I could have had the temerity. Just because I'm most interested in novels of character, doesn't mean that everyone is or should be. Forgive me. You will, naturally, write what you want most to write, what compels you, what you feel most deeply about. After all, we write first and foremost for ourselves, before the work ever gets to any potential readership. You are absolutely right on that score.

  Frank, I'm not only NOT lonely up here—my quiet country life is like a four-ring circus! My problem is not *isolation*; it *is* not having enough time to contemplate, think, pace the floor, try to get into this damn novel that I feel is there somewhere. I have an unfortunate tendency to get myself involved in Good Causes—I do not mean that in any trivial way; I mean things I really believe in. Peace organizations; the constitutional debate; women's causes; you name it. I believe that I can't write in any didactic sense, nor do I want to, although all my novels have political or social themes, if one reads them carefully. But as a citizen, I have responsibilities, and sometimes they weigh a little heavy. Also, the damn correspondence—when I open a letter that begins: "I am a Grade 13 student . . " my heart sinks. It is another good, intelligent kid who wants info from me because he or she is writing an essay on my work. I can only respond to so much of it; frequently, I reply very briefly, saying (courteously, I hope) that people must trust their own assessments of novels, and try to see what their own responses are. I am also involved with Trent University to some extent, and have accepted the position of Chancellor for the next 3 yrs. I do believe in Trent, as it is a small liberal arts college . . and there are damn few of them these days. I also have some very dear friends, both here and in T.O., and my two adult kids in T.O. Frank, lonely, I ain't! There are moments when I would like to rent a cosy igloo in the Far North, with no telephone and no mail delivery! However, we struggle on. . . .

PS. Once again, please believe that you don't need anyone's advice . . you will simply go on and write what is in you to write. In the end, that is the only thing that matters.

I'm wondering if I'm following a certain path here, a similar path—the myth of the writer. The myth of the writer, in my sense, is someone who divorces himself or herself at an early age, gradually so, though, and comes back and writes the story of the people that formed him or her. While not being able in real life to thank these people, [writers] do it through art, but only through a very long struggle with the people themselves and the art form.

Lakefield,
5 Sept 81

Dear Frank—

I enclose a copy of my letter of reference to the Canada Council, and will offer up prayers that you get the grant. I'm delighted that your second novel [*Black Madonna*³] is coming out in the spring. It's a very good title. I really look forward to reading it. Don't feel strange about applying for a grant—you've earned it. But I know what you mean—of course we would have to go on writing anyway, but I believe the arts should be to some extent funded by government—I'd sooner have my tax money spent on that than on nuclear arms, I can tell you! I have had 3 Can Council grants, and won't, I hope, ever have to apply for another, but they do exactly as you say . . . the money buys time so serious writers can write.

After thinking about a novel for about 3 years, I've finally got going . . (after 5 false starts . . rather depressing). It sure doesn't get any easier. I'm making slow progress, but I'm not about to give up. As for work hours, I have never been able to work 8 to 10 hours a day. Of course, when my kids were young and still at home, the most I could ever work was about 4 hours a day, but even now, when I don't have to make meals and do laundry for other people, I still can only work about 3 or 4 hours on weekdays. I'm then exhausted. I guess when I was younger I could work up to about 6 hours a day, sometimes, but the tension of writing, and the involvement, seems to me to be so great that after about 4 hours I am wiped out, usually. Actually, I think 3 or 4 hours at a stretch is pretty damn good. It's the regularity of it that counts. A novel is such a long haul. You'll be okay—I have no doubt of that. But meantime, a writer has to eat.

I hope the film of THE ITALIANS gets made. I know what you mean about film people . . anything I've had to do with same certainly confirms your feelings . . their language indeed knows no bounds. They talk to you as tho' you were a mixture of Shakespeare and Tolstoy, and one has the feeling that ten minutes later they may well forget your name or whether you're a writer or the fast-food purveyor. Ah, well. . . .

I see her as a spiritual writer because she's concerned with the soul of people . . . and she dealt with sexuality in a forthright way, too, that wasn't adverse to soul.

Lakefield,
15 June 82

Dear Frank—

I'm appalled to see that your letter is dated 10 March 82, and I hope you will forgive me for not having responded sooner. In fact, Oberon did send me a copy of BLACK MADONNA when it first came out, and I have only just now read it, because I have been struggling to get into a novel and have been reading nothing serious until recently. I am not at all in despair but this one is taking me a long time . . it gets more difficult as I get older, I guess.

BLACK MADONNA is a very very good novel, Frank. I was delighted to see that it got good reviews and reviews in the most important publications . . *Globe & Mail*, [Toronto] *Star*, *Books in Canada*, *Maclean's*, etc. I don't want to sound cynical, but reviews in those publications do indeed matter, damn it. The reviews I saw seemed to me to understand the book quite a lot.

It is an incredible novel, I have to tell you. As with THE ITALIANS, I was astounded at your ability to portray female characters. This is a rare quality, believe you me. Your portrayal of Joey was splendid, but did not surprise me as much as your portrayal of Maria/Marie, and of the old woman herself. What was astonishing and wonderful in the novel, Frank, was that Assunta came across so strongly . . . and to portray a virtually unverbal woman and make her live in the reader's mind is really amazing. The presence of her dead husband is also strong. But through her children, Joey and Marie, you present this woman as a tragic figure . . terrible and impossible to live with, but *real*. I felt so strongly for her and for both Joey and Marie. The issue I would take with some of the reviewers is that they did not apparently see how important it was for both J and M to come to terms with their parents, honour them, and let them in a sense go while always knowing the parents were part of them. I think it is a fine and good novel, Frank, and the characters will live on in my mind. It is also an honest novel . . it speaks of your own truth, from the sight of your own eyes, and to my mind that is the most important thing. We must bear witness to our own people and our own lives. Which does not mean writing totally autobiographical novels, naturally, as you know. I have to say that your portrayal of Maria/Marie moved me a great deal. You showed her with great compassion but also with terrible honesty .. I hope she will (because the people seem real to me) understand that she is doing in another way the same kind of damage to her child as was done to her. I guess that character moved me the most. Anyway, thanks. It is a very good novel.

Much love to you and yours. . . .

I was in her presence a few times, but every time I felt very good afterward. I felt good as a writer, and I felt that I was doing something very worthwhile. . . . And that would hold me for a year or so. . . . It's almost as if she had this tremendous sense of who and what a writer is, and she took it from within herself and she gave it to you.

Lakefield,
9 March 84

Dear Frank—

I've just finished reading THE FATHER.[4] It is a *Very Good* novel . . . it is so moving and so accurate in the matters of the childhood and the family and the heart. The portrayal of both the mother and the father seems to me to have been done with such caring, such pain. I have to compare Magdelena [the character's name is Maddelena] with other strong mother figures, others who are so difficult, so hard, so needful . . . I think of Hagar in my novel THE STONE ANGEL. But your Oreste, the father, is .. how can I express it, Frank. You have created a character that is so memorable, so understandable, so complex . . . how could any reader fail to love him and also to see how difficult he was to his family, his son? The last scene is one of tremendous revelation, rejuvenation, and grace. . . . This is the third in your fictional tribute to your people .. I don't think anyone else has done exactly that. You are the only novelist to have set down the things re: the Italian immigrants and new Canadians of that community, and oh Frank, you have done it so very well. I am proud of you, if I may say so. Gosh, THE FATHER did move me to tears and that must be the test of a novel. It is not easy, and living and writing isn't easy, nor is earning a living. I think the [Canada] Council has to be stupid .. if you want me to write another letter of ref, I will gladly do so. . . . You know, Frank, you would have done this without any words from me at all, but I seem to feel glad that about 14 years ago I told you you should write about what you knew. My own dear stepmother told me the same thing when I was about 8 years old! I hope you know that you are a *pioneer*, in terms of writing about the new Italian-Canadian communities, with passion, sadness, love, hope. . . .

[P.S.] The test of a good novel is if the reader remembers always the protagonist—I think I will *always* remember Oreste, although he wasn't presented as the protagonist. I feel I *know* him. He lives.

(Editor's note: The Laurence–Purdy correspondence is voluminous, and has been collected and edited by John Lennox of York University.[1] Since that book is available, I refer readers to it, and include here, from a taped interview, some of Al Purdy's thoughts on Margaret Laurence and her work, as well as a poem he wrote about her.)

She was a very religious writer. When [I] say religion, I think it actually did take in not a conventional deity, but a deity of some kind. I'm not sure how it could be described.

She had very strong beliefs. She was a very strong-minded woman. Her beliefs were almost implacable. . . . The morality has to do with the family, with children, with the sacredness of children, and that children are somehow sacred people that mothers look after. She was very angry at me in one letter when I said something to the effect that "If you want to write, you've got to travel. You ought to. Why don't you pick up and go if you want to go." [But] she would have [had] to leave her children, and she said "Damn you!"

When she was in England she was a much more passionate person about writing itself.

Anybody who takes on the censors seems to me very important in a sense. . . . If you looked at Lawrence's Lady Chatterley's Lover, *a lot of people would think that was dirt. Well, Lawrence was this moral person who was advancing a strongly felt moral cause. I don't think Margaret ever thought of herself as doing that. That was one of the reasons why she was hurt so. Lawrence was actually trying to create a revolution, somehow. But Margaret was not. She was just trying to say what she thought had to be said.*

She was a trail blazer morally and socially. I don't think of her as a trail blazer technically, as a writer I mean.

I'm not sure how important the tribe [was]—that she was right about that. We're all related to each other, yes, but the question of how important [this is], I don't know. . . . you learn from everybody. You learn all your life. You have to. And I suppose that is part of it with her. But no, I don't agree with her that tribe is as important as she thought it. You know, to say "tribe" is to think that we're all related. Of course we're all related. We're all doing the same thing. We know each other. We know what we've done, and so on. . . . But I've met some miserable lousy writers, and miserable bastards as human beings. So I don't feel very much related to people like that.

I think that Canada was fatal for Laurence. If she had stayed in England, she would have written more novels, her drive would have still been there. When she came over to Canada somehow the reception she got— so many people loved her and liked her and thought she was a great writer. Yes, she was. But that . . . destroyed her appetite for writing to some degree, I think. Whereas, if she had stayed in England, she would have still had that drive, that push. . . . certainly Laurence was needed in Canada. Women particularly needed a woman writer to look up to and to love.

For Margaret[2]

We argued about things
whether you should seek experience
or just let it happen to you
(me the former and she the latter)
and the merits of St. Paul
as against his attitude to women
(she admired him despite chauvinism)
But what pitifully few things
we remember about another person:
me sitting at her typewriter
at Elm Cottage in England
and translating her short story
"A Bird in the House" into a radio play
directly from the book manuscript
in just two or three days
(produced by J. Frank Willis
on CBC his last production)
and being so proud of my expertise
Then going away to hunt books
while my wife recuperated
from an operation
Returning to find the play finished
Margaret had taken about three hours
to turn my rough draft
into a playable acting version

fingers like fireflies on the typewriter
and grinning at me delightedly
while my "expertise" went down the drain
And the huge cans of English ale she bought
Jocelyn called "Al-size-ale"
and the people coming over one night
to sing the songs in *The Diviners*
(for which I gave faint praise)
And the books she admired—
Joyce Cary's *The Horse's Mouth*
Alec Guinness as Gulley Jimson a Valkyrie
riding the Thames on a garbage barge
—how Graham Greene knew so much
that she both loved and cussed him
for anticipating her before she got there
and marked up my copy of his essays
These are the lost minutiae
of a person's life
things real enough to be trivia
and trivial enough to have some permanence
because they recur and recur—with small
differences of course—in all our lives
and the poignance finally strikes home
that poignance is ordinary
Anyway how strange to be writing about her
as if she were not here
but somewhere else on earth
—or not on earth
given her religious convictions
Just in case it does happen
I'd like to be there when she meets St. Paul
and watch his expression change
from smugness to slight apprehension
while she considers him as a minor character
in a future celestial non-fiction novel
And this silly irrelevance of mine
is a refusal to think of her dead
(only parenthetically DEAD)
remembering how alive
she lit up the rooms she occupied
like flowers do sometimes and the sun always
in a way visible only to friends
and she had nothing else

JANIS RAPOPORT

I was pleased to see women characters written so dynamically, so well integrated, so . . . well, action-oriented is the wrong word, but . . . they do things. And they felt true to me, really, basically, very true.

Elm Cottage,
5 Feb 68

Dear Janis—

I'm returning your novel, as I thought you might want it, and I'm not sure when I shall be able to get into London. I want to try to finish the first draft of the novel [*The Fire-Dwellers*] I'm working on, before I do anything. Christmas, and then 2 weeks in Spain, have meant that I haven't done any work for quite some time.

Re: KALEIDOSCOPE[1]—please remember that anything I say about it is only the opinion of one person, and what concerns you most is not the opinions of friends but of a publisher. . . .

My general impression is that you have the first draft of what could become a worthwhile novel, but you need to do some more work on it. I think it would benefit from a certain amount of cutting, editing, and rewriting. For heaven's sake don't be discouraged. When my first novel went to St. Martin's Press in N. York (they subsequently published it), they sent me the report of one of their readers, who said things like "the purple prose and overdone oratory of the last chapter left me only reasonably nauseated"—or words to that effect. I rewrote a hell of a lot of it, and survived to bless the guy. Anyway, as I say, don't take anyone else's remarks about your work too seriously—your own considered opinion, when you're at a slight distance from the first writing of it, is what counts. . . .

She told me she didn't want to leave [England]. She couldn't handle being in a big city, she wanted to be in a small place. And she wanted to have another place where she could be isolated.

156

Dear Janis—

I've been wanting to write to you, and to quite a few other friends, literally for *months*, but life has been terribly busy—more of that later. Anyway, altho it sounds an unlikely tale, I was about to sit down and write to you when your letter arrived today! ESP. I'm absolutely delighted to hear about your book with Press Porcépic [*Jeremy's Dream*[2]]—that is just great news! . . . . You must be enormously busy, with the writing and the kids.

    I spent last term at Western, and it was hectic as all hell, but I enjoyed it. Life at Trent is not quite so hectic, thank goodness, but I have been trying to get my house in Lakefield fixed up. It's a lovely old 2-storey yellowbrick house, 3 bedrooms and a study, liv rm, kitchen-diningroom. At the moment it is full of carpenters, painters, paperhangers etc. I hope to move in on May 1st. . . . I'll keep the cottage on the river, for summers.

    I'll be in Toronto about mid-May, but probably won't be able to see anybody, as I have to do a bunch of publicity for the novel, which should come out about then. I hate that sort of thing but cannot refuse entirely. I'm a bit uncertain about this pre-publication publicity which the novel seems to be getting—hope people won't think the book is an anti-climax! . . .

    I'm really looking forward to seeing your book of poetry.

Love to you all. . . .

WILL READY

(Editor's note: Ready was a writer and University Librarian Emeritus and Professor of Bibliography at McMaster University from 1966 to 1982. Laurence began to correspond with him in 1966, when McMaster University Library started collecting the manuscripts of her fiction.)

Elm Cottage,
8 Nov 66

Dear Will:

... Thanks ... for sending me your review of A Jest of God. I had not seen it before—stupidly, when you wrote asking if I'd seen the [Hamilton] Spectator review,[1] I thought you meant the English Spectator. Anyway, thanks for what you said about the book—I'm very glad you liked it. Or rather, I'm very glad you took from it what I hoped was there.

When I was cleaning out the garage the other day, I found the manuscript of my first published story, "The Drummer Of All The World," which was published in Queen's Quarterly in 1956.[2] I am sending it to you, in case you may want it. I think that the original manuscripts of everything else have disappeared. ...

Sincerely. ...

Elm Cottage,
22 Oct 68

Dear Will—

Thanks so much for both your letters and for sending me THE TOLKIEN RELATION.[3] I found it absolutely fascinating to read, especially as you gave a *real* picture of Tolkien himself, not the idealized sketches that one so often finds in books which deal with living writers. I must say I admire very much your style in this book—it seems to me to be so fresh and so incisive, so unlike much of the heavy-hearted and heavy-handed lit. crit which one reads. I must tell you also that after reading the book, I decided my education had been sadly neglected and that I must read LORD OF THE RINGS. Oddly enough, that very week I happened to be in London and happened to be passing the Essex bookshop on the Strand, and there in their window was the paperback of Tolkien, all three books collected together for the first time, for the amazingly small price of thirty shillings! I went in and bought a copy, and they told me they had just received them that day—obviously, I was fated to read the trilogy! . . . I've never even read THE HOBBIT, although both my kids have, and my daughter read LORD OF THE RINGS about a year ago.[4]

Thanks for sending me the clipping of the movie review [of *Rachel, Rachel*]. The film opened in London a couple of weeks ago, and has had very good reviews here. I went to see it with some qualms, as you can imagine, but I felt really good about it—they have done a splendid job, and have remained very true to the characters.

Your book on THE CANADIAN IMAGINATION[5] sounds most interesting, and I would love to see it when it comes out. I am sending you a copy of my book on Nigerian literature, called LONG DRUMS AND CANONS. It comes out this month. I will also send you the manuscript of the book as soon as I get some brown paper to wrap it in! I've been wondering about the manuscript of my novel [*The Fire-Dwellers*], Will—do you think it would be ethical for me to let you have it before the novel is published? Perhaps I ought to wait and mail it to you when the novel comes out in the spring. . . .

Elm Cottage,
8 Jan 69

Dear Will—

. . . I've finished LORD OF THE RINGS, as I think I told you. I was fascinated by it, and found myself gradually drawn more and more into the whole epic and more involved with the characters. I did feel it was too long and drawn out in places, but this is only a personal preference. Tolkien must be a very strange man indeed. Personally, I thought your book was extremely useful in understanding Tolkien's writing, although I can understand how you feel—nothing is ever quite the way one would have wanted it to be, when it is published, but I think this is inevitable. I'm glad you've got a new novel,[6] and I hope you'll get some word about it soon—I agree, the waiting is well nigh unbearable. That is always the worst time for me, much worse than reading the reviews. . . .

ps. I sent the manuscript of THE FIRE-DWELLERS registered sea mail.

Elm Cottage,
May 25, 1969

Dear Will—

. . . The reviews [of *The Fire-Dwellers*] in Canada have been so far split right down the middle—those who seem to relate to my character, Stacey, and those who seem to want almost to *kill* her—astonishing to me, really, as I thought the novel would be reviewed just as a straight novel but did not suspect it might be reviewed with many overtones of the sex war!! Some men reviewers do not seem able to *look* at her. I have been reassured by the men reviewers such as Bill French in the Globe, who wrote about the novel very perceptively and without apparent threat to the male ego. How peculiar all this is. . . .

Elm Cottage,
8 Feb 73

Dear Will—

This is a vastly delayed communication. . . . I feel, in fact, that I have barely surfaced for about two years, because of this damn novel I've been writing.

It is now finished. Or at least, finished for now. It may need some work done on it, once the publishers have seen it. Or, of course, they may all express such mammoth indifference that no further work will be needed—just a small bonfire in the back yard. Do not mistake me—I do not say that out of false modesty, of which I have none. I think parts of it work, but as a whole, I just at this point cannot tell, because I have been so deeply involved with it for what seems such a long time that my judgement is not to be trusted. I came back here (after a summer in Can) and put into typescript the 28 notebooks of novel, doing a lot of cutting and rewriting as I went along. I then thought— Hm, maybe I should set it aside for a month or so? I always think that. But never do. The next rewrite was started the next day, as it always is. My daughter is now typing the thing out in fair copy, although I am sure I will have to do more work on it, *if* my editors feel it is worth publishing. We will see. I have also, and very strangely but happily, written 4 songs for the novel, and a Canadian friend here who is like a member of the family and who composes songs, has written the music for my songs [Ian Cameron]. My songs, I may say, have been composed in the persona of one of the characters in the novel, and maybe there will be another song composed by his daughter. All this may sound a bit peculiar, but probably not to you! I mean, you are accustomed to peculiarity and tend to take it as it comes, and you understand that sometimes an unexpected gift is given, from somewhere, undeserved and even unasked-for (yes, I *do* know what this means, and I know the word for it, and if anyone thinks that *grace* is unconnected with writing, they are crazy, but it is difficult to give expression to, to explain—one doesn't have to explain and doesn't want to try). Anyway, Will, for the time being this novel is out of my hands. I have the feeling that it is a peculiar novel, and am desperately uncertain about it—I always am, but this time more than ever, because it is a kind of culmination for me, the wheel (Manawakan-type wheel) come full circle, or something like that. We will see, in time, how it all works out. It *is* very connected with the ancestors, and with time and place, and with geography both inner and outer, and all of these seem to come together for me in this book in terms of Canada (not Canada as a theoretical thing, but as a place where I came from, the true land of my ancestors, as I now see, the *other* and more distant ancestral land being Scotland, but for me so far away that I wasn't formed by it.) The main protagonist, I need hardly say, is NOT (repeat, NOT) me, but we are, as usual, spiritually related. . . .

I was DELIGHTED to see the article about you in *Maclean's*.[7] Well overdue, I thought. Canada is still a kind of strange place Re: some of its talents—you are a bit like George Woodcock in my opinion—after some years, the country wakes up and says "Ye God! Who have we here? Has this incredible guy been here all along?" And people like you and George smile sardonically, I suppose, and even smile quite gently, and don't bear a grudge although people like myself *do*, in a sense, on your behalf, owing a great deal to you both and knowing that your scope is essentially much wider than mine. . . .

I shall be going back home (yes, HOME) in the spring, and will be staying there. . . . I shall have to return here and sell Elm Cottage, which really breaks me up. How I wish I could sell it to the Canadian govt or a brace of Canadian universities, for a hostel for young Canadians or a home for Can English academics on sabbatical. . . . It has been Unofficial Canada House (me as Low Commissioner) for some years—the number of young Can writers, poets, song composers, and others, who have stayed here, you just wouldn't believe. . . . If I had my way, dream-wise, I'd have it remain accessible to Canadians, and I'd persuade Can House in London to furnish the bookshelves with all the Can novels and poetry and biography etc which they have stashed away in their basement, not on view, and I'd keep it as 2/3 of an English acre which is forever Canada. But that is only what *should* happen, were we able to do things for the best, which we aren't. . . .

Love to you all. . . .

Department of English,
The University of Western Ontario,
21 Nov 73

Dear Will—

I feel AWFUL that I haven't written to you before. Have been meaning to do so for months, literally. What has happened, of course, is that I am rushed off my feet here. Am enjoying it, tho, and seeing quite a lot of young writers, one at a time, and finding that quite a few of them are very promising. Also have been going to a lot of seminar classes in Can Lit, and visiting high schools and community colleges, etc. etc. So feel rather exhausted at end of week. . . .

I feel embarrassed about the manuscript of THE DIVINERS (my novel). I discover that I really will have to have my typescript until I get the galleys to proof-read. But also have another little problem—a lot of the rewriting was done on a xerox copy and not on the original typescript, so don't know which to give you. Maybe both? But original typescript is an incomprehensible mess, in some ways, as chunks lifted out and destroyed whilst first rewriting going on. Anyway, I'll sort out all this and ultimately you will probably receive about a ton of paper from me. . . .

Champlain College,
Trent University,
6 Jan 74

Dear Will—

When in doubt, tell the entire truth! I am still having problems about the manuscript [of *The Diviners*] for McMaster, and it is only within the past few days that I fully realized myself what the truth *is* in this matter. I had told you that possibly I should let you have both the original typescript and the xerox copy because it was the xerox copy upon which much of my revision and rewriting and cutting were made. . . . I didn't take any steps to get the cheque [you sent me] cashed because I was uncertain about the manuscript. I now see that the cause was this—there are sections in the original typescript which I rewrote and incorporated into the xerox copy when I was doing massive revisions and cuts, and at that point was working totally from the xerox, so these sections still remain in all their awfulness in the original typescript, and the blunt truth, Will, is that it is not worth $500 or anything else to me to let ANYONE SEE THEM, EVER! And if I pull them out, there will be huge gaps and an absence of transitions throughout the manuscript.

I think therefore that the only course is for me to return the cheque to you. . . . You can, however, if you want it, have the xerox copy in the spring when the novel is out—I think I should keep it until then in case there are last-minute enquiries from the publishers. Perhaps I could deliver it to you personally in the spring, if you want it. Even then, I will have to include a note with it, saying that those parts which have been cut but which are still legible because I only drew a line through them, must not ever under any circumstances be printed in a critical article, essay, thesis, or anywhere else. I'm sorry to sound so fussy, but I find I cannot bear to contemplate those bits which I have carefully taken out, because they didn't belong, being at some time or other printed—it seems to make nonsense of the painstaking job of revision, the object of which is to make a better novel. With my other manuscripts, I have mostly drawn very heavy felt-pen lines or blue-pencil lines through the portions I've cut, but this time the cuts were so extensive and the time was so short (because of my move from England) that I just drew one line through whole paragraphs. . . .

Anyway, I'm sorry about this, and I know that probably some students would like to see the original typescript as it stands, but I wouldn't want them to! . . .

Lakefield,
17 March 77

Dear Will—

. . . Your letter arrived just when I had been going to write to you. . . . (The reason I've been so long in writing is that I've been flitting here and there in . . I guess . . the cause of Canlit, and have just got back from a splendid trip to Saskatoon, where I took part in a prairie writers' workshop at a high school and also had the opportunity to spend a day visiting Batoche, Fish Creek, Duck Lake, the sites of the 1885 Métis uprising, and was able to pay my respects at the grave of Gabriel Dumont, that heroic man, and repeat silently there his own prayer . . do you know it? . . "Lord, strengthen my courage, my faith and my honour, that I may profit all my life from the blessing I have received in Thy Holy Name.")

. . . I have begun to go back, Will, to the church of my people, which is the United Church (my folks long ago were of course Presbyterians, but joined church union with those parts of the Methodist church which went along with the concept). I wanted to do this for about two years here, and felt—it sounds odd, but it's true—shy. I finally did make it, and felt as though I had come back home, again, in yet another way. Well, life is strange and sometimes wonderful. . . .

Dear Will—

Thanks so much for LOSERS KEEPERS.[8] A wonderful title! I
enjoyed it very much indeed, and as you thought, I did like
Jerome so much. . . . I think the play will indeed make a splendid
masque. I love [Bess Ready's] illustration for the cover, and I love
her concept of the Holy Ghost/Dove as a crazy bird. Why oh
Why do many people think that faith has to never crack a smile?
Personally I rather like my own concept of the Holy Ghost as a
great blue heron, also. . . .

    I am working, but slowly, slowly. I have come to the
conclusion, as so often before, that I am really a very slow thinker.
Once I really get into the writing, I write rather quickly, but the
beforehand period is the worst—one insight a week and I feel
lucky. There are moments when I want to say, "Please, do I *have*
to do this?" But I guess the answer comes back, "You must try."

    Do you think you could possibly do me an enormous
favour? If there is difficulty, don't worry—it's not essential, but
it would be very helpful. Do you think you could obtain for me
the Roman Catholic Book of Prayer (or whatever it is called),
including the Order of the Mass and the various prayers. No, I
am not considering converting—I guess I am an incurable
Protestant! But I find myself increasingly wondering why it is
that the various Protestant churches give so little recognition to
the female principle in life. I have ambiguous feelings, because
my own church, the United Church, has long had women
ministers. . . . And I know that the R.C. church does not ordain
women. On the other hand, the various prayers to Mary as
Mother of God strike some kind of deep chord within me.

    I have two little books for little kids coming out this fall.
One . . . is called *The Olden Days Coat*, and is kind of a nice little
story, I think, with a 10 year old girl protagonist. . . . The other . . .
is one of a series, by different writers, aimed at both the school
and the trade market, and meant for beginning readers of 5 and
6 years old. I sweated blood over that one! I have never done a
read-it-yourself book for little kids before. It is called *Six Darn
Cows* and is about two farm kids. . . .

    Re: your play again—I, too, am a Celt of sorts, being
Irish on my mother's side and Scots on my father's, with a slight
admixture of Sassenach blood, through one of my grandmothers

who came of U[nited] E[mpire] L[oyalist] stock. The sense of sorrow (and laughter as well) is in me, also, I believe. However, my grandfather Wemyss, whose family came from Fifeshire in the Lowlands of Scotland, believed firmly that we were directly descended from the Picts, the little people of Scotland, and always said (or so I was told by my family; my grandfather Wemyss died when I was only three weeks old) that the name Wemyss meant "cave-dweller". I have found in recent years that in the Gaelic the word "weem" does indeed mean a Pictish earth-house. How about that? I do like it a lot, I must say.

Love to you. . . .

Elm Cottage,
15 Feb 65

Dear Mordecai:

Thanks for your letter. I've got only one story which might possibly be okay for your purposes. Will submit it as soon as I have a chance to type it out—possibly within the next week or at most two.[1]

Kids and myself are extremely well, and I now rank as a country dweller, which means only two things—I can light and *keep going* both a coal and a wood fire, and I know what to do to prevent the pipes from freezing.

I'd like you and family to come out here sometime, but I suppose that as you are also country dwellers this wouldn't hold too much attraction. Could we meet in London for lunch one day?

All the best. . . .

Elm Cottage,
14 March 67

Dear Mordecai:

I'm writing to you on behalf of the Canadian Universities Society of Great Britain. PLEASE DON'T STOP READING HERE. The thing is that I have somehow allowed myself to get roped into organizing speakers for the Literary supper which is held every year—I haven't done this before, and God forbid that I ever do it again, but now I have to go through with it. As this is centennial year, we thought it would be a good idea to have Canadian speakers. There will be three speakers, and usually each speaks for about ten minutes. The audience is not tremendously literary, so nothing academic or highly analytical is required.

The supper is to be held at the National Book League on the evening of May 18th. The topic is CANADIAN VOICES 67, and

I thought that some of the following questions might be dealt with: a quick look at the Canadian fiction, poetry and T.V. drama of today; how have things changed over the past decade?; how do we compare with other English-speaking countries?; where are the Canadian voices in these fields heard? nationally? internationally? or are they in fact heard much outside Canada at all?; is there a distinctive Canadian voice or are we culturally North American and scarcely distinguishable from the U.S.A.?

Would you be willing to give forth with ten minutes of personal opinions on Canadian fiction? I would be grateful if you would.

Things are settling down for me, after a hectic year. I spent the summer in Canada—I had the intention of going there for a holiday, but Jack McClelland thought otherwise, and as I have a novel out in September, the whole thing turned into a lunatic kind of publicity tour which made me feel like a campaigning politician and all but killed me. When I got back here, I had the chance of going to Egypt for *Holiday* magazine, so I spent a month there. I took my kids along, and we had a wonderful time. Ever since then, I've been writing the two articles for the magazine.[2]

Saw a chapter of your own new novel in *Tamarack Review*.[3] When does it come out?

Please agree to speak on May 18th. . . .

Elm Cottage,
1 Feb 68

Dear Mordecai—

When I looked through my files, I realized that only two of my Canadian stories have not been published in some kind of anthology. One of these is a story [possibly "The Loons"] I don't much like, so I'm not sending it to you—it was read on the CBC and later published in *The Atlantic Advocate*, and if you really want to see it, I'll send it, but it isn't a very good story. I'm sending you "Horses of the Night", which was published in *Chatelaine*, as you can see (although *not*, as they say, "written especially for this issue . . ").[4] It hasn't appeared anywhere else. It may be rather long for your purposes, but I'm afraid it's the best I can come up with at this point.

Good luck with the collection. . . .

Elm Cottage,
5 Feb 68

Dear Mordecai—

Am enclosing another story. Upon re-reading it, maybe it's not such a bad story after all. Anyway, see what you think. Could I have it back, please, ultimately, even if you decide to use it? It seems to be the only copy I have. Would have it copied out for you, but I hate copy typing and I thought you would want it quickly anyhow. . . .

[P.S.] you don't need to return HORSES OF THE NIGHT—I've got another copy.

Elm Cottage,
2 Aug 68

Dear Mordecai—

I meant to write some time ago to say how much I liked COCKSURE,[5] but got sidetracked by life as usual. Today, however, reading Leslie Fiedler's semi-idiotic article in *The Running Man*, I've at last been prodded towards the typewriter.[6] What he means by "an anti-genteel defence of the genteel tradition" I can't think, but I have been thinking for some years that this guy has an enormous flare for the prophetic and meaningless phrase, and I think his ability to make significant-sounding statements that will become instant cocktail party-or-whatever chitchat is truly admirable but totally unimportant. If he's an old friend of yours, I'm sorry. . . . I can't stand to see somebody damn a novel with faint praise, or to say that the writer is actually terribly effective but not in any of the ways he intends to be. "It is another aspect of his work which makes Richler more dangerous than he seems, perhaps even to himself." I don't have a clue how you feel, but if it were me, I would feel—thanks for letting me know what I think, and where did you get the hot-line to my psyche from? I was glad to see that he gave a boost to Leonard Cohen's BEAUTIFUL LOSERS,[7] which certainly ought to be published in this country, but it would have been nice if he'd got the detail right—the two male lovers don't jerk each other off in the car; the dominant partner refuses the mutual-admiration society method, saying this is between him and God. For what it's worth, but that's the way I read it. I don't know. Such an article shouldn't make me angry—it's futile—but it does.

Anyhow, I thought COCKSURE was a terrific send-up of my part of the world. Especially liked the progressive school, and the (to me) really touching bits with the kid who said he really wanted to get into his mum's bed because he was scared, and also the beautifully done film ending with the girl unable to see that reality is real (sorry—references probably not too exact; someone has borrowed my copy). There were parts where I thought the Star Maker bit didn't quite jibe with the rest of the fictional world which was (to me) largely an only-too-real one, but this was a personal objection to two tones which didn't entirely fit. Mortimer I thought was splendid—I know him very well. His wife reminded me of myself, not so much in the progressive-sex bits as the progressive-race bits, and if you have ever once been a white liberal, you never forget how it was, way back when, even when you have changed and no longer can imagine yourself agreeing with people, just because the colour of their skin was different from yours (I could write a long weary diatribe on the subject, but why bother?). These days the whole question of Africa etc etc leaves me having no opinions on the subject whatsoever).

Also liked PLAYING BALL ON HAMPSTEAD HEATH—read it first in *Can Winter's Tales*.[8] How is the other novel coming along? It's really that one that I look forward to. Saw one chapter in *Tamarack Review* and thought it looked very very good. . . .

I understand you're going to Montreal as writer-in-residence this coming year at Sir Geo Williams. . . . What I want to ask you is this—what in hell do writers-in-residence do? Don't mistake me—I'm not asking frivolously or ironically. The U of T asked me to go as w-in-r next year (1969) and maybe I will if I can get my kids' grandmother to come and stay with them here. . . . But what bugs me is—what do you *do*? I can see myself sitting in a well-appointed office doing absolutely nothing for 6 or 8 months. I have never been part of an academic setup, so don't know any of the ropes and tend to be more intimidated by large buildings etc. than perhaps I should be. But I feel that if I do manage to go, I may be scared out of my mind or else feel in my old Presbyterian way that I ought to be doing something for the money they're paying me. I don't expect you to reply at length, but I would sure as hell be interested in any comments. The whole role (w-in-r) seems to me, to tell you the truth, to be quite ridiculous, but I think I would like at this point in my life to get away from home for awhile, that's about it. . . . it would be nice to go to Toronto for some months, even if only to discover all over again that I couldn't bear to live in Toronto.

Have finished a novel, which has been Praise God accepted by my 3 publishers in Can, Eng, and USA. . . . It's once again an unlikely character—this time a middle-aged white anglo-saxon Protestant mother of four. Maybe I'm wrong in saying "unlikely"—maybe this is just about as far-out as you can go. Let's face it—some of my best friends are middle-aged white anglo-saxon Protestant mothers. Many are real, *too*, although this disturbing thought seems to have recently been forgotten in fiction. Better close as I can feel my Scot's ire mounting. . . .

Elmcot,
10 Sept 68

Dear Mordecai—

Many thanks for your letter of Sept 4th. . . .

Sorry to bother you with something which I ought to have asked when I wrote before, only then I wasn't thinking of my short stories because had finished novel, etc. Can you tell me what finally happened about those stories for Penguin collection of Can. writing? The thing is that I submitted several to you, at a time when I was pretty much involved in novel, so don't really remember what I sent you, or when, or what. I think I sent two— "Horses of the Night", and "The Loons". The latter was shorter and therefore maybe better for your purposes. I am being slightly sneaky when I say this, because I would now like to submit the former, "Horses of the Night," for the next *Winter's Tales*,9 not because it would entail more [money] but because I hope ultimately to finish another few stories which will complete a collection all set in the same Canadian town, with the same characters, and it would be better for me to have this particular story come out in *W.T.*, for the sake of timing, etc etc. . . .

Thanks for the comments re: writer-in-res. I am somewhat reassured about it. If I do get there, will no doubt worry all the same. If there aren't any worries I have to invent them. But I'd like to go, nonetheless, maybe only in order to live in Can for a few months, without too many long-term commitments.

Saw your story in last *Tamarack*[10] and thought it one of your best short ones. Was very involved personally and somewhat split re: Egypt–Israeli war, as had just spent month in Egypt writing article for *Holiday* (which won't be published, needless to say). Relieved at Israel's victory, but couldn't help thinking also of bloody Egyptian soldiers . . . left to walk around Sinai till they dropped. Naturally, it happens everywhere. A plague on both your houses? I knew Chris Okigbo slightly, who was killed in Biafra. Also Wole Soyinka, Africa's best Eng-writing writer, maybe dead, maybe if not dead would be better so after 1 yr in Kaduna jail. Anyway, that wasn't what I meant to say about your story. What I meant to say was about the ending, Jake standing to lose either way. That seems very pertinent—not sure why. Issues not being as clear as they seemed 20 years ago, maybe. Issues haven't that much changed—I'm 42 not 22, that's all. . . .

Elm Cottage,
7 April 72

Dear Mordecai—

Congratulations and all that, re: Gov Gen's for *St. Urbain's*. When I read it, I said in my best prophetess voice, "Well, it should get him the G-G, but probably the swine won't give it to him, as he got it for *Cocksure*." Very glad I was proven wrong. Don't believe in such statements as "Mr. Richler's best novel to date"—this kind of categorizing seems meaningless to me, but I did think Wow in every possible way, when I read it.

Best to you. . . .

Lakefield,
15 Feb 76

Dear Gabrielle Roy—

Joyce Marshall gave me your address, so I'm venturing to write to you. Joyce said you had mentioned that you'd like to meet me, and I was so very pleased to hear it—it's a cliché, I know, but I have admired your work for a long time. You know how there are sometimes scenes from novels which continue to inhabit the mind forever after? For me, one such scene is the one in *The Tin Flute*[1] in which Rose-Anna is told that Daniel has leukemia, and not told that it will be fatal. There are many other scenes (and characters) in your work which remain with me always, but somehow that is one scene which has in a sense grown in power in my mind throughout the years—when I first read it, I was in my early twenties, and did not yet have my children; later, when my daughter was a month old, in England, she developed a mysterious illness with convulsions . . it turned out that she had had her yellow fever and smallpox injections too close together and in the wrong order (we were going out to West Africa), a fact which medical science only discovered several years later. At the time, they didn't know what was wrong with her, so they told me she probably had spinal meningitis—it was, in a sense, the reverse of Rose-Anna's experience, for they neglected to tell me that the disease was not always fatal. In my terrible pain, believing she would die, I remembered Rose-Anna. Although the circumstances of my life and Rose-Anna's could hardly be more different, I have always felt I knew that woman awfully well. There is a part of her in me, the part that never ceases to be concerned over one's children, even though mine are now 20 and 23.

I have recently received from Joyce the NCL edition of THE ROAD PAST ALTAMONT.[2] I had read it when it first came out, and loved it, and felt I shared something of that Manitoba background and could understand and feel it so well. I think Joyce's Introduction is splendid—probably unique, in a way; I don't remember ever having read such an essay before, in which the translator can speak from an unusually close position to the work and can therefore talk of it with a special kind of knowledge.

Since I finished THE DIVINERS, several years ago, I have virtually written nothing except some articles and a lot of book reviews. No real writing. I'd like to try to write a children's book. I'm a bit hesitant about beginning, but no doubt will do so. I am assured by Sheila Egoff, in her book about Canadian children's literature, THE REPUBLIC OF CHILDHOOD[3] (Republic? Why not Dominion??), that animal fantasies are looked upon with scorn by the young of today. . . . Anyway, mine will be an animal fantasy because that is what I want to write. I have done one children's book—an animal fantasy, JASON'S QUEST, which Ms. Egoff calls "the most disappointing book in all of Canadian children's fiction." If one is going to fail, by all means let us do so grandly! However, one cannot in the end be guided by critics or even potential readers.

If ever you have the time, I would like so much to hear from you. Don't, however, feel any obligation. I really just wanted to write and send you my greetings and my thanks for your work.

Sincerely. . . .

Lakefield,
23 March 76

Dear Gabrielle—

Thanks so very much for your letter, which delighted me. It *is* strange that we should hesitate to approach other writers—I had the same sense of diffidence before I wrote to you. But we are, after all, members of the same tribe, all of us. There is this growing sense of true community among the Anglophone writers in Canada, over the past couple of years, owing mainly, I believe, to the Writers' Union. I don't doubt that the same is true among Francophone writers. If only we could get together more, across the language barrier.

Speaking of languages, two of my novels, THE STONE ANGEL and THE DIVINERS, are going to be translated into French, by the publishing firm Le Cercle du Livre de France, in Montreal. THE STONE ANGEL is being translated by [Québécoise novelist] Claire Martin, which pleases me very much, needless to say. The only other of my novels to be translated into French as yet is THE

174

FIRE-DWELLERS, which was done by a publisher in France. At the time when they had just taken the book, Naim Kattan [of the Canada Council] was in Paris, and tried to persuade them to get a French-Canadian translator, but they wouldn't. Alas. So I am very pleased that these other 2 books are being done by a French-Canadian firm.

I'm glad to hear that you want to write a children's book. There is such a desperate need in this country for good children's books—not that that is any reason for writing one! I haven't yet begun mine—I sense that it is not quite ready to be written, as yet, but I hope it will be soon. I've just completed work on a collection of essays and articles, written over the years [*Heart of a Stranger*], and I think McClelland and Stewart will publish it in the fall. A good many of them are travel articles. Not deathless prose, but fairly interesting, I hope. Jack McClelland and I are having our usual amiable battle over the title . . he doesn't like my title, and I refuse to allow him to choose one, naturally. I have called it after one of the articles . . "Where The World Began", which refers to my world beginning in a small prairie town.

THE DIVINERS is coming under fire in my own community here, I am sorry to say. It was on the Grade 13 high school course, and a parent complained that it was "obscene" because it contains some so-called four-letter words and a few sex scenes—the first are essential to the idiom of particular characters, and the second are essential to the narrative line and the revelation of character. A local school trustee, who is a fundamentalist, has got into the act and stated in the Peterborough Examiner that only "true" Christians have the right to choose material for English courses (this would, I suspect, exclude not only those of the Jewish faith, but also Roman Catholics, Anglicans, etc etc!). He admits he reads only the Bible (I can't quarrel with his reading of that—it is a book I frequently read myself) and "religious writings". He has not read THE DIVINERS because "one does not have to wade in the muck to know what it is all about". I realize that people like this will always, alas, be with us, but I cannot help feeling hurt at having my work so vastly misunderstood. There have been some very heartening and supportive letters in the papers, and also some very nasty ones. The nasty ones all state that the people who are writing them have not read my novel, but they somehow "know" it is corrupting the young! It will be taken to a Textbook Review Committee, so we shall see. But the fundamentalist trustee is lobbying against it as hard as he can. In fact, at its deepest level, it is a novel about God's grace. But even if [the] trustee

175

read it, I doubt he would see that. Well, we must survive such unpleasant episodes.

I'm sending you a copy of the novel, together with a little record of the songs. The music was composed by a friend, Ian Cameron.

I hope your health is improving, and that you will be able to get outdoors when the spring arrives. . . .

With all best wishes. . . .

Lakefield,
9 June 76

Dear Gabrielle—

Please forgive me for not having replied sooner to your two good letters. I shall tell you presently of some of my activities these past two hectic months. But first, thank you for your response to THE DIVINERS. It means more to me (your comments, I mean) than I can possibly say. As for the pathetic fallacy—I've often used it myself. It was just one of those things that Morag learned about at that age, and [she] probably used the form herself later on! I myself tend to think very anthropomorphically, and attribute feelings of deep parental concern to the swallows, which they may not have, or not in the same way as I imagine. Yes, they do, though!

During April and May, it seems I had about six deadlines for book reviews, one of them a fascinating and definitive history of the Japanese in Canada [*The Enemy That Never Was*, by Ken Adachi[4]], but a book of some 445 pages of fine print, and although I am normally a pretty fast reader, this one took days to read. I also went out to a number of Canadian literature classes at Trent university and various high schools where they were studying one of my books. I worked for a solid week, together with several others, on the final draft of the Writers' Union standard contract, which our members can use as guidance when signing a contract with a publisher. I attended the Writers' Union conference (3 days) in Ottawa. I also, in between all this, had to try to keep up with the flow of business correspondence, plus doing final revisions of a manuscript of my own . . a book of essays, to be called HEART OF A STRANGER (the title is from Exodus) which will be published in the autumn. Then, in the middle of May I went out to High Prairie, Alberta, 225 miles north of Edmonton, to visit with my brother and his wife and their two daughters, for a week. What beautiful country it is! Great stretches of farmlands, with those vast prairie fields all set out in sections and quarter sections, and the soil that true black colour that always has seemed the only proper colour for soil to be. In between are forests of poplar, spruce, pine. It is much more northerly than my own (and your) part of the prairies, but it still felt like home. I think you are right— I am basically a prairie writer, even though I have written of other places. My emotional attachment to the prairies remains very strong. . . .

So I have been having a busy time, but it's all been interesting and worthwhile. I'm now out at my summer cottage, which is about 20 miles from Lakefield, on the same river, the Otonabee. The river is the same as I described it in THE DIVINERS—I wrote most of the novel here and the river just seemed naturally to flow through the book. I hope to have a reasonably restful and quiet summer here. . . .

With very best wishes. . . .

Lakefield,
2 Nov 76

Dear Gabrielle—

I must apologize for having been so long in writing to thank you for ENCHANTED SUMMER. . . .[5]

I can't tell you how truly enchanting I found the book! The river—"your" river—is so much more vast than the little Otonabee where I have my cottage, but nonetheless, so very much in the book reminded me of my own summers, and so many aspects of the book really spoke to me. I love Monsieur Toong— I, too, love to listen to the bullfrogs in the river in the spring of the year. Our bullfrogs here are, I think, Anglophone, as contrasted to your Francophone ones! Ours say "Gronk!" Scarcely as mellifluous as the Francophone "Toong", but perhaps with a certain dramatic emphasis. I loved very much, too, your description of the killdeer . . anxious parents that they are. So many times when I've been out walking near my cottage, I've met with the same nervous birds, hysterically trying to lead me away from their nest. How accurately you describe it, and how poetically at the same time! As for the possible charges of being "anthropomorphic" in our attitudes to birds and animals—in THE DIVINERS, Morag muses on this possibility in her attitude to the beloved swallows, and comes to the conclusion that I have come to—so what? If we interpret birds and animals through our own perceptions, why, those are the only perceptions we have, and probably the birds and animals interpret *us* through their own types of perception, too. I so much like, also, your stories about your cat. I have been wanting to write a story about my cat, and for a long while I thought I would do it as an animal fantasy, but just lately I am beginning to wonder if I won't simply tell the story as it happened—of course, I would have to portray her with "human" feelings, but really, people who feel that animals have no feelings recognizable by us are just mistaken, in my opinion, or they have never really observed animals very closely. . . .

I have now shut up my cottage for the winter, as the weather had begun to be too cold for enjoyment out there, so I'm back at home now. The winter season, as usual, promises to be busy, but I'm trying not to take on too many commitments. I need time to think about what I want to write next—it is still so vague and unformed in my mind, but perhaps it will come. . . .

Love. . . .

Lakefield,
17 Feb 77

Dear Gabrielle—

. . . When you last wrote, it was the eve of the Quebec elections. I don't even presume to make any comments—I have not the right. I do feel, however, that Lévesque is a man of integrity. I wish with all my heart that in Anglophone Canada (and yes, in the prairies which you and I both love so much) that more people could have realized, really realized, long ago, the way in which people in Quebec feel about their history, their language, their heritage, their identity. I only pray (and I use that word advisedly) that it may not be too late. I have never been in the slightest doubt about how Francophone Canadians feel about their language. It is the same way I feel about mine, even though for me, as for millions of Canadians not of English background, it was not the language of my ancestors. But I never knew Gaelic (or as the Scots say, "had the Gaelic"); English is my birth tongue, and I love it. And yet I am always aware of the irony . . here I am, writing to you in my language, not in yours. I am as much to blame as any other "Anglo". The ideal would be for me to write to you in English, and for you to reply in French. And you could do it, that way, with full and complete understanding, but I could not. And yet I feel—it may be too late for me (and for all those middle-aged civil servants taking crash courses in French), but surely we could begin with the children? A family irony of mine . . my daughter, educated in *England*, is pretty fluent in French. But surely primary school is the place to begin, and not from duty, but from a desire to know one another. Also, I believe that translations of books, from English into French, and from French into English, is one area which can help. I know that some of the younger Quebec writers aren't anxious to have their books translated, but one can hope they may change their minds, ultimately. I believe that, national considerations not withstanding, writers should be as widely read as possible. When I think that without translations, to speak realistically, I would have been deprived of your work, and of the work of many others, it doesn't bear thinking about. And there are so many translations yet to be done, both ways. . . .

There are times when I find I cannot think too long at once about all the problems which beset us. One turns, as you did in ENCHANTED SUMMER, to things which are simple (and enormously complex as well) and beautiful and perhaps joyful. Also, to the humorous stories . . and my life seems to abound in these, thank God. It abounds in lots of other things as well, but I really do believe that laughter is a kind of gift of grace . . I mean laughter that is warm, of course, not malicious (but that isn't true laughter, is it?). . . .

Love, and God bless. . . .

Dear Gabrielle—

Thanks so much for your letter. . . .

Yes, Quebec. It seems that everyone is terribly concerned and indeed heartbroken, but it is so difficult to know what to do. I myself feel that the views of many anglophone Canadians are not being adequately or even accurately presented to the Quebec people by the federal government. To express, as I and many of my friends do, the passionate hope that this country may remain *one*, does not imply a faith in the status quo, of course, and I wish that this could be communicated. I am sure we need a new constitution and have needed one for a long time. The talk of "repatriating" the constitution seems to me to be an exercise in futility—all we really need to do is announce that our constitution is *our* country's business and ours alone. I expect Britain would be quite glad to be rid of it, but in any event, what could Britain do even if some diehard imperialists there disapproved? Nothing, obviously. Gary Geddes, poet and editor, is putting together a collection of essays etc on the whole question, and hopes to put it out in both English and French. I can't believe it will do much good, actually, but one must keep on trying to communicate. I enclose a copy of the essay I am contributing.[6] I found it very hard to write, and although I rewrote it about 10 times I am still not too happy with it. It is quite emotional, but how can one write about this subject without being emotional? I hope you do not mind that I have mentioned you, with great respect, in the essay. . . .

After travelling, it seemed, all spring (to Vancouver—Simon Fraser University; Fredericton—conference; Saskatoon—writers' workshop; etc.) at last I am out at my cottage. What a relief to be here! I am in future going to refuse all invitations to conferences etc—I shall never get back to writing unless I allow myself the time and space to meditate upon it. . . .

Lakefield,
27 Oct 77

Dear Gabrielle—

I feel badly at having taken so long to write to thank you for
GARDEN IN THE WIND,[7] which I read in the summer while I was
at my cottage. How incredibly you have found your way into
the minds and hearts of the people in the stories! Yes, it is
something we have to try to do, and when it is people of very
different backgrounds and cultures with whom we are dealing,
it takes a very special leap of the imagination. I found all four
stories so very moving in so many ways. First, of course, they're
profoundly moving because you do lead the reader into the hearts
of your characters, and we feel *with* them. And secondly because
so much of the stories' content reminds me of my own prairie
days. Like all prairie towns, mine also had a Chinese restaurant,
and I can remember the days when no Chinese wives or children
were there—only later on did I realize how terribly lonely it must
have been for those men. Lee Ling, the proprietor of the first
Chinese café, in my town, was a truly wonderful man . . . kindly
to all children, as I recall well. My father always did his legal
business, and every Christmas Lee would give our family a
turkey, a box of chocolates and a box of lichee nuts. After my
father died, Lee continued to give our family these Christmas
gifts, every year until Lee himself died. I have always found that
very remarkable. Your story of the Doukhobors I found
fascinating . . . there is a kind of Old Testament prophet feeling
about those people. Oddly, I had just finished reading THE
DOUKHOBORS, by George Woodcock and Ivan Avakumovic[8]
shortly before I read your story, so it had a special dimension for
me. I loved "Tramp at the Door" . . the reader knowing all along
the true state of affairs and yet realizing more and more the real
truth that the mother comes to see only at the end. Perhaps the
title story moved me most of all—one has often thought how
lonely and yet how incredibly persevering must have been all
those women like Marta, living out of their language areas, often
with husbands grown despairing or numb, seeing their children
move out, move on. To me, you have captured all this perfectly
through Marta's eyes. Anyway, many many thanks for having
written these beautiful stories.

I am trying to feel and think my way into another novel . . .
how slow the process often seems. One must be patient, and make

a space in one's life so as to be able to find, gradually, what it is that one is perhaps being given to do with the writing. Often this is difficult . . I read somewhere this summer that all too often the *important* gives way to the *urgent*. This strikes me as true, and yet it is so hard to avoid it. I'm not doing any more travelling about, readings, seminars, lectures, etc. I did have a restful summer and did a lot of reading and thinking. . . .

Lakefield,
26 Feb 78

Dear Gabrielle—

This will be a brief letter, as I have a horrifying stack of business letters to catch up on. But before I tackle them, I did want to write and tell you how wonderful it was to meet at last! I only wish we had had more time, but at least it was so good actually to be able to talk for awhile. I would so much like to visit you some time. Would there be any chance of persuading you to visit me?

I was so amused to learn that we had received letters from the same students! Teachers, however, really should know better than to advise their young charges to write to authors with all kinds of complicated requests. One begins to feel like an agency.

I had a lovely trip home on the train. One realizes, going across the prairies by rail, what a *huge* country this is. I covered only about half of it, in terms of miles, and yet it took nearly 2 days and 2 nights. Also, although the prairies in winter may be difficult to cope with, how incredibly beautiful they are! And, of course, not empty at all, as non-prairie people envisage them to be. I wonder how all the wild birds survive—dried berries on bushes? On the way out . . . I saw two small antelope standing near the tracks—my Calgary nephew told me these are "pronghorns", the fastest animal on earth, he says. The cheetah, he informed me, is faster in short stretches but the pronghorn can keep up speed for long distances. I love facts like that! On the way home, I looked out at dusk, and there was a prairie jackrabbit in all his winter white, bounding across a field. He stopped and looked at the train, and became almost invisible against the snow. I hadn't seen a prairie jackrabbit in years and years. . . .

Dear Gabrielle—

I do feel ashamed that it has taken me so long to answer your last letter, and also so long to write and CONGRATULATE YOU ON WINNING THE GOVERNOR GENERAL'S AWARD FOR YOUR LAST BOOK!!! [*Ces Enfants de ma vie*]. I was delighted. Do you know when we may look forward to an English translation? It is at times like this that I feel the worst at not being able to read French. The winner in the English language for fiction was Timothy Findley's novel, THE WARS. . . . It's a splendid novel. Of course, the press gave its usual minimal coverage to the event. I think the Canada Council must also take some responsibility, too, for making the announcements so late. But it always annoys me to see the very little bit of publicity the Governor-General's Awards get—one would hope that such an award might increase sales of the books, but how can it if no one hears of it? In our local Peterborough paper, the only mention of the awards was a brief report stating that one of the French-Canadian writers had refused his award. . . .

It was wonderful to meet you in Calgary in February, at last! . . . The whole question of the literary lists seemed to me to have been played up far too much. Malcolm Ross had intended that the lists would be announced at the beginning of the conference, not the end, and that they would serve only as a talking point—they weren't intended to be definitive lists in any way. However, this was misinterpreted by the media. . . .[10]

I am out at my cottage now, looking at the beloved river, and I wonder if you are now at your summer place, overlooking your beloved river.

I have been here for less than a month and can hardly believe it is July already. I don't think the tensions of the winter have quite dropped away from me yet but each day I feel a little calmer and more relaxed. When I'm too busy, as I always seem to be in the winter, I find I can't do any real thinking and hence no real writing. These summers are important to me. . . .
Please take care, dear Gabrielle. . . .

Dear Gabrielle—

... Thank you so much for sending me a copy of CHILDREN OF MY HEART. I have not received it yet, but will be delighted to have it. . . . When I received your letter, I was on the point of writing to you! I had been sent a copy of CHILDREN OF MY HEART and had just finished reading it a few days ago. McClelland & Stewart had sent me a copy. . . . I wanted to write right away and tell you how much I loved the book.

Justice was done when you were awarded the Governor General's award for the book in French. I think Alan Brown's translation must be a very faithful one, for the book seems—I don't quite know how to express this—it seems almost perfect, flawless. I was so moved by the stories of all the children, and by the portrayal of the young teacher, scarcely more than a child herself, trying to understand her charges, loving them, sometimes bewildered by them. I was in tears at many points throughout the story, especially when reading about the little Ukrainian boy with the lark's voice, and about Médéric . . . that final tale I found so very moving and evocative.[11] In the town where I grew up, there were one or two young men like that . . having to act so tough and yet being so unhappy within the confines of school, and happy only when in touch with the land and its creatures. How beautifully you have portrayed Médéric, and how delicately you have explored his feelings and those of his teacher towards him. When I was a child there was an isolated Ukrainian settlement somewhere near Riding Mountain (I have forgotten the name of the place, but on our way to Clear Lake [summer cottage] we could see the onion spires of the Greek Orthodox church at a distance). The local legend was that the settlement had been started by a Hungarian nobleman who had come to Canada, bringing all the Ukrainian peasants and serfs from his old-country estate (the Ukraine then being part of the Austro-Hungarian empire). He had tried to impose a feudal system on "his" people, until they discovered that they did not need to be serfs of his in the new land. I wrote a story about this, when I was in college, long ago.[12] Médéric's father might have been just such a man.

I can't begin to tell you how much I loved CHILDREN OF MY HEART. There is something so crystal-clear and flowing and pure about your writing, like a mountain stream. And it is the quality of gentleness and tenderness in it, combined with the knowledge of life's pain and sadness, that speak to me. . . .

God bless, and much love. . . .

Lakefield,
7 March 79

Dear Gabrielle—

. . . I have just got home after a week away, during which time I spent two days at St. Andrew's College in Aurora, Ontario . . a private boys' school (high school). I was exhausted when I finished, as I had NINE sessions with students of various grades, in groups of 25 to about 50 . . in two days! However, the boys were enthusiastic and bright, so I enjoyed it as well. My father attended that school before World War One, and they very kindly looked up the old records of his attendance . . I was astonished that the old records still existed. I learned that he had kept his old school informed about some events in his life, and there was one entry that moved me very much . . "July 18/26 . . birth of a daughter, Jean Margaret". He must have been very pleased at my birth, to inform his old high school! He died when I was only nine, so I felt somehow that seeing the old record was like a kind of message all across those years. . . .

Lakefield,
15 Jan 80

Dear Gabrielle—

I feel so badly that it has taken me so long to thank you for your children's book, *Courte Queue*. . . .[13] I wanted to wait until I could get my daughter to translate it for me. . . .

I found your children's story very moving indeed. Parts of it are very sad, but I think that children recognize sadness and need to become acquainted with it in books. I am sure all children are quite often sad, and can identify with those feelings. I think the mother cat's bravery and tenacity are marvellously portrayed. I also liked the illustrations—I can see what you mean about their seeming French rather than Canadian, but I think they are awfully well done.

I am trying so hard to get started at another novel. I hope I will be able to stay home and work now. . . . During November and December, I had to go in [to Toronto] often for publicity for my little kids' books. It seems that something is always coming up—in March I am giving a paper at a Royal Society symposium. Why did I ever agree?! Never mind—the ideas won't go away. . . .

Lakefield,
3 March 80

Dear Gabrielle—

It was wonderful to talk with you on the phone! How glad I am that you called! I do so much hope the new translation of *The Tin Flute* comes into being. . . .

I'm sending you a copy of *Les Oracles* (*The Diviners*). It has turned out to be a very thick book . . more than 500 pp. in the French edition, so I am looking for a book envelope large enough! . . . I am quite certain the translation is an excellent one. . . . I have to admit, dear Gabrielle, when I wrote in the book for you, I was sorely tempted to cheat! The thought crossed my mind, briefly, that it would be nice to autograph it in French. But how could I? Obviously by copying *your* inscription to me in *Courte Queue*!!! I almost instantly perceived, however, that this would not be an honourable thing to do!

My writing goes so slowly and so badly, of late. I have three times made a false start at a novel, and so far have torn up about 50 pp of handwriting. However, my handwriting is somewhat large and scrawling, so it isn't as much as it sounds. I am pretty sure there is a novel there, somewhere, if only I can find it, or at least find my way into it. It has often been this way with me, but I tend to forget, and to think that it has never before been as difficult as this time. It does, though, in some ways, get more difficult each time. One must forget any potential readership, or the critics, or anyone except the characters themselves. This was easier some years ago than it is now. In a sense, it was easier to write when my books were relatively unknown. When people say to me (as they often do), "I'm just waiting for your next book," my heart positively sinks. I want to say to them, "Don't hold your breath while you're doing it, because it may be a long time." However, we go on in some way or another. It is a strange profession that we chose, Gabrielle . . . or rather, that chose us.

I don't know at all if you would be interested, but I am also sending you. . . . a reprint, in *The United Church Observer*, of a dialogue-sermon I did with my old friend, Rev. Lois Wilson at Chalmers United Church in Kingston, last year. We did a dialogue instead of having a sermon at a Sunday service. We spoke of things that we had often previously discussed. It was taped, and *The United Church Observer* reprinted it.[14] It does represent my true feelings, but, being a writer, and seeing it in print rather than having it as the spoken word, I look at it and think how inadequately I have expressed myself. I would like to take my parts and rewrite them! . . .

P.S. Good news . . Joyce Marshall will be coming to Trent University for the next academic year, as writer-in-residence. . . . I told her she had only one worry—she must try very hard not to be *too* conscientious!! I believe that a writer-in-residence should earn her or his salary, (and in this not all writers agree with me), but I know that my own tendency was . . as Joyce's will be . . to take on far too much and to become exhausted. . . .

Lakefield,
25 Sept 80

Dear Gabrielle—

I have thought of you so often this past summer, and have been meaning to write for ages. Now that I'm actually doing so, it's good to be able to send you the enclosed little book. There is a wonderful story about this book and how it came into being. It is always so good when one can tell a happy story, in this terrifying world of ours.

It began more than 20 years ago, when we lived in Vancouver. My son was then 4 and my daughter 7. At that time, we attended the Unitarian Church, and our kids went to the Sunday School there. One Christmas I wrote a re-telling of the

Nativity story, for use with small children. I wanted to tell it in such a way that small children would understand and be able to connect with it. I really wanted to emphasize the birth of the beloved child into the loving family. Of course, I took some liberties with the story (such as saying Mary and Joseph didn't mind whether their baby turned out to be a boy or a girl! But that seemed so natural—I had one of each, after all, and it seemed to me that children of today would relate to the concept of the *child* being wanted, whether boy or girl). Of course, many variations of the story have occurred for hundreds of years—in paintings, tales, carols—many of them with very little reference to the story as it is told in the gospels (e.g. the carol . . I Saw Three Ships Come Sailing In). Of course, I took the main elements of the story from St. Matthew and St. Luke—but the two gospel stories differ quite a bit from one another, too.

When I left Vancouver in 1962, and went with my children to England, I somehow lost my only copy of the story. It remained lost to me for 15 years. Then, in the Christmas season of 1977, I was invited to the home of friends who live near Lakefield. There I met a woman who also lives near here. She asked me if I remembered my re-telling of the Nativity story, so many years before. I told her I certainly did, and that to my sorrow, I'd lost my only copy when I left Vancouver. Then—to my delight and astonishment—she told me that she and her husband had lived in Vancouver during the years we were there, and she had a copy of the story, which she used to read to her children when they were young, each Christmas! Imagine! She sent me a copy of the story, and so it came home to me after so long. I thought this must mean something, so I rewrote the story slightly, and added to it a little, and then I asked the Toronto artist, Helen Lucas (whom I had recently met—another wonderful happenstance) if she would consider doing some pictures for it. She did, and we submitted it to Knopf and to McClelland & Stewart. Both accepted it, and the book you now see is the result! I am thrilled with it. I think Helen's pictures have exactly the love and tenderness—and yes, some humour too—that I hoped to convey in the text. The picture of the infant Jesus is like a sunburst.

I do have very special feelings about this book. It does seem as though it was meant to be. The fact that it had been lost to me for so long, and that when I found it I had just met an artist who I *knew* would be exactly the right person to create the pictures. The fact that [the woman], who returned the story to me, had lived in Vancouver at that time, had gone to the Unitarian

Church (I had not met her in those days), had a copy, and had actually settled in the same part of Canada as myself, and the fact that mutual friends had asked us to their home on that day in the Christmas season! With my dour Protestant upbringing, I am not much of a believer in miracles, and yet—a number of small seeming miracles have indeed happened to me in my life, and I am grateful.

I sold my cottage this spring. Not because of financial need, but because it was getting to be a bit too much of a responsibility to have 2 places, and also because it had, I came to see, served its purpose in the 10 years I had it. I could not write there, now, because I think in my mind the river at that place was too much connected with the writing of *The Diviners*. The same river flows through this village, and is only half a block from my house, so I can see it any time, but from a different viewpoint. This seemed to be the right thing to do. I seemed to have a need to simplify my life. Goodness knows, it wasn't all that simple all summer—I had a steady stream of visitors. I enjoyed them very much, but didn't get much writing done. I still have not found my way into the novel I want to write. I think it will come, but when? Patience is difficult for me, and I am fed up with making false starts at it. This often depresses me, as does, greatly more so, the state of the world. Still, many good things do happen. . . .

Lakefield,
9 Jan 83

Dear dear Gabrielle—

Please forgive me for my long silence. I have thought of you so very often, but have not written to you.

No excuse! I have spent the past two years in trying, without much success, to write the novel I have been attempting to do for so long. Maybe I will do it—maybe not. We will see. It has been a good time for me, in terms of my own life and friends and children, but not such a good time in terms of my work, which still seems to evade me, much as I try. I do not tell many people about this anguish, because they would not understand and because it is my own private concern. . . . Well, Gabrielle, I am trying and not giving up, and I am doing a lot of other things . .

work with anti-nuclear groups, work with young children in enriched (?) programs here in my county, and so on and so on. I am not without work or without concerns. But my writing seems to puzzle and foil me. Perhaps it will work out .. I hope so. I seem to stand in need of grace. I feel, however, that the early church fathers (I would have liked the "mothers" there, too) were right in saying despair was a deadly sin. I am not in despair, but I am not, either, seeming to be able to write as I would wish to. We will see. I read recently your book "The Fragile Lights of Earth"[15] .. loved it; loved your early writings about the many peoples in the prairies; loved your humorous account of how you got the Prix Femina! Thanks so much for that book. I hope you are reasonably well and going on. I love you so much, always, for what you have given me in your writing, and I take courage from you.

Love, and blessings for the new year. . . .

ANDREAS SCHROEDER

Lakefield,
28 March 75

Dear Andy—

... I thought the [Writers' Union] meetings in Van were just
terrific, and it was so good to see you all again! Like wow! I know
what you mean—it really is like a new infusion of energy. And
yes, you have found a family again. I began to feel that way, years
ago, as I got to know a lot of Canadian writers, and I've never
stopped feeling it—even more, now, with the Union. It does feel
great, because we have all needed this sense of tribe for so very
long. You know, we're really lucky here, at this point in our
history, writers I mean, for that one thing alone. The American
writers, apparently, don't feel it—maybe they're too many, too
spread out, too various? I don't know. But we *are* lucky in that
way. . . .

Love. . . .

For her [the Writers' Union] was the first sort of organizational
maturing of Canadian literature. She was quite anxious about it. . . .
She was being asked to come back and head up a family. . . . I never
cease being astonished at how many friends she had and how little she
seemed to benefit from that. . . . She never somehow really quite believed
that she deserved all this and that she had it coming or that she should
be allowed to accept it. She wasn't being asked to come back and do
something simply on the basis of being a lovely person. She was actually
being asked to give us what she was best at, because she was best at
mothering. She wasn't strong at philosophizing and at theory and at
political techniques. . . . She got tremendously emotionally involved.
All her thinking came from the heart.

Lakefield,
1 May 75

Dear Andreas—

... Bless you, Andy, for what you say about the faith. As we
discussed in Van, both at the party and when the whole thing
was over ... one of the best things about the Union has been
precisely this feeling of tribal belonging—and the fact that it now
extends from Newfoundland to Vancouver Island—I find that
enormously heartening, in the face of so many awful aspects of
politics, publishing, writing, and life. I get the sense that Amer
writers don't have that any more, if they ever did—strangely
enough, our farflung geography, which for many years made
writers feel so isolated, is now what is pulling us together. In
many ways, Andy, for those in our profession in our country,
we're living in pretty exciting times, it seems to me. . . .

ps.2. what you say about a lot of people being fond of me—you
know, Andy it has just occurred to me that when I lost a marriage,
I really *did* gain a whole tribe. That, my work, and my kids—
these keep me alive. At one time, isolated, I wouldn't have
believed there could be so many people whom I would truly
love and care about.

She most definitely ended off a sequence in her life [with The Diviners*].
You know, woe betide the writer who does that sort of thing with
resounding finality. . . . I don't know whether she just got frightened
and didn't believe in herself enough to tell everybody, after a year or
two of doing the mothering thing, to basically shove off. She had to go
through the furnace again to get the next stage of her writing life going.
It could have been that. And as I mentioned earlier, she had a remarkable
sort of self-deprecatory perspective on herself, and just really had no
faith in herself.*

Dear Andy—

. . . I'm not going to be at the AGM. This has nothing to do with my feelings about the Union . . I wish the Union awfully well, I need hardly say. But I just cannot take part in any more conferences. I think I have paid some of my dues, re: the union, in the past. I am not Mother Earth. In fact, I do not feel that at present I can call myself a writer, as I have been unable (not through lack of trying) to write what I would like to write, for some years now. For some time, if I am not mistaken, I did try to help other and younger writers. Now I need help. A shocking thought? Mum isn't strong? You bet she isn't, and it is not a shocking thought. The help I need is just understanding, and knowing that I wish you all well but have to stay home. . . . I am not in despair—like the early Church fathers (who have much to answer for, in my view, but they did have *some* insights) I believe that despair is one of the deadly sins. I am living in hope, but. . . .

I th[ink] about Margaret and . . . that whole phenomenon of somebody's dedication to books ultimately killing her. . . . There were other elements and ingredients in it, of course, but still the fact that she couldn't write any more was probably the largest part of what just dragged her down. And then the other stuff [the censorship issue], which otherwise I think could have been sustained or resisted or whatever needed to be done so that it wouldn't damage her . . . [was] able to do maximum damage to her as well. So here was an immensely tragic figure, one of the best-loved writers in the country, who was lonely as hell.

GLEN SORESTAD

Lakefield,
15 Feb 76

Dear Glen Sorestad—

A very belated note to thank you for WIND SONGS.[1] It seems to me that you catch *exactly* the feeling of the prairies, the sense of the land itself (why do non-prairie people think of it as unvaried? even the fact of the seasons is the wildest kind of variety), of the people .. the discouragement and yet the sheer will to survive, and of the ancestors—and there is a sense, of course, in which Riel and Dumont, Big Bear and Poundmaker, become our ancestors even though we have not yet earned the right to call them that, I know. Some of your poems, like some of Andy Suknaski's, moved me to tears—and I do not say that in any sentimental way whatsoever. . . .

I've just recently become acquainted with *NeWest Review*, which I think is extremely good. I would like to see it available in Ontario etc bookshops—it should be spread around, I think, as much as possible. The issues I've seen have some incredibly good stuff in them.

All the very best. . . .

Lakefield,
10 Jan 77

Dear Glen—

Thanks so much for PRAIRIE PUB POEMS,[2] which I enjoyed a great deal, despite the fact that in my day ("in *my* day, young 'un") women weren't allowed in prairie pubs, so my knowledge of them is all from the outside! Your book helped to give me insights previously not available to one of my sex! . . .

Lakefield,
2 Feb 77

Dear Glen—

Heavenly days! The Ides or whatever of March are nearly upon
us! I received a letter not long ago from David Carpenter at the
U. of Sask re: my visit, and it seems that you and he have sorted
out a good plan of operation.[3] Also, I am so pleased that you
both are not too other-wordly to evade the crass question of
money. It is so damn nice, Glen, to read both your letters, in which
you both clearly recognize the need to fund this sort of thing and
are going about it in practical ways. You wouldn't believe the
number of universities which expect me to come and deliver all
sorts of hard work for nothing! I don't do it, of course. Well, there
are prairie people for you—we understand that people shouldn't
have to work for no pay, possibly because we've seen so many
who have had to, and in our various ways have been them,
although with us in *no way* like the farmers of the drought, and
maybe partly it is a kind of folk-memory which makes me now
wild with rage when well-heeled institutions expect me to work
for nothing. . . .

Main thing is—ARRANGEMENTS. . . . I don't quite know
what your program will be, Glen—will there be other writers
there, and if so, could we combine on a panel or whatever? I'm
willing, pretty well, to follow whatever you visualize, except that
what I can do will not be a lecture or a talk but an *exchange*, with
students or whoever, or panel discussions with other writers and
the "audience" to be brought in as participants. I know you know
that is my style for such events and the only way I can cope.

So I leave the organization of Mar 10 and 11 up to you
and David Carpenter, with the one stipulation that I can't do
more than 1 session in the morning and 1 in the afternoon each
day. I also leave the financial thing to you and David. . . . I am
trying these days to say $300 per session because I am so aware
(a) that writers have been for years ripped off, unwittingly, by
various institutions, and (b) that I must never work any more for
nothing, because of my union and because of the way this may
affect the younger writers in our country, ie. they'll get ripped
off. I am, of course, of course, not suggesting that either you or
David Carpenter wants to rip me off—*au contraire*, as we say in
bilingual Upper Canada. (I am developing a dark sense of
humour). But just try to see what you can do, and it will be okay

195

by me.

Batoche in March?? Ye Gods, I must have been out of my skull. But I visualize the pilgrimage all the same. . . .

Love to you all. . . .

Lakefield,
12 Feb 77

Dear Glen—

I feel *awful* about this, and probably you and others will never speak to me again, but after receiving your letter, it is not the money which is worrying me—I certainly would not want to be paid more than the other writers, and I believe that in these circumstances all writers should be paid exactly the same. But golly, Glen, I had NO IDEA of the nature of the event, or I would never have agreed to come in the first place. This was undoubtedly my own fault, as no doubt you said it would be a Workshop and somehow I just didn't realize what would be involved. I didn't really visualize anything except perhaps one session or two with your students, plus the reading or seminar session at the university. I didn't even know there would be other writers there. But according to the program, I would have *ten* sessions over the three days, one following another in quick succession. I do know that many writers can cope beautifully with this sort of situation, but I just can't. Also, I really never give readings from my own work, because on the few occasions when I've done so, I simply shake and tremble for hours beforehand and all throughout the ordeal, which for me is just sheer hell—I know it sounds crazy, but I simply cannot overcome this feeling and reaction. After *one* seminar session of one hour, I am left absolutely drained and practically incapable of speech. I am so damn sorry, Glen, but really I did not know what would be involved or I would have declined courteously from the very beginning. I realize that now this is going to throw out all your plans, and those of the university, but honestly, I just cannot attend after all. I feel terribly apologetic about it, but really and truly, I would be *dead* after all that. I just cannot bring myself to do it. My psychic energy isn't what it once was, but it was *never* sufficient to cope with all these sessions. Maybe this is because I have never been a teacher, and undoubtedly to a teacher the schedule doesn't seem anything unusual. But when I look at it, I can feel a dreadful sense of panic. I am so sorry, Glen, I really am. I feel like a heel, but there is just no way I can come.

ps. also, a re-arranged schedule wouldn't work, as I wouldn't want to go and do less than the other writers.

Lakefield,
16 Feb 77

Dear Glen—

Further to our phone call today—it'll be just fine if I do a total of 4 sessions, 1 of them at the university. I'm sorry to be so chicken about the larger number of sessions, but I just know my limitations. . . .

Lakefield,
25 March 77

Dear Glen—

. . . I was so grateful to you and Sonia [Sorestad] for that really memorable day at Batoche and that area. When I came home, I spent three days re-reading a lot of things re: the rebellion and re: Gabriel [Dumont]—it put it all into a kind of fresh perspective to have actually seen the place.

All the best to you all. . . .

Lakefield,
16 Jan 78

Dear Glen and Sonia—

. . . I have read [Rudy Wiebe's] new novel,[4] and loved it. I

197

think he wanted to use the voice of Pierre Falcon, Métis bard, or rather, the voice of the spirit of Falcon, in order to have an *inside* kind of narrative voice . . i.e. to enable him (Rudy) to feel the story from the inside. It was a curious technique, in a way, but it worked for me, in the main. It's a splendid novel. . . .

Lakefield,
28 Nov 82

Dear Glen—

Thanks for the poems and note. I loved the poems . . they give a real sense of country. . . .

All fine here. I'm working hard; trying to find where this novel is going, if anywhere; involved in a number of disarmament groups plus things like Energy Probe; enjoying being Chancellor of Trent; whipping into T.O. nearly every week, alas, but at least I get to see my daughter and various friends; and so on and so on. The quiet country life. . . .

Love to you both. . . .

P.S. I have to tell you this marvellous story, and you are free to pass it on, because I just love it. I went out to Calgary by train, and someone from the Banff Centre met me there and drove me to Banff. I love the train . . the service that Via Rail provides is now awful and the meals are dreadful. But as yet they can't spoil the scenery. We went through my heartland, southern Manitoba, in the morning light. I sat (in my posh accommodation, a *bedroom*, not one of those dinky little roomettes) and gazed out the window, I hadn't seen the prairies in August for a long long time, at least not at ground level. One sees zilch from a plane. The fields of wheat and oats and barley and rye were almost ripe . . the various shades of gold, copper (words are inadequate), flecked with green. The creeks and rivers I remembered so well. The huge sky, an incredible blue. The bluffs of poplar, scrub oak, Manitoba maple. The wolf willow. I sat for hours, thinking how beautiful this country is, and also thinking of the other side of it . . the way in which, despite all the modern machinery in the world, farmers are still at the mercy (or otherwise) of the weather. I went into the dining car for lunch. I sat at a table with two American women, very friendly, very nice, and I mean they really were nice. I liked them. One of them said to me, "Are you a native-born Canadian?" I said "Yes." She then said, "Well, then, perhaps you can tell me and my friend. . . . when do we get to the *more interesting* country?" I said, "Well, you have to understand—I was born and grew up here. For me, this *is* the more interesting country."

DAVID WATMOUGH

Essentially, I felt I was coming to an introvert country from an extrovert one [the U.S.]. Well, people like Margaret Laurence somewhat dented that pattern. . . . I just found [in her] a dry, shrewd, quick, radical prairie spirit.

Lakefield,
2 Dec 74

Dear David—

Thank you for ASHES FOR EASTER.[1] And apologies for not having written sooner. David, it's a beautiful book, and I use the word *beautiful* even tho it has been vastly over-worked. I mean, I like it very much and think that there are two relevant things here—(a) when you read one of the monodramas, it reads (you read) so bloody well that the voices come across so intensely that it just amazes me; I can see that these are prose perceptions written to be read aloud; but also (b) David, you know—they read *awfully* well on the printed page. You've done a kind of two-fold thing— prose which should be read aloud but which should also be read by the reader in quiet by oneself. I have always had a kind of feeling about my own fiction that it should be read aloud, and yet also read on the page. When I write the damn stuff, I often read it aloud—cannot bear for anyone else to be even in the same *house* with me, at those times, never mind the same room. But if you write, as some of us do, with a very strong feeling for the *voice* which is speaking the whole thing, surely one must have this sense of the spoken and heard, as well as the thing that is seen on the page. Anyhow, you do it. I feel you've got such a sense of what I can only call the voice speaking. And I can hear it even when I'm reading it. Thanks. . . .

    Life here is hectic as always. I begin to think that I must like a hectic life, or I wouldn't lead it. But sometimes I don't like a hectic life at all, and just withdraw into my house and contemplate and write letters, as today. Don't know how you feel about it, David, but I feel less lonely when alone than almost any other times. . . .

    I hope you are bearing it heavily in mind that any BC

writers who feel the sense of connection with other Canadian writers which I myself feel should give thought and join the Union. I'm not pressing you, David. I'm probably becoming a bit more political (having been always very political, small "p" for most of my adult life) in my middle age. Have done my five books out of my time and my place, and now what? Well, have just turned down an offer from a Toronto TV production firm to do a script on Canada's immigrants—funded by Imperial Oil. Not for me. They screw up our natural resources; the Amer govt even goes so far as to say that if Canadians are a bit firm re: oil exports, they may bring in the military (David, [President] Ford *said* it; if that happens, I can tell you where I will be, but maybe you don't need to ask; I am anti-war in an almost absolute sense, but if anyone attacked my land, I would be in arms); then Imperial wants Can writers to go along with them and write a series on Canada's immigrants, designed to give Imperial a good public image about being concerned about Canada. We have got to be very careful about the people for whom we work, or so I believe.
. . . God bless, David—keep well and keep working. . . .

I don't think she was distracted [by public life]. At least if she was distracted, she knew bloody well she was being distracted. . . . Because Canadian writing began in such a kind of instant coffee, Nescafé way in the 1960s, people tend to think of it in terms of "You haven't had a book in two years. Where are you? Dead?" You cease to be a Canadian, or you've gone away, or something. Well, if you look at the cosmic view of literature, there's actually no reason why people shouldn't go [away] for ten years. . . . Thomas Hardy never wrote a word of fiction in the twentieth century. He was writing poetry from 1900 on. Didn't die until 1928. So I think we put writers through a rather cruel hoop. . . . There can be a long hiatus and then another whole spate of work.

Lakefield,
12 Feb 76

Dear David—

Never mind Ashes for Easter—how about Ashes for Valentine's Day . . cigarette ashes, that is, heaped on my head for not having written sooner? . . . life has been like a three-ring circus these past months. Not bad, just hectic. First—thanks so much for sending me . . . your new book [*Love & the Waiting Game*[2]]. . . .

No problem at all re: writing letter to C[anada] Council. . . . It is *meant*. The monodramas do indeed stand up equally well as performances, ie with the dimension of the human voice and with your incredible ability to speak in a variety of voices, and as short stories on the printed page. They are indeed beautifully crafted and moving. I didn't add to the letter, but probably should have done, my appreciation of your sense of pace—the timing is so good, the narrative flow is neither turgid, nor neurotically speedy—it's just right, at least to my eyes. . . .

I have been having a really peculiar time recently—THE DIVINERS was for a time banned in our local Lakefield Highschool, because some (2) parents apparently phoned up one of the Peterborough school superintendents and complained, and the guy got his secretary to phone Lakefield school and hoick the book off the course (Grade 13). Not only did the Eng teachers throughout the country rise up, but also the media and a lot of community people, in the book's defence, and it is now back on the course. But in the free-for-all, a whole lot of interesting stuff has happened—an airing, for one thing, about *how* books are taken off courses . . there is a proper procedure, involving the Board of Education and a review committee, neither of whom was consulted in this case. A parent phones and says "My kids shouldn't be reading those dirty words" or something, and this superintendent panics and phones the school principal and says . . take the book off the course. Little did he think he had stirred up a hornet's nest. The Tor papers covered it (and there have been all kinds of inaccurate reports, because it has been so hard to find out the real facts . . I'm not sure I know them even at this point myself—but the papers stood up loud and clear agin this kind of censorship) and even the Van Sun phoned me, because an item went out on CP. Well, David, it has been an odd experience. The book is now back on the course, however, and I still don't know who in my village hates me. I'm not surprised, of course. I grew up in a small town. I'm not even wounded, although I was a bit shocked, at first. But the amount of positive support has been incredible.

God bless, and love. . . .

She had a far broader sense of the world than many people who have lived in a much more worldly mode than she did. That's why I think that had she gone on writing, had she lived longer—well, after you drain a certain motherlode in you, which comes from life experience, you move on to another.

Lakefield,
12 May 76

Dear David—

Thanks so much for your good letter. . . . First, it was super to talk with you in Ottawa. . . . And I'm so glad you are in the Union—you had some very practical and sensible things to say at the conference, and it is a great help, too, to have someone who like you and Pierre [Berton] . . . have had long experience in ACTRA [Association of Canadian Television and Radio Artists].

Second, I wanted to tell you how much I really loved your story in *Saturday Night*.[3] The character of the woman, both when in her prime, so to speak, and when old, is unforgettable. Also, the way in which you convey the sense of time is just fantastic—you know, fifteen years doesn't sound much if you say it quickly. But it's the difference between a boy of 15 and a man of 30; the difference between a still-sexual woman of 55 and an old woman of 70. Chilling in a sense, and yet in another sense, when one has thought a lot about these things, as I think both you and I have, there comes a kind of calm. I will probably rage against the dying of the light, but only with one part of me, I hope—there is a sense in which one appreciates trivial good things (not so trivial, really) even at this stage in life, in a way that one did not when younger. Or didn't notice. Last evening two very small girls came to my door with a rather tatty looking tray of weeds and wildflowers. They were selling wildflowers for the Heart Fund, they said, 10 cents a bunch. I picked a bunch of yellow ones (a form of buttercup I think, altho I haven't yet found them in my Weed Book), and asked them what these were. "Well," one tad said, "we don't really know the name, so we call that one Yellow Beautiful." Total seriousness, not flippant at all. It made my day!

Glad to see Pat Morley's good review of LOVE AND THE WAITING GAME.[4] She has done a good job. It's nice when one is understood. The Pentecostals and others in the Citizens Decency League are still gunning away at me, here, but the hell with them. . . .

It doesn't start with Laurence. It starts in the nineteenth century— that Canadian writing has been indigenously feminine. The usual question in Europe is, why is it so? Why is Canadian culture matriarchal? . . . I think there's a whole range of voices, but the larger question has been to try to explain that in cultural terms—why we are a feminine culture, why those voices have been so tunable in this country, why we've heard them instantly as our own. It has a whole lot to do with being a colonial country living next door to a patriarchal culture and an imperial country. Women have long known how to cope, I think, with domineering husbands, and there have been various strategies of subversion. Politically, I think we've been in that position. We've felt it for a long time. And Laurence unconsciously felt those kinds of things.

Lakefield,
27 June 77

Dear David—

Please forgive my long silence. Since we talked, at the Union conference weekend, I have been travelling here and there in idiotic manner, working under the usual nervous tension that I experience when I have to make public appearances, give talks, etc. I seemed to be home only long enough in between trips to do the laundry, draw a deep breath and go off again to pastures new. I didn't want to answer your letter hurriedly, for the obvious reason that it moved me very much . . more of that presently.

. . . I went up to Sudbury, where I had promised to go because the United Church minister there is a guy I went to United College with, and I hadn't seen him in 30 years, nor met his wife. It turned out that we had so much to talk about, and the years fell away. Not only catching up on news, but talking viewpoints and outlooks towards life. . . . I had a seminar session with some of the young people, then [he] and I had an interview-type session with members of his congregation present that evening. I found, as I had at Bloor Street United in T.O., that it somehow meant a lot to me to be able to talk about some of the biblical references in my work, and some of the—well, I guess my own concepts of grace, or how I feel about it as a gift given not because deserved but just because given, by life, by some mystery at the core of life which mankind sometimes calls God, in our need to put names to and define unnamed forces and indefinable ones, perhaps.

Anyway, I then had to go to Simon Fraser U in Burnaby, B.C., where I had seminars with students, and gave a public lecture .. looking at Can writing as Third World writing, and our attempts to find our own voices in the presence of imperial and colonialist aspects of our culture .. don't know that everyone would agree with me, but I feel rather strongly about it. . . .

Now, as to your letter, David. Thank you for sending me a copy of your uncle's letter,[1] and a copy of your reply to him. Oh, David, if I thought I suffered from the attacks of the Pentecostals in this county, I did not suffer at all in comparison to how you must have felt. Suffering may indeed not be qualitative, but David, when I read your uncle's letter, and your own reply—trying so hard to explain to him things which to you were self-evident, trying so hard to be patient and even gentle, and in the face of the enormous hurt you must have felt, trying to be fair both to yourself and to him, I just felt so badly for you— and of course for him, as well, that so much love on your part must perhaps be unknown to him or unacknowledged, that he should shut himself off in that way, under the guise of virtue, from the human contact which is love.

In your letter, to your uncle, there are several points that I thought were especially important from my point of view, and I daresay many writers have wished they could explain some of these things to readers who misunderstand. The first is the "dangers of mistaking character outlook for authorial position". Precisely. How many times have I tried to get that outlook across, when talking about fiction? It is also part of the kind of misunderstanding that does *not* see fiction as the author's perceptions of life transformed into fiction and given life through *fictional* characters, but must see fiction as essentially and totally autobiographical and fictional characters as impossibilities. This is, of course, a common enough misunderstanding of the whole nature of fiction. A book like THE BURNING WOOD[2] or THE DIVINERS can quite possibly be seen as spiritual autobiographies; this does not mean they are autobiographies in any external sense, as well we know but as many people do not know, and this lack of knowing does hurt, as I have experienced. Linked with these comments is your comment on language—meaning of course in this case the so-called obscene language. What you are essentially saying when you say that most of it is spoken by Indians, and that is the way they do speak, is that (as I have tried, also, many times, to explain with THE DIVINERS and such characters as Skinner and Christie) you are using the speech and idiom appropriate to particular characters, as you have observed it in real life, and to do otherwise would be a *betrayal* of those characters. Your use of TURVEY[3] as a case in point is a good example. This very point is one which I tried to explain to an old aunt of mine who, as I probably told you, said she had not noticed *anything* about THE DIVINERS except the "four letter words"!!

However, I believe, as you do, that the most important thing for a writer is to try to be true to one's own vision, with as much compassion as one can muster, and praying that one will gain some understanding of *others*, which means *all* others, as well you know, including people such as the Indian characters in your book (and the Métis in mine) who are so very different in their many concepts from oneself, and for whom one feels such a sense of terrible sympathy and a sense of historical injustice having been performed against them. It also—oh David, here is the crunch, eh?—includes people such as your most bigoted fundamentalist characters, and in my novel, such basically authoritarian and imperialist characters as Morag's husband, Brooke. To try to understand someone with whose viewpoint one feels basically at odds is very hard. In the future, more of that may be demanded of me, and I hope I can face the problem as directly and honestly as you have done in THE BURNING WOOD, and as I believe Rudy [Wiebe] did in PEACE SHALL DESTROY MANY.[4] Of course, in both your case and Rudy's, there was the familial thing, in a sense .. which perhaps made it in some ways easier to understand the fictional characters but perhaps more difficult to be fair to them. I don't know. I don't in fact believe that Rudy's synthesis, either in his earlier novels, or in BIG BEAR,[5] is as you say "torn in two". . . .

Finally, it seems to me that the comment of one of your Mennonite students is of basic importance .. that "not one character is left unredeemed or unforgiven". . . . Just so, and partly this is, I think, because of your own Christian background but more than that, probably, because you do have, or work towards, compassion as a human individual, and you do not set yourself up as a judge. I feel this is a very tricky area for a novelist, because as a human being I feel in myself not only that rush of sympathy towards most or all of my characters, but also the undoubted and recognized need in myself to battle spiritual pride. In my case, spiritual pride does not, I think, especially take the form of the danger of judging others (altho God knows this has to be watched as well) but of feeling myself to be a liberal-minded kind-hearted kind of person . . I discovered this danger in Africa, myself as a well-meaning "white liberal"!! One can probably only approach other people, whether "real" or "fictional", as individuals first and foremost, not as representatives of a racial group or ideological group. Talking of groups, I have occasionally in my life known a few Communists who seemed to me to embody some of the Christian virtues more than many declared Christians did. I don't think the Lord of the Universe, a concept too large really for the finite mind, would say them Nay. Of course, my feeling about many religions (and I would include Communism as a type of religion although of course I know many people would disagree with me) is that there are many positive and negative aspects in each, as in each of us. Well, we struggle on, I guess. . . .

God bless, and all best wishes. . . .

Lakefield,
30 June 77

Dear David and Darlene—

I am sending you a small gift for your son, something he will maybe like to play with when he is about 8 or 9 months old. . . .
    I'm also sending you a kind of poem (I'm not a poet) which I was moved to write last year for my son's twenty-first birthday.[6] I guess you will understand all the ambiguities of the line breaks. In the end, *we leave our children alone*, "leave me alone, I'm alright, then", we don't pester them. But also we have to leave them, because we in our turn become the ancestors who must die and yet mythically remain. A responsibility. Everyone must, as all mankind has ever had to do, accept their alone-ness, their individuality and their responsibility for their own life. But also one really is never alone—the sense of family, of tribe, of friendships, the sense of connection with others who are not only members of one's human tribe but also creatures of all the earth, and it is probably only the creatures of this earth that we can reach out to and try to make some contact with, but that is enough

to be getting on with.

It seems to me that, if we pray, we pray for ability to love, ability to forgive, ability to forgive our own selves, and for strength, strength to cope with whatever comes our way. Not easy. We cannot pray for grace, it seems to me—that is something given, and if it *is*, then we have to accept it and . . well, just accept it, which is not so easy either. . . .

There's plenty of evidence in The Diviners *that she'd exhausted Manawaka, that she couldn't go back to it. She'd wrapped it up, she'd tied up the threads. . . . although she was trying to move to a different territory, new ground, she never really told me where she was setting her anti-nuclear novel. But I think it was the kind of novel that she never would have been able to write. I know she admired MacLennan's* Voices in Time, *and I think she wanted to write a book like that. She was most concerned with that kind of political legacy [at this point], but I don't think her gifts and her skills and her intellect went in that direction.*

Lakefield,
7 July 77

Dear David—

. . . I'm not able to do much thinking about a novel, but that's okay, too. The odd thing is that now that I am half a century old, I feel not more rush but less, in terms of things to get done. It will come in its own time if it is meant to be so. Of course, it won't come without my help—but I do have a kind of sense of calm about it, which is nice for a change. I need to discover a lot more before I would be ready to write it, but I feel that this may indeed happen. . . .

Love to you all. . . .

I see her moving away [in The Diviners*] from mere self-referentiality to a concern for other storytellers, for the inheritors. She regretted very much that that title had already been used. She was much more concerned with the legacy of story, not her own possession and not her* *own talisman and not her own empowering tool, but as a gift which is given to be used and reused and changed and transformed. So I think that the writing about writing is transformed . . . into a kind of social purpose, a kind of creation of community, and a kind of empowerment of others.*

Lakefield,
14 Aug 77

Dear David—

Thanks so much for your letter. . . .

    I was very interested in your article, THE INDIAN OUR ANCESTOR,[7] and thought you made some very good points. I agree that lit. crit. can be creative, and I agree that reading should and must be creative . . alas, how few people really know how to read in any depth, which is one problem that the fundamentalists have with novels . . they tend to see only the individual words on the page and to miss much of what is going on underneath the words. I like your comment that the myths Christie tells "are stamped with the character of Logan" . . very true, and you are the first critic to have pointed that out.

    Critics can also sometimes point out things to the writer, things which were in a sense unintentional or which came from some subconscious place and which are seen by the writer to be true. Thus, I really had not thought of the clan of Morag's adoption being that of the "young Archie Macdonald", although of course I naturally knew about Archie. I had thought mainly of the plaid pin having belonged to Hagar, so that Morag is linked with that ancestry in her own place of belonging—this, incidentally, simply happened within the story like a kind of revelation; I suddenly *knew* what had happened to the knife and the pin. But of course it is quite true that the Currie family was a sept of the Macdonald clan!! So you see, even now, I can be surprised by aspects of my own work. Incidentally, a friend of mine was at that time writing a book about Archie Macdonald, who was one of her ancestors, so I really knew quite a bit about him. When I finished the first draft of THE DIVINERS, I was telling her a bit about Christie's tales to Morag, and how they were myths based on the historical reality of the first Selkirk settlers. She had researched that whole area very thoroughly, both in this country and in Scotland. She said, looking at me oddly, "Of course you know there *was* a piper on the march from Churchill to York Factory, but do you know what his name was?" I said no, I didn't. "His name was Gunn," she replied. Wow! It knocked me out! I can't explain it, but I accept it gratefully.

Anyway, it's an excellent critical article, even tho I would take issue with some things about your views of BIG BEAR. . . .

When she came back [from England] she found that the country itself had changed, that there was an emergence from colonial mentality, and as she had been growing and changing the country was different too. I think that attracted her. She wanted to come home, and there were plenty of signs, even in The Diviners, *how she wanted to find ancestors and roots again. . . . Her literary work wasn't over yet either. I think the general purpose of post-structuralism is freedom, pure and simple. I think she saw a social purpose to that kind of freedom. She was arguing not only for female characters, not only for the country itself, [because] her whole attempt to empower others was also related to her political campaign against old, autocratic governments, against old ways of nuclear thinking and military thinking.*

Lakefield,
1 June 81

Dear David and Darlene—

. . . I was told by several people, first by Marian Engel, about your announcement re: the Nobel prize perhaps going to me sometime. David, I AM HORRIFIED. I do not *want* the Nobel prize; I have not written enough to justify it, ever. I understand, of course, the ways in which awards are given—maybe in 4 years' time it will be time for "Canada". Rats. When the Nobel was given to Patrick White of Australia a couple of years ago, I thought justice had been done. He really is in a class by himself. He is totally amazing, and continues to write complex and fantastic novels. But that kind of writer is rare. Obviously, if any writer in the anglophone world should get the Nobel, it should be Graham Greene, William Golding, or . . . well, we could talk about that a lot. I think Naipaul probably deserves it, but I really take issue with his reaction. He says, as reported by you, that if he does not win this prize he cannot be happy. WHAT THE HELL! He is a fine writer, and if he isn't happy already, that does not have anything to do with prizes or awards. . . . David, I am as happy as I can be, in this terrible and frightening world of ours, right now. I do not *want* any more awards, prizes, etc etc. I just want to stay at home in L'field and try to press on and write at least one more novel and maybe some more kids' books, and pay my taxes and make enough money to live on, and see my friends and my kids. The hell with anything else. I have not done enough work to deserve the Nobel, and I know it well. I am not falsely modest . . in fact, I'm not modest at all, but I know what I have done, and what it is amounts to a lifetime of work, 15 books including 7 books of adult fiction, and that is quite honourable. As Adele Wiseman, my nearest and dearest friend and fellow novelist once said to me, "Kid, we're not in it for the immortality stakes." True. Who knows what will last, and is it not spiritual pride to hope our work will? It does not matter. What matters is to do the best we can, in the time that is given to us, and to live our lives as well as do our work. All I really care about now, at the age of 55 (mid-July) is that I may be able to write one more novel, and to pay my own way in the rest of my life, and to connect with my kids and my friends.

Much love to you all four. . . .

[I remember her] simply as somebody who gave a voice to a generation that I knew too, and that I'd never seen in written speech before. I know she felt that was her strongest legacy when she discovered her grandparents' voices. She made it possible, along with Sinclair Ross, for other people to try to fill up their postage stamp of soil with writing too.

I think the first time I heard about her was during the time she was writer-in-residence at the University of Toronto, and she came up to Peterborough. . . . We were invited to dinner with Margaret, but I don't think I knew who Margaret Laurence was at that time. I remember thinking, because I was told she was a writer, "I can't go to this dinner party and not have read any of her books," so I read The Fire-Dwellers. *. . . I wore a black sheath dress and they put Margaret beside me. . . . I've always been kind of half-way overweight, and Bill Morton came up and said, "What would you like to drink?" and [when] I said, "A gin and tonic," I thought, "Oh, my God, I'm Stacey!". . .*

I remember Peg Morton saying that she identified with Stacey and that practically every woman she knew had identified with Stacey. Now that would be women with young children—they all said the same thing, "Stacey's me," no matter what their lives were like, what their husbands were like, how they behaved with their husbands . . . they were all inside Stacey's head.

The Shack.
21 July 78

Dear Budge—

. . . I'm doing a lot of reading . . as usual in the summer, very eclectic stuff, including Norman Penner's *The Canadian Left*, John Porter's *The Vertical Mosaic* (difficult, but fascinating), and a whole pile of fundamentalist literature (I use the word "literature" *very* loosely here!) Golly! Some of the latter is so hate-filled it scares me. One guy, writing about Anita Bryant's crusade vs homosexuals, is just plain *obscene* . . talks about "perverts" trying to corrupt our youth etc etc, and says snidely "not that I particularly want to be beastly to the bisexual, or nasty to the nance." Oh Christian love! . . .

At last my mind seems to want to come to grips with a new novel in a practical way . . I mean, I'm thinking *story* and *people*, not just vague *areas*. Pray for me and it.

I've realized that a lot of Christians will hate my re-telling of the Christmas story, because I don't present Jesus as THE SON

OF GOD. That seems a difficult concept for a small child. I thought it was better to begin with the story as a *family* story. But I'm sure a lot of people wouldn't agree. Did I ever show it to you? I'm enclosing a copy, to see what you think. Also, some would object to the fact that I don't have the angel telling Mary she'll have a *son*. But heck! I've always rather resented the implications of that particular part of the gospel story, and I think one has to remember that it was written at a time and in a culture where women were not valued much. Of course to the fundamentalists the story would be blasphemy, I daresay, in my re-telling, but then, if it is ever published, it sure ain't aimed at them! . . .

Much love. . . .

The censorship issue took up so much of what she would call psychic energy. She really was deeply hurt both on a personal and professional level [because] it meant people were not reading her books properly or, in the case of a lot of people, those who were leading the censorship movement, weren't reading her books at all. . . .

She was a very . . . intense person. . . . She really linked the censorship of other people to her own experience, so she not only grieved about the censorship of her own books but the censorship of others' books as well. . . . If she found something outrageous her fury was terrible. If she found something sad her grief was heartbreaking.

Lakefield,
22 Sept 83

Dearest Budge—

I tried to phone you just now but you weren't home. I am writing instead because I just have to express myself RIGHT NOW! I have just read "The Metaphor".[1] Budge, it is truly one of the most moving stories I have ever read. I cried at the end. One cared so much about both the teacher and Charlotte. I would bet, too, that so many people, whatever period in time they attended High School, will be reminded of some teacher to whom they were in some way cruel, possibly going along with the cruelty or giving it silent acquiescence because of the dread of the mockery of their peers. With Charlotte, it was worse, because Miss Hancock's gifts to her had been so valuable, almost a life-saving of the girl, a gift whose value she only half-realized at the time, in Grade 7, and which she sought, through her own embarrassment, to deny in Grade 10—and the scene where she realizes the full force of her own betrayal is *brilliantly* done. Never over-stated, but done with such passion. The comparative metaphors—the mother and the teacher—conveyed so very deeply the girl's dilemma and her perceptions, and of course, in giving Charlotte "metaphor", Miss Hancock also gave her potential wisdom and the ability to perceive both others and her own self. There are so many levels of the story—no one who is a skilled reader can fail to know that the story speaks to all our lives, to the times when we might have conveyed love and did not, and then it was too late. Perhaps, too, some thanks for the times when we have indeed conveyed that love before it was too late. Perhaps the story will even prompt someone, somewhere, to write to an old teacher who gave her (or him) so much that wasn't even recognized until years later. I have so often thought that is the terrible thing about teaching—so many teachers must never know how their gifts have been so valuable to certain of their students. I feel especially strongly about this, as you no doubt know, because of my great debt of gratitude to Miss Mildred Musgrove, my High School teacher of English, and thank God I have been able through the years to acknowledge this publicly many times while she is still alive. But I take no credit—I was able to do that, and I am glad. But I also recall another High School teacher . . a young woman (not much older than ourselves at 15) who taught Home Ec but who also (in Neepawa in those days) was made to teach another course . . I can't recall, even, what it was. Perhaps History to Grade 9 and 10, and of course she was terrified, and I think that Mona and I even felt sorry for her, but in the presence of the great hulking boys whom we hoped to impress, we sure didn't stand up for her. All these years later, I'd like to say Sorry to her. Well, I think your story must touch a whole lot of people, of whatever age, in many many ways. The other (or one other) aspect is the mother, whose portrait is so very well done. The touch with which you portray her is so sure and delicate—she is not an ogre; we have all known many of her; her name is legion. Her children are supposed to rise up, and call her blessed, and probably some of them even do, God help them and her.

I am so glad that Charlotte slapped the face of the smart-ass handsome boy! That was so convincing—that is exactly what would have happened. And only under those circumstances of shock and loss and sense of having betrayed Miss Hancock. The ending was absolutely and totally right. It is a story full of grace in both senses of the word. The teacher was, at least in my perception of the story, a kind of fool of God, as St. Paul once described himself. . . .

Anyway, Budge, I just wanted to express right away my feelings about the story. I think I do have a sense of the short story as a fiction form that is incredibly difficult to do well because of its length—everything has to be just right. And you really achieved that. There are not many short stories that convey that sense of being totally self-contained while at the same time reaching out with so many reverberations like a skipped stone on a calm lake, widening circles. Thanks for it. . . .

Much love to you all. . . .

I feel that like most writers who are serious about what they do, she felt compelled to write, driven to write. . . . When I'd read The Diviners *I wondered if she didn't have the feeling that she had lost or was about to lose the divining gift. . . . But she wouldn't have stopped writing because she felt she'd said enough. . . .*

I think the causes she embraced were another factor in her not writing as much any more. . . . She had a strong sense of community and she was very willing to speak to schools. . . . She was a real nurturer of young talent, of new talent. . . . She may have felt, although I don't think she actually said this to me, that keeping the world from destroying itself was more important than her writing—that is to say, if someone asked her to come and talk about "the bomb" and she was in the middle of a chapter she would go and talk about "the bomb", I'm sure.

35 Heath Hurst Road,
London, N.W.3,
29 Nov 62

Dear Mr. Woodcock—

I enclose the review of W.O. Mitchell's novel [*The Kite*[1]]—I hope
it is all right and that it will be about the right length. . . . The
great difficulty with life at home, from a writer's point of view,
seems to me to be the inevitable involvement with a relatively
large number of activities—whether these are worthy causes or
community responsibilities or friendships, each may be
rewarding in itself but taken as a whole they seem to diminish
one's time to a point where one can begin to feel a little desperate.
It is the anonymity of London that appeals most to me, I think. I
have a number of friends here, whom I see from time to time,
but I can spend many more hours a week here in working at
writing, without the guilty feeling at the back of my mind that I
ought to be doing something else. I have begun work again on
the novel which I had done in rough draft [*The Stone Angel*?]. I
hope something may come of it—one never knows. I have had
one encouraging thing happen, however—there seems to be quite
a good chance that Macmillan may do a collection of my West
African short stories [*The Tomorrow Tamer*] next year. I have spent
the past few weeks typing them out, and am now keeping my
fingers crossed until I hear Macmillan's reaction.

I would so much like to hear from you again, when you
have time to write.

Sincerely. . . .

Elm Cottage,
11 Oct 67

Dear George—

Thanks for your letter—I'm sorry it has taken me such a long time to reply. The summer has been absolutely hectic, with a great many very welcome visitors and my kids on holiday and myself trying to continue writing a novel [*The Fire-Dwellers*]—finally in despair I abandoned the novel, temporarily, as concentration was all but impossible under these circumstances, and wrote a children's book instead [*Jason's Quest*]—a thing I always vowed I'd never do, but which I thoroughly enjoyed doing, for some obscure reason. Anyway, I'm back at the novel now, and in fact this is the fifth time I have tried this particular novel, so if I can't get it this time, I'm through with it. I keep on believing that it is there, somewhere, though.

I would very much like to write something for *Canadian Literature*—may I wait and see what comes along once I've got the first draft of this novel completed? I've got a few ideas about an article I'd like to do, and when I can put my mind to it, I'll write and outline the subject and perhaps you could tell me then whether or not you'd be interested. . . .

Elm Cottage,
25 Nov 67

Dear George—

Many thanks for your letter. . . .

There isn't a chance in hell that I could get an article done by mid-January. If I ever get this novel done at all it will be a kind of miracle. Don't dare look any further ahead than that. However, if I do manage to get through this lot, then we'll see. At the moment the only kind of article I could write would be one which gave good advice to my youngers—don't write novels; go into Insurance. . . .

All the best. . . .

I think she was very much a transition figure. I've always seen it as a MacLennan decade followed by a Laurence decade. MacLennan was really the old-fashioned didactic writer. He had messages to deliver and [was] really a theme writer. But you come to Margaret and the whole thing shifts. There are still the big themes there, there is still a certain amount of didacticism, she is still preaching at us. At the same time,

*there are experiments and a much deeper understanding and develop-
ment of character.*

> *She had a good imaginative grasp of a prairie culture that
bloomed quickly and died, and what she's really telling us about, even
more than Sinclair Ross, is the death of that culture. As a social historian,
she's excellent.*

Elm Cottage,
17 July 68

Dear George—

Thanks very much for your letter of July 5th. I would be very
glad to attempt an article for the Tenth Anniversary issue of
CANADIAN LITERATURE, along the lines you mention. I don't
know if I will be able to turn out anything which would be of
sufficient general interest, but I'll try. Who could resist the
invitation to talk about oneself? Actually, it isn't quite that simple,
as you know—one is not always aware of each stage in the
changing of one's attitudes, for one thing, and for another thing,
many of the events etc which have really been of the most
importance in relation to writing are those related to one's private
life, which one feels strongly does not belong to anyone else.
However, I'm willing to have a go, and will try to write the article
sometime this autumn.

I'm happy that my new novel has been accepted by the
publishers in England, Canada and America, so this is a great
relief to me. I guess it will be published next spring. . . .

Elm Cottage,
18 Sept 68

Dear George—

A brief note, to say thanks for your article in THE NEW
ROMANS[2]—I was impressed and moved by it, and thought it the
best thing in the book. I wonder if you might consider sending it
to THE NEW STATESMAN here? It seems to me that it really must
be reprinted outside Canada. I like very much the fact that it is

written in relatively low key (ie no exaggerated emotional outpourings), and has such a strong grasp of history and such a somehow eminently sane point of view. I've never read a better summary of the whole Amer dilemma and its relation to Canada. I know it may be presumptuous of me, but I do urge you to send it to some publication such as THE STATESMAN here, and a comparable one in America (don't know what it would be, there).

I'm battling into an attempt at an article for you, for CAN LIT. I find it hard to write about my own writing—rather like talking about one's sex life or finances in public, and I'm not by upbringing uninhibited in these verbal ways. I guess that's why I prefer fiction, for myself, rather than any other form of writing— I seem more able to tell the truth in fiction. However, I think I'm progressing with the article, and if in the end it seems merely corny to you, don't worry—I won't feel hurt or anything.

My new novel [*The Fire-Dwellers*] will come out in the spring, I gather. At last all the final revisions are done, much to my relief, and it is really out of my hands. I want to get down to a few stories now, if I can. I've got a book on contemporary Nigerian literature coming out in England next month [*Long Drums and Cannons*], but feel a total lack of interest in it, owing to the terrifying situation now in Nigeria. The book seems at this point quite irrelevant to what is going on there now. . . .

Elm Cottage,
26 Sept 68

Dear George—

. . . Thank you so much for your reassurance re: my book on Nigerian writing. Yes, I guess it is possible that some relevance will return, although it is difficult to believe so, at the moment, at least within the next generation.

I'm sending you the article I have written for *Canadian Literature*.[3] I don't know if it is any good or not. I find it hard, as I told you, to talk about my own writing. One wants to do a kind of juggling act—to speak truthfully, on the one hand, and yet to avoid making public the areas which must remain private. One also wants to avoid sounding pompous or flippant, as these are the easy but to my mind disagreeable masks of self-revelation. Anyway, if the enclosed isn't okay, I won't mind if you don't use it. . . .

Dear George—

Thanks very much for your letter and for writing to the [Canada] Council on my behalf. I do appreciate it greatly.

I am, as always, astounded at your capacity for work and at how much you accomplish. I'm delighted that the book on Herbert Read is nearly finished.[4] I sympathize, also, with the labours of condensation—that will be my problem when I have the first draft of this novel done [*The Diviners*]. It is simply too long, but I think I have to let it take its own course for the time being, and try to cut it later.

I would very much like to write an article for Can. Lit, on the theme of fiction in life and art. I think probably I would not be able to do it until I have the first draft of this novel done. Also, by that time, I may with luck have discovered a few more things about the subject!

Once again, very many thanks.

Very best wishes. . . .

Lakefield,
12 Aug 75

Dear George—

I have just finished doing a review of your book on Gabriel Dumont for *The Canadian Forum*.[5] I had intended sending you a copy, but have sent it to Mel Hurtig [publisher of the book] instead. . . . I asked Mel to send you a copy. . . . I guess the Forum will run it in October. . . .

There isn't any way that anyone could really do justice to that splendid book in a review. All I hope is that I have communicated my own enthusiasm for it. It was a privilege to be able to review it, and I felt inadequate to the task. I found the book fascinating, moving, powerful.

It's a period of our history which has haunted me for a long time, and some of that haunting I tried to put into THE

DIVINERS, the sense of the dispossessed and of the ancestral myths. Culloden in my mind has been connected for some time with the dispossession of the Métis, an irony of history. It connects, too (although naturally one cannot go into all this in a review) with other wars of a tribal society vs a technological society— the wars of the British against the Mahdi in the Sudan; the Ashanti wars in West Africa; the war that Mohammed Abdullah Hassan (called by the Brits "The Mad Mullah") fought for 20 years in Somaliland against the British. So many parallels, and in so many ways. If I had your grasp of history, and your ability to put down events both movingly and analytically, I'd write about it. As it is, I have to suggest some of these themes through my own medium, fiction.

Odd that you mentioned the only other true "hero" in our history—Norman Bethune. There must in me, I guess, be that strain (Celtic, probably) which recognizes the epic here. In my cottage, there are two posters. One is of Riel, a poster from the Manitoba Métis Association, which says (around a very bad reproduction of a fairly early pic of Riel), "Nous Sommes La Nouvelle Nation". The other is of Dr. Bethune, a poster which was (if you can believe it) printed in China, and which makes Bethune look a bit Chinese, and which I obtained in devious ways. But in my study, in my Lakefield house, there is above my desk another picture—a silkscreen print done by Susan Newlove, and given to me by her. It is called simply "The Plainsman", but it is Gabriel, and it is based on that famous photo of him, with Le Petit [his rifle] across his arm.

Thanks a whole lot for writing that book. We have long needed it. . . .

Lakefield,
28 Jan 78

Dear George—

A number of people phoned me to ask if I'd heard your broadcast on my work, on "Audience", CBC. Alas and alack, I had not. Adele Wiseman heard it, and summarized for me some of your statements, which I find fascinating and totally valid—is it possible to deal with the underlying universal themes (such as the elements of earth, air, fire, water) without being conscious that one is doing so? I believe, of course, that it is. We are responding as writers to things very deep within not only our own psyches, but also within the general human psyche. . . .

All well here. Am deeply thinking about another novel, but I still have much to learn before I begin it. I don't mean I'm doing research . . but I am thinking a lot about it, and also doing strangely eclectic reading which I somehow sense will be in some way relevant. Spent a strange summer, reading things like Jung's MEMORIES, DREAMS, REFLECTIONS, your and Ivan Avakumovic's THE DOUKHOBORS and a lot of weird Pentecostal pamphlets!! Where is it all leading? Maybe I'll find out. I also want to write some stories for very young children, and hope I can do that. I am not really *into* (as the kids say) writing the apparently fashionable stuff for kids, all about how it's okay if mummy and daddy get divorced and mum is on Valium. My ideas, apparently, tend more in kids' stories to a celebration of the things and creatures I have loved, especially out at my cottage by the river, the trees, birds and animals, although of course one cannot write about them without also acknowledging the danger in which all life exists. We will see.

Hope all is well with you. All the very best. . . .

Lakefield,
11 April 78

Dear George—

Thanks so much for your article.[6] I found it simply fascinating! Of course, I knew about the 4 elements and 4 humours (if memory serves, these came rather heavily into a 17th century thought course I once took at university from Malcolm Ross!). But I have to admit there was no conscious use of those themes—from your article, they seem so clearly to be there that one wonders if these things can indeed happen at subconscious levels. So much of writing does take place in mysterious ways that I am prepared to believe it. An odd thing—before I began writing A JEST OF GOD, I started THE FIRE-DWELLERS and got about 100 pp done and realized I had to write A JEST OF GOD first—the other just wasn't happening the way it should, so I threw out what I'd actually done on *The F-D* and did *A Jest of God* first. So the 4 were actually written in that order . . *The Stone Angel, A Jest of God, The*

222

Fire-Dwellers, and *The Diviners.* Strange. . . .

[Her life and work after The Diviners*] all comes together in a Christian context. It's very much like the progressions of religious people. They create when they reach the end of youth or in middle age; then in their later years they go into devotional exercises. Hers is a classic pattern.*

Lakefield,
5 June 80

Dear George—

I am going to apply for a Canada Council grant—I think, for the 3-year one—and I am wondering if you might be kind enough to write a letter of reference for me. . . .

I am starting a novel, and although I have made several false starts and am proceeding slowly, I believe it really is there to be written. It is ironic that just when, *at last,* I think I can write another novel, I may have to concentrate on doing articles etc— if, indeed, anyone will buy them! Things are tough all over. However, I actually feel fairly optimistic because the characters in my mind do seem very real to me. You know, it doesn't get easier to write as one gets older; it gets more difficult. I think I also find the fact that quite a lot of literary criticism has been written about my work is rather intimidating to me. One has to forget everything except a direct connection with the characters. . . .

She didn't have the life-saving ability to shut off what other people said. She took everything to heart.

Lakefield,
18 June 80

Dear George—

Thanks so very much for agreeing to write a letter to the Canada Council on my behalf. I am very grateful. . . .

Yes, it surely is a bad situation right now, although I suspect that serious writing has always been in a fragile situation. When I think that *any* of your books are out of print, I want to rage endlessly and proclaim that there *has* to be an answer to that problem. It is *terrible*. Well, I guess we press on and try to take comfort from the fact that we have, indeed, been able to do the kind of work we loved doing, and not so many human beings have been that lucky. Personally, I feel that if some of my books have spoken something to 3 generations .. the one before me, mine, and my children's generation .. then I've been pretty fortunate. As one gets older, of course, one worries a bit about the money to live on, but I guess in our highly privileged society (wrongly privileged, of course) this should be the last of our worries. I delivered the convocation address at York University in T.O. last week—it was really on the theme of *not* giving way to despair in a terrifying world, of believing in the necessity of proclaiming and working for such beliefs as many of us hold dear. You will know what I mean, because it has seemed for many years to me that your perceptions of these things are much like my own, and heaven knows we have not saved the world nor really been too effective in defeating the hawks (I really hate the name of that noble bird used in that context!). Still, we go on. In fiction, of course, one tries to approach the human condition by trying to portray some few individuals within it.

Anyway, many many thanks, not just for this ref, but for all you have taught me (unknowingly, probably) throughout a lot of years.

Lakefield,
26 March 81

Dear George—

I did get the Arts Award from the Canada Council, and I just want to thank you very very much for supporting my application. This does give me a year's sense of financial security. . . .

Anyway, the novel that has been brewing in my head for about 4 years may get started. I think so. At least I am getting into the New Regime schedule, i.e. working in the mornings and early afternoons, from 9 a.m. to 2 p.m., sometimes with terrifying doubts, but I must stick to it. I think that what has frightened me most, George, is (since I came back to Can in 1973) the volume of critical articles analysing my writing. One tends to read it all and get scared about all the in-depth stuff (much of it referring to things I really did intend, and passionately, to put in the writing). But if one thinks of the critics, the reviewers, and even God bless them the readers, one is *paralysed*. So I am trying, as I have before, simply to connect with the characters and to become a story-teller telling *myself* a story that I want to hear and find out what happened. Pray for me, please, as I know you do.

All best wishes and love to you and Inge. . . .

R.R. 11,
Peterborough, Ont.,
19 July 71

Dear Dale—

I am saying "Dear Dale" instead of "Dear Dale Zieroth", which is the usual interim ploy between the business and the personal, the opening introduction to someone you haven't met but actually intend to call by their first name sometime. I think maybe you and I should call each other by our first names right now.

To go back a bit. Some six months ago, when I was still in England (where I have usually been living since 1962, with visits to Canada, plus one year as writer-in-residence . . whatever that means . . at the U of T), Al Purdy sent me his collection *Storm Warning*.[1] I read it, naturally, as I read all the things written by young writers in Canada, with enthusiasm, love, interest, suspicion, etc. Quite a few of the poems hit me, and one that hit me more than most was a poem called *Father*, which really struck deep. I thought "this guy has got to have been a prairie farmer . . can't be, though . . I am as usual immersed in my own ancestral fantasy." Looked up writer; it was you. GOOD LORD . . where did you come from? Neepawa, Manitoba. I couldn't believe it. If you had been a lousy writer who came from my hometown, it would just not have mattered and I wouldn't have felt like saying anything. But you were so good that it really knifed me. I sat down and wrote you a letter. I then re-read it, and thought, "This guy is going to think I am a nitbrain, to have written to him simply because we come from the same town". (It was *not* just that; but I felt the threads were beyond me to get across to you). So I tore up the letter and never sent it.

Next Episode: Last weekend, Don Bailey and [his wife] Anne were here. I had no idea they even knew you. But Don . . . happened accidentally on purpose to mention your name; I responded with . . "My God, you know him?"; he said, "Dale & Marge are about our best friends." We then went through the strange exchange. I told him I had written a letter to you but had been too basically reticent to send it; he told me you had (at least, this was Don's story) written a letter or so to me in your head.

Hence this letter. Belatedly.

Don said that when you drove through Neepawa, you said, "This is where the world begins." The virtue of poetry is that it can say things in such a concentrated way, the things a novelist has to take 250 pages to say. Yes, this was where the world began. And you are the world, or as much of it as you know, and this was where you first gained consciousness, knew that you were yourself. And it happened very young.

I couldn't wait to get out of that town. I was 18 when I left it, and 23 when I paid my last real visit, when my mother [father's second wife] still lived there, and when I and my husband were about to take off for England, in 1949. I never went back, until once, briefly, in 1966, when friends drove me out there for the day and I only went to look (why?) at my grandfather's brick house (one of the first in the town; both my grandfathers lived there most of their adult lives), and at the cemetery where my mother and father have lain since I was four and then ten years old. I never went to look at my maternal grandfather's grave . . his memorial was that brick house. It was still standing; much smaller than I recalled; the hedge had not been trimmed for some time . . the old man (hated, in the past, by me) would not have liked that, and I at that moment did not like it either.

The ancestors reverberate.

I was brought up . . Irish (from Ontario) on one side, and Scots on the other, to honour mainly my Scots ancestors. It was quite awhile before I really knew that the real land of my ancestors was a small town in Manitoba. This, by the way, is not sentimentality. The real ancestors were not glorious. They were great, though, in painful and convoluted ways. As I think you put across in your poetry.

I've lived in a lot of places. I could no more go back and live in Neepawa than I could become the Queen of Siam. No way. But . . very oddly . . it has all become fiction. This is what interests me now. The ways in which the past becomes the present becomes the future and all are intertwined. Once I lived in a Brick House in a small town. Now I live wherever I live, and can make that home, but the Brick House and the town now live in me, in my skull. At last, without being too much bugged by it (only after having written quite a lot) I can now give them houseroom. . . .

God bless. . . .

I was perennially poor as students are, so I started reading [A Jest of God] in the bookstore in The Bay. If this was any other bookstore I think they would have stopped me. But, you know, it's The Bay, and they sort of don't care. It's like a big department store. There's always someone running around. So I read the novel there in instalments, coming back to it, reading a chapter and a little bit more on a daily basis. . . . The part that I remembered more was the part that wasn't about Neepawa [but] was about away. Because of course I wanted to get away.

R.R. 11,
Peterborough,
3 Aug 71

Dear Dale—

Thanks a lot for your letter. I was very touched re: your recounting of reading an early story of mine, and also reading *A Jest of God* in the H[udson] B[ay] C[ompany] book section. Incidentally, that story you read in the magazine must have been one of my African ones, published in the old *Saturday Evening Post* in 1960[2], so you must've been about 14. It doesn't seem all that long ago to me, of course! Anyway, what really got to me about what you said was that you seemed to have nearly the identical reaction to my writing, especially when you read *A Jest of God*, as I did when I first read Sinclair Ross's novel *As For Me And My House*.[3] I must've been about 17 or 18, and it was the first thing I had ever read which was deeply out of a background similar to my own. The first time it ever occurred to me that maybe you did not have to have been born in London Eng or New York USA or the Amer Deep South, to write a novel which people would read with comprehension. If I have passed any of that feeling on to the next generation, yours, the feeling of value and worth for one's own people, then I am really happy. For me, it's a kind of repayment for a debt I owe to people like Sinclair Ross. In time, Dale, you'll do the same.

You didn't miss much by not hearing me at United College that time. I come across better in the printed word. Sometimes I feel that (as James Thurber once said) I ought just to write to people and never actually talk. That isn't quite true. It's good to talk with friends. Public talking I hate, and am very nervous and think I am going to faint on-stage, altho never actually have.

I have *Storm Warning* and *Soundings*[4] . . Al Purdy sent me the former, and it gladdens my heart that you don't like young writers knocking him down. He has got so goddamn much sympathy for young writers and has done such a lot for them. Also, this is not, in a profound sense, a competitive trade, writing. We aren't all saying the same thing; none of us are. We may work in similar areas, but the idiom, the eyes, the view are always different. Nobody needs to feel threatened by anyone else. I get more and more fascinated by the work of young Can writers, in poetry and more especially in prose (because that is my territory). I don't think I am going to write novels forever; this may be my last; after that, I hope to God some publisher will take me on as reader or editor, because the stuff that is being written now is really interesting and it appears to me that there are not enough publishers' readers or editors in this country who know one goddamn thing about it all. I was so glad when [John] Newlove went to McC[lelland] & S[tewart] . . at last, somebody who knows what poetry is all about! . . .

I sort of thought you came from around Neepawa, because about 6 months ago an old High School teacher of mine, a really great lady who taught Eng in Neepawa High School for about 35 years, came to Eng[land] and visited me for a day and I asked if she had known you, and she said "He could not have gone to school in Neepawa or I would remember him" . . . quite right, she would've, I think. (Okay, so now tell me you went to High School in Neepawa).

This novel of mine is coming at a terrific pace, and I am worried it will be about 900 pages long, and I hate long novels unless they are as entertaining as Richler's last one [*St. Urbain's Horseman*]. However, I think now I may see a way of paring it down to essentials. I am about a third of the way through the first draft. It will take about 2 years to finish, if God is good. My problem is always that I am so impatient . . when I really get inside it, I do not want to do anything else or think of anything else, but even in my shack here, one has to mow the lawn from time to time, and say an occasional word to neighbours. When I get back to Eng, the situation will be much more complex, and the distractions will be multitudinous, so I want to get as much done this summer as I can. Anyway, I am into it, and it won't go away, so now I must try to learn patience. I never will, tho. . . .

I have sent you and Marge a copy of *The Fire-Dwellers*. Anyone who will cheat the HBC over a book deserves a free one, for once! I have read books myself that way, in bookshops, mainly in London the first year I left my husband and was there broke with my kids. The ploy with sales clerks is to lay down the book one has been reading, as tho one had only been waiting to get the clerk's attention, and then ask about some book so obscure or non-existent that they are certain not to have it. . . .

All the best to you both. . . .

I read her to find out what people did with their lives, lives that were either falling apart or were challenged or wrecked or were at a point where they had to make decision[s]. I read her for those things, and I found out lots of answers. For me she was a writer that I went to if I wanted to be nurtured in some way, which is what makes her . . . an old writer as opposed to a new writer. I mean, contemporary authors seldom nurture at all, it seems.

Elm Cottage,
12 Dec 72

Dear Dale—

Sorry it's taken me so long to answer your letter. I got back to England the middle of October, and settled down right away to getting the novel put into typescript. I finished the first draft this summer, 28 notebooks of handwriting, so the job of getting it into typescript is vast. I'm about a third of the way through now, and am trying to cut as much as possible, but alas, this is proving more difficult than I thought it would, as most of the parts were indeed put there for a purpose. It will be much too long, but I don't quite know how to do anything about that. It is full of a lot of strange bezaz—plot summaries of novels, bits of history, even songs. Yep. I have just composed 2 long ballad-type songs! Even got a tune for one of them, and I think a friend is going to write a sort of Country and Western tune for the other. This is perhaps very foolhardy of me, I mean to compose songs in the name of several of my characters, but it feels like the right thing. Of course, it adds to the already huge length of the damn thing, too! So I'm working pretty hard, and in general feeling pretty good about things. I hope to get the novel rewritten by next spring, and then to type it out in triplicate next summer. I wish I could get someone to type it for me. . . . It would be much more fun for me to write a kid's book next summer, if possible. . . .

One of the wonderful things about reading [her] books is recognition, recognizing states of being and people . . . reading a novel that had a Ukrainian in it, even if it was just somebody passing through or had that kind of odd name or Métis. That was a whole kind of thing that said my life was legitimate. . . . She planted that seed very early on, and a lot of things came out of that. The first real poems I wrote were about my father hunting and those kinds of poems. I sometimes feel that those poems might not have been written if it hadn't been for Margaret Laurence being there. . . .

Elm Cottage,
21 Feb 73

Dear Dale—

Thanks many times for sending the book for friends—a number of the poems I'd read before, and some I hadn't. It serves to confirm what I already knew—that however often you may think you just don't *want* to write, a deeper truer part of you needs to write and has to write, because from somewhere it has been given to you. It will BE ALL RIGHT. YOU WILL SEE.

I actually do know what you mean by the poet in you is jealous of the fiction-and-play writer. I'd be kind of surprised if you turned out to be a fiction writer, basically, but who knows? I do know one thing—damn near every novelist *does* want to be a poet, as you say, and damn near every poet wants to be a novelist. This is an irony which I've discussed many times with Al Purdy. He has sometimes said to me that he really would've liked to write a novel, and I have said to him innumerable times how strange and in a sense envious (not really) I feel when I read one of his poems which particularly strikes me and which deals with some of the areas I'm dealing with (as often happens with his writing and mine), and I think—jesus, it takes me 397 pp to say what this guy has said in 20 lines. But in fact none of us really has that much doubt about our areas, and I believe that more and more the (probably false) boundaries between fiction and

231

poetry and drama will be broken down; I visualize novels which include poems; poems which include music; everything which includes everything else, in whatever ways the artist (I hate that word) has felt compelled naturally to do. So if you find yourself branching out and wanting to do different things—oh Dale, that is just fine! Everything you feel you really want to do joyfully in these areas is fine. Down with fences.

Well, I'm speaking as usual out of recent personal feelings. I HAVE FINISHED MY NOVEL!!! Three drafts and it is now done. My daughter is typing it in fair copy for me. . . . I may have to cut it further later on, when I've distanced myself from it. I also at this point have no idea whether any of my 3 publishers will accept it—this is *not* false modesty, of which I have none, but the realization that this is a kind of peculiar novel, so deeply ingrained with the Manawaka background, and yet moving out from it, taking a lot of crazy chances in the sense that the protagonist is a writer (woman, age 47), and she is *not* me, but we are sisters, and so on. . . . A dear Canadian friend, who is a poet and composer, has done the music for [four] songs, and I think the music is really good. . . . what I'd really like as well is to have a 45-record, with all the songs on it. This house is filled with recording equipment. . . . I find all this kind of exciting. . . .

She was an "ordinary person", and she was a great writer. . . . That's what was inspiring about her: she made it possible for people who might not normally have thought that they could be a writer to suddenly think, "Yeah, I can be a writer, and I'd better get at it and start writing". . . .

Elm Cottage,
24 March 73

Dear Dale—

Thanks a lot for your letter. I wish you would not feel yr writing is irrelevant—it *isn't*. Of course you feel there's something lacking in it—there is always something lacking, namely that the poem or novel which is in the head is always better, more piercing, more direct, more everything than the one that gets down on paper. I can see in a way how you feel about you'd rather be a plumber. I often feel I'd rather do damn near anything than be a novelist. I also know quite a few young writers who, like yrself, are busy at the moment fighting their own need to write, knowing, of course, that in a way you may not have chosen the poetry, but apparently it has chosen you. If that sounds mystic, let it. For years I went around decently pretending that writing was just like being a typist or whatever—a conscious choice which could at any moment be reversed. Not any more. I've had too many years in this dilemma to pretend I really have a choice. I'll quit writing when it quits me, not before. That will happen someday, too. And I'll feel like hell about it, for awhile at least. Old-er isn't safe—it's much more unsafe. At least I think so. The beginning of having to come to some kind of terms not only with life but with eventual and unavoidable death. But heavens, neither young, old-er or Ancient is safe. Boring if it were, likely, altho one longs for inner and outer peace. Precisely where yr poetry *is* relevant is that you *do* know that plumbers and etc have dreams and inner life and fears and all the rest no less than your own. That's something some writers never see. I think the poems you sent are the core (or maybe beginning) of something quite exceptionally valuable. Not just to poets or other writers, either.

... Of course one doesn't feel the "leaving a legacy of poems" bit—if you wrote for that, it would be, as Arthur Miller once said about the same thing, like carving your name on a block of ice out in the street on a hot July day. You don't need a poetical "histericomy", pal, you need a course in Spelling!

So—take heart, eh? We need you. ...

Love to you and Marge. ...

She became something that people rallied around. I don't think she ever wanted that. My sense is that she was more shocked by it than anything, at first. And then outraged by it. And then just kind of worn out by it, worn down by it.

Lakefield,
16 July 75

Dear Dale—

For nearly a year your last letter has been waiting, amidst many

233

others, to be answered. . . .

My life in the past two years has been incredibly hectic. I sold my house in England and moved back to Canada permanently in August 73. I came out to the shack (where I am at present, for part of the summer) for August, and during that time, I bought a lovely old two-storey yellowbrick house in Lakefield, a little village just north of Peterborough. I rented it for the winter . . . and then zoomed on to the Univ of Western Ontario, where I was writer-in-residence for that one term until Christmas, and where I, quite frankly, worked my ass off. I then returned to Toronto for Christmas, just in time to read the galley proofs for *The Diviners*. Then on to Trent Univ, at Peterborough, where I was w-in-r until Spring of 1974. . . . On May 1st, 1974 I moved into my Lakefield house. . . .

This past year has been incredible for me. . . . as w-in-r at Trent, seem to have gone out to dozens of high schools and community colleges. I am now saying No to all that, as I began to feel I was turning into a performer, not a writer. *The Diviners* has done well, and got the Gov-Gen this year, which pleased me a lot. I also got the Molson award, which is $15,000, so that will be a big help with the kids' university expenses, etc. I've also done quite a bit of work with the Writers' Union. I ended up, about mid-June, totally exhausted, and have been here at the shack ever since, trying to unwind and get back to writing. So far, all I've done is to catch up on correspondence, plus write a few reviews, etc. I'm not in any tearing hurry re: writing, tho, at this point. I finished *The Diviners* just 2 years ago and it left me totally drained. It took three and a half years to write, and took an awful lot out of me, to say the very least. . . .

I wonder how your writing is coming along? I got a copy of *Clearing*[5] when it came out, and thought it was splendid. . . .

I think she wanted to establish something, not with her books or not in the world, but with herself. I think that she wanted something to be settled, to be redeemed, or whatever. And I don't know if she ever did get that. . . . It wasn't bitterness. She wasn't bitter. She wasn't disillusioned. . . . I sense this [was] just more of a feeling that she didn't get to where she wanted to go in herself, somehow.

Lakefield,
8 June 76

Dear Dale—

Forgive me for not having replied sooner to your letter. The past 2 months have been unbelievable for me. I've done about 6 book reviews, worked on the Writers' Union contract, attended the union conference in Ottawa, worked on the union educational project, finished final revisions on a manuscript of my own (a collection of essays and articles to be published in the fall), tried to keep up with business correspondence, gone out to various Canlit classes at Trent and in local high schools, and finally, spent a glorious week with my brother and his family in High Prairie, Alberta. It's been a busy but a good time.

Neepawa last fall was really really great. One thing they gave me was an architect's scale drawings of my Grandfather Simpson's brick house (the Brick House in the stories). A team of architects from the U of M had been there about a year before and had done drawings of a lot of old houses, the Town Hall, the Land Titles Office, etc. And the Simpson house was one of them. Lawrence Hurrell, the mayor (with whose brother Dennis I'd been in love in Grade One!) persuaded the university to let the town have an extra set of the drawings of the house. I was really touched. Also, you recall I was worried about not remembering people's names? I had no problem at all. I guess if you live in the same town for the first 18 years of your life, you don't forget. . . .

Fine things are happening in the prairies re: writing, or from prairie writers like yourself who aren't resident there. I've recently read Andy Suknaski's book WOOD MOUNTAIN POEMS,[6] and am going to review it for the Montreal *Gazette*. I've also become acquainted with *NeWest Review*, edited by George Melnyk—do you get it? It's really good. Operates from Edmonton, and when I was there I met George. . . . Also saw Rudy Wiebe, of whom I'm extremely fond. . . . I've also recently read some of the poetry of Glen Sorestad . . his chapbook WIND SONGS. And George Melnyk gave me a record called PRAIRIE GRASS PRAIRIE SKY with songs by Geoffrey Ursell and others. . . .

. . . I hope very much that the writing spell continues. What you call The Grave Doubt is what I call The Black Celt. But it passes. . . .

Love to you all. . . .

235

Margaret Atwood—b. Ottawa, 1939—is one of Canada's most accomplished and acclaimed writers of poetry and fiction, with over a dozen books of poems and eight novels published. Already a winner of the Governor General's Award for poetry for *The Circle Game* (1966), she confirmed her reputation as a critic with *Survival* and as a writer of prose fiction with her second novel, *Surfacing*, both published in 1972. In 1986 she again won the Governor General's Award, for her novel *The Handmaid's Tale*. She was president of the Writers' Union of Canada 1981–82 and president of International PEN, Canadian Centre (English-Speaking), 1984–86. Her most recent works are the novel *The Robber Bride* (1993) and a collection of new poetry, *Morning in the Burned House* (1995). She first met Margaret Laurence at the Governor General's Award ceremonies in Ottawa in 1967.

Don Bailey—b. Toronto, 1942—has published three books of poems, eight short-story collections, and a novel. He has received an ACTRA Award nomination for Best Television Drama, and is the author of numerous television and radio scripts. His latest collection of stories is *Window Dressing* (1994), and a new novel, *The Grace of No Regret*, will appear in 1995. He first met Margaret Laurence when she was writer-in-residence at the University of Toronto in 1969, and for a number of years had a cottage next to hers on the Otonabee River near Peterborough. In 1989 he published *Memories of Margaret: My Twenty Year Friendship with Margaret Laurence*.

George Bowering—b. Penticton, British Columbia, 1935—teaches English at Simon Fraser University. He has published over two dozen books of poetry and six works of fiction, and has won the Governor General's Award for Poetry for *Rocky Mountain Foot* (1969) and for his novel *Burning Water* (1980). He is also a noted critic of modern and postmodern literature, and his 1971 essay on *A Jest of God* remained one of Margaret Laurence's favourite commentaries on her writing. His most recent works are *George Bowering Selected: Poems 1961–1992*, and *The Moustache*, a memoir of Canadian artist Greg Curnoe. He first met Margaret Laurence at a Writers' Union meeting in 1974.

Ernest Buckler—b. Dalhousie West, Nova Scotia, 1908, d. 1984—lived most of his life in rural Nova Scotia, and contributed early stories to *Esquire* and *Saturday Night* magazines. Best known for his classic novel *The Mountain and the Valley* (1952), he also wrote a second novel, *The Cruelest Month* (1963); a "fictional memoir", *Ox Bells and Fireflies* (1968); and a collection of short fiction, *The Rebellion of Young David and Other Stories* (1975). He won the Leacock Award for Humour for *Whirligig* (1977). Buckler and Margaret Laurence first began to correspond in 1974.

Silver Donald Cameron—b. Toronto, 1937—taught English literature at several Canadian universities, but left academe in 1971 to become a full-time writer. He has won four National Magazine Awards, and is the author of more than fifty radio dramas, four of which have been ACTRA Award finalists. His TV drama *Peggy* was a Gemini Award finalist for best short drama. He has been vice-chair of the Writers' Union of Canada. Some of the best-known of his twelve books are *Faces of Leacock* (1967), *Conversations with Canadian Novelists* (1973), the novel *Dragon Lady*, and *Wind, Whales and Whisky: A Cape Breton Voyage* (1991). A new work, *Sniffing the Coast: An Acadian Voyage*, appeared in 1993. He first met Margaret Laurence in England in 1965 when he interviewed her for *Canadian Literature*.

Marian Engel—b. Toronto 1933, d. 1985—was the first chair of the Writers' Union of Canada, and very much influenced the collective movement of Canadian writers to deal with their publishers. She won the Governor General's Award for her novel *Bear* (1976), and published six other highly respected novels. These include *Monodromos* (1974), *The Glassy Sea* (1978), and *Lunatic Villas* (1981), which employ a variety of landscapes and relationships to reveal the complexities of women's lives and accompanying gender issues.

Hubert Evans—b. Vankleek Hill, Ontario 1892, d. 1986—enlisted in the Canadian army in 1915 and was wounded at Ypres in 1916. Evans's writing career spanned 56 years. He published his first collection of stories, *Forest Friends*, in 1926 and his last book, *Mostly Coast People: The Collected Poetry of Hubert Evans*, in 1982. In between there were four other story collections, three novels, two books of poems, two works of teenage fiction, and a biography. He was given the Canadian Authors' Association First Annual Award for Distinguished and Enduring Contribution to Canadian Writing in 1966, and an Honorary Degree (LL.D.) from Simon Fraser University in 1984.

Timothy Findley—b. Toronto 1930—had an early career as an actor, and has worked for three decades as a writer of fiction, plays, and scripts for film, television, and radio. He won the Governor General's Award for his novel *The Wars* (1977), and received national and international critical praise for four subsequent novels, including his most recent, *Headhunter* (1993). In 1990 he published the first of his memoirs, *Inside Memory*, and his third play, *The Stillborn Lover*, was published in 1993. He was chair of the Writers' Union of Canada 1977–78 and president of International PEN, Canadian Centre (English-Speaking), 1986–87. His first meeting with Margaret Laurence was in 1969.

Gary Geddes—b. Vancouver, 1940—was founding editor of the Studies in Canadian Literature series, Quadrant Editions, and Cormorant Books. His anthologies—*20th-Century Poetry & Poetics*, *15 Canadian Poets X 2*, and *The Art of Short Fiction: An International Anthology*—are widely used in Canadian universities. He has published over ten books of poetry, including *Letter of the Master of Horse* (1973), *The Terracotta Army* (1984), *Light of Burning Towers: Poems New and Selected* (1990), and, most recently, *Girl by the Water* (1994). He teaches at Concordia University in Montreal and lives on a farm in eastern Ontario. As a teacher at the University of Toronto in 1969 he first met Margaret Laurence when she was writer-in-Residence there.

Graeme Gibson—b. London, Ontario 1934—wrote two early novels, *Five Legs* (1969) and *Communion* (1971), which had a strong influence on a generation of young Canadian writers. He has since published two more novels, *Perpetual Motion* (1983) and *Gentleman Death* (1993). Gibson's influence on Canadian cultural politics has been profound. He was the initial organizer and a founding member of the Writers' Union of Canada, and its chair 1974–75; a founding member of the Book and Periodical Development Council and of the Writers' Development Trust.

From 1987–89 he was president of International PEN, Canadian Centre (English-Speaking); he was chair of the committee responsible for organizing International PEN's 54th World Congress, and co-president of that Congress. He first met Margaret Laurence at one of the organizing meetings of the Writers' Union in the early 1970s.

Harold Horwood—b. St. John's, Newfoundland, 1923—has published three novels, the best known of which is *White Eskimo* (1972), and a collection of short stories. He has also published sixteen books of non-fiction, including two biographies, most recently *Joey: The Life and Political Times of Joey Smallwood* (1989). His other works comprise several books of popular history and two books on the philosophy of evolution. He was a founding member of the Writers' Union of Canada. Recently he was awarded a grant by Telefilm Canada to produce a screenplay of one of his novels. He first met Margaret Laurence at Silver Donald Cameron's house in the early 1970s.

Myrna Kostash—b. Edmonton, Alberta, 1944—is a non-fiction writer, scriptwriter, and playwright. She has published an autobiographical work, *All of Baba's Children* (1977), *Long Way from Home: The Story of the Sixties Generation in Canada* (1980), *No Kidding*, a stageplay (1987), and *Bloodlines: A Journey Into Eastern Europe* (1993). Her essays and articles have appeared in numerous anthologies, and she has had several television and film scripts produced. Her work won a Silver Medal, National Magazine Awards in 1985. She was 1993–94 chair of the Writers' Union of Canada. She first met Margaret Laurence at Elm Cottage in 1969.

Robert Kroetsch—b. Heisler, Alberta, 1927—is one of Canada's most influential postmodern writers and critics. He published five novels between 1965 and 1975, and won the Governor General's Award for *The Studhorse Man* in 1969. His *Completed Field Notes* (1989) contains two longer poems—"The Ledger" and "Seed Catalogue"—which, along with others, emphasize the archeological site and citing of history, as poetry is created from the extra/ordinary discourse of daily life. His voicing of theoretical concerns in his creative work is complemented by his critical commentaries in such volumes as *Labyrinths of Voice:*

Conversations with Robert Kroetsch (1982) and *The Lovely Treachery of Words* (1989). His most recent novel is *The Puppeteer* (1992). He first met Margaret Laurence at a Writers' Union meeting in 1973, but for years had been "gauging [his] own sense of the West against hers."

Dennis Lee—b. Toronto, 1939—was a co-founder of House of Anansi Press in 1967, and an editor there until 1972, and brought to the fore the work of many younger writers. The politics of his poetry, rooted strongly in anti-colonial values, can be found in *Civil Elegies* (1968), which won the Governor General's Award. A generation of young adults know him for his children's poetry, especially *Alligator Pie* (1974). His critical work *Savage Fields: An Essay in Literature and Cosmology* (1977) provides perhaps the most challenging and significant analysis to date of works by Michael Ondaatje and Leonard Cohen. His most recent books are *Riffs* and *Ping and Pong* (both 1993). He first met Margaret Laurence in 1969.

Norman Levine—b. Ottawa, 1923—lived in England from 1949 until the 1980s, but was the first writer-in-residence at the University of New Brunswick, 1965–66. Now he divides his time between Canada and Europe, living and writing in France. He published two early works of poetry and a novel, but is best known for his eight volumes of short stories, including *One Way Ticket* (1961), *Thin Ice* (1979), and *Something Happened Here* (1991), and for his novel *From a Seaside Town* (1970). A new edition of his highly praised autobiographical work, *Canada Made Me* (1958), appeared in 1993. He and Margaret Laurence first met at his home in St. Ives, Cornwall in 1971.

Hugh MacLennan—b. Glace Bay, Nova Scotia, 1907, d. 1992—is arguably the most widely read Canadian novelist of the 1940s and 1950s. His ardent nationalism shaped his fiction through four decades as he dealt with colonialism (*Barometer Rising*, 1941), Quebec–Canada relations (*Two Solitudes*, 1945), ethnicity, class, and puritanism in a small Maritime town (*Each Man's Son*, 1951), and the politics of personal and collective human experience (*The Watch That Ends the Night*, 1959, and *Voices in Time*, 1980). He won three Governor General's Awards for his fiction and two others for collections of his essays. He was a Rhodes Scholar, obtained a Ph.D. in Classics from Princeton University, and taught English Literature at McGill University in Montreal. Through the quality and quantity of his work he greatly influenced the next generation of Canadian novelists, including Margaret Laurence.

Joyce Marshall—b. Montreal, 1913—had many short stories broadcast on CBC Radio between 1950 and the 1980s, and was the first reader for the *Anthology* program on CBC Radio in the early 1960s. She has published two novels—*Presently Tomorrow* (1946) and *Lovers and Strangers* (1957)—and a collection of short stories, *A Private Place* (1975). She is also known as a translator of Québécois works, especially those of Gabrielle Roy, such as *The Road past Altamont* (1966, La route d'Altamont), *Windflower* (1970, *La Rivière sans Repos*), and *The Enchanted Summer* (1976, *Cet Été Qui Chantait*, for which she won the Governor General's Award for Translation). In 1977 her passionate essay against Quebec separation, "A Difficult Country, and Our Home", was published in Gary Geddes' collection *Divided We Stand*.

John Metcalf—b. Carlisle, England, 1938—came to Canada in 1962 and taught school in Montreal for a number of years. He has published three volumes of short stories, two novellas, and two novels (*Going Down Slow*, 1972, and *General Ludd*, 1980). He has had an important impact on Canadian literature through his editing of many short-story collections, including *Here and Now* (1977, with Clarke Blaise), *First Impressions* (1980), *Second Impressions* (1981), and *Third Impressions* (1982). As a skilled critic he confronted the literary establishment in *Kicking against the Pricks* (1982). He was a founding member of the Writers' Union of Canada and has been writer-in-residence in several Canadian universities. He first met Margaret Laurence in Montreal in 1970.

Claire Mowat—b. Toronto 1933—graduated from the Ontario College of Art and worked as a commercial artist for a number of years. In 1983 she published *The Outport People*, about Newfoundland and her experiences there. This was followed by *Pomp and Circumstances* (1989), which chronicled her adventures as lady-in-waiting to Lily Schreyer, wife of the governor general. She has written two novels for young readers, *The Girl from Away* (1992) and its sequel, *The French Isles* (1994). She and her husband, author Farley Mowat, first met Margaret Laurence at the home of publisher Jack McClelland in Toronto in 1966.

Farley Mowat—b. Belleville, Ontario, 1921—one of Canada's best-known writers whose many works has been translated in thirty-three languages, he has won a Governor-General's Medal, the Leacock Medal for Humour, the Mark Twain Award, the Etoile de la Mer (France), a Gemini Award for Best Documentary Script, and many other prizes. He gained international notoriety with the publication of his first book, *People of the Deer* (1952), which strongly criticized Canada's treatment of the Inuit people, and over the years has continued to write what he calls "subjective non-fiction" about the interaction of people, animals, and the environment, such as *Never Cry Wolf* (1963), *A Whale for the Killing* (1972), and *Sea of Slaughter* (1984). His volumes of memoirs range from children's books to the recounting of his World War Two military experiences in *And No Birds Sang* (1979). His most recent work is *Born Naked* (1993), a memoir of his first sixteen years. With his wife Claire he met Margaret Laurence in Toronto in 1966, and refers to Laurence as "the greatest writer we've ever had".

Alice Munro—b. Wingham, Ontario 1931—is a writer whose portraits of small-town and rural Ontario both delineate and transcend region through their essential focus on young women growing up and older women struggling to come to terms with their existence. She has profoundly influenced the short-story genre in Canada with the publication of six collections, four of which have won Governor General's Awards: *Dance of the Happy Shades* (1968), *Something I've Been Meaning to Tell You* (1974), *The Moons of Jupiter* (1982), and *Friend of My Youth* (1990). Her novel *Lives of Girls and Women* (1971) breaks new ground in its exploration of gender issues and in its use of linked narratives. Her most recent collection of stories is *Open Secrets* (1994). She first met Margaret Laurence in Vancouver in 1960.

F.G. (Frank) Paci—b. Pesaro, Italy, 1948—emigrated to Sault Ste. Marie, Ontario in 1952, where he grew up. He now lives in Toronto, where he teaches and writes. His portraits of Italian émigrés and first-generation Italian Canadians constitute an important part of the Canadian literary mosaic. He has published six novels, beginning with *The Italians* (1978), the first in a trilogy which also includes *Black Madonna* (1982) and *The Father* (1984). His most recent work of fiction is *Sex and Character* (1993). His work has been widely anthologized. He first met Margaret Laurence when she was writer-in-residence at the University of Toronto in 1969.

Al Purdy—b. Wooler, Ontario, 1918—is a writer whose range and depth of poetic expression are virtually unrivalled in Canadian poetry. He rode the rods during the Depression, served in the RCAF during the Second World War, and then settled in Ameliasburg, Ontario, whose landscape and people have served as his primary poetic matrix for over thirty years. His first book was *The Enchanted Echo* (1944), and since then he has published over two dozen volumes of poetry, the best-known being *Poems for All the Annettes* (1962), which received the Governor General's Award, *Wild Grape Wine* (1968), *In Search of Owen Roblin* (1974), *The Stone Bird* (1981), and *Piling Blood* (1984). His *Collected Poems* (1986) also won the Governor General's Award. He has published a novel, *A Splinter in the Heart* (1990), and has played a significant role as an editor of work by younger Canadian poets in *Storm Warning* (1971) and *Storm Warning 2* (1976). He and Margaret Laurence first met in Ottawa in 1967.

Janis Rapoport—b. Toronto, 1946—is the author of four books of poetry, the most recent of which is *Upon Her Fluent Route* (1991). Her poetry has appeared in several anthologies and educational texts and has been broadcast in Canada, the United States, and (in translation) France. She has also written three plays, and has had *Dreamgirls* (1979) performed across Canada. She has been playwright-in-residence at Tarragon Theatre in Toronto, writer-in-residence at several Ontario libraries, associate editor of *Tamarack Review*, and editor of the cultural magazine *Ethos*. At present she is an instructor in creative writing at the University of Toronto. She first met Margaret Laurence in London, England in 1967.

William Ready—b. Cardiff, Wales, 1914, d. 1982—was educated in Wales and at Oxford, lectured at the University of California at Berkeley 1940–41, and served in the British army in the Middle

East, North Africa, the Aegean Islands, and Italy. After the war he came to Canada and obtained an M.A. from the University of Manitoba. During the 1950s he held positions at Stanford and Marquette universities, and later at McMaster University. His books include *The Great Disciple* (1951), *The Tolkien Relation* (1969), *Notes on The Hobbit and The Lord of the Rings* (1971), and a play, *Losers, Keepers* (1979).

Mordecai Richler—b. Montreal, 1931—an outspoken satirist of racism, class bias, nationalism, and pomp and circumstance everywhere. He has written essays, articles, and nine works of fiction, at least three of which—*The Apprenticeship of Duddy Kravitz* (1959), *St. Urbain's Horseman* (1971), and *Solomon Gursky Was Here* (1989)—have established his reputation as one of Canada's foremost novelists. He has twice won the Governor General's Award, and has received an Academy Award Nomination for his screenplay of *The Apprenticeship of Duddy Kravitz*. In 1992 he published a controversial essay on the limitations of Quebec nationalism, *Oh Canada! Oh Quebec!* He met Margaret Laurence when both were living in England in the mid-1960s.

Gabrielle Roy—b. St. Boniface, Manitoba, 1909, d. 1983—is the most important Francophone writer for English Canada, as her work was translated through five decades. She was nationally and internationally acclaimed for *Bonheur d'occasion* (1945), which won the Prix Femina in France and was translated as *The Tin Flute* (1947), and substantiated her status with such novels as *La Petite Poule d'eau* (1950), translated as *Where Nests the Water Hen* (1961), *Rue Deschambault* (1955), translated as *Street of Riches* (1957), and *La route d'Altamont* (1966), translated as *The Road past Altamont* (1966). She won the Governor General's Award three times for her fiction. Margaret Laurence considered Roy a vital literary ancestor and valued colleague. They became close friends through correspondence which began in 1976 and met two years later in Calgary at a literary conference.

Andreas Schroeder—b. Hoheneggelsen, Germany, 1946—emigrated to Canada in 1951, settling in British Columbia. He has made his living as a poet, novelist, translator, journalist, and broadcaster. He has taught Creative Writing at several universities and has chaired the Writers' Union of Canada (1976–77), and was founding chair of the Public Lending Right Commission. His thirteen books include poetry, *File of Uncertainties* (1971); *Dustship Glory* (1986), a documentary novel; and a translation of Mennonite Low German short stories, *The Eleventh Commandment* (1990, co-authored with Jack Thiessen). He first met Margaret Laurence at a Writers' Union meeting in 1973.

Glen Sorestad—b. Vancouver, 1937—moved to Saskatchewan when he was ten, and taught in the English department of a Saskatoon high school 1969–81. In 1975 he and his wife, Sonia, co-founded Thistledown Press, which quickly became one of the leading small presses in Canada. He has served on the executive of the Association of Canadian Publishers and the League of Canadian Poets. He has published nine books of poetry, beginning with *Wind Songs* in 1975, and his work has appeared in many North American anthologies, magazines, and journals. His most recent book is *West into Night* (1991). He first met Margaret Laurence at a Writers' Union meeting in 1973.

David Watmough—b. London, England, 1926—was raised on a farm in Cornwall, and has lived professionally as a writer since university. His early life in Cornwall greatly influenced his fiction, especially the single, extended work (through ten volumes) of the "Davey Bryant" chronicles. The first of these was *No More into the Garden* (1978), and the most recent is *The Time of the Kingfishers* (1994). He has published other fiction as well, including the collection of stories *Love and the Waiting Game* (1975) and the novel *Thy Mother's Glass* (1992). His reputation as a performer of his own work, in for example the monodramas in *Ashes for Easter* (1972), emphasizes the variety and complexity of his creative expression. Although they began to correspond in late 1974, he did not meet Margaret Laurence until a Writers' Union meeting in 1976.

David Williams—b. Souris, Manitoba, 1945—is a professor of English at the University of Manitoba, a short-story writer, and the author of three novels, *The Burning Wood* (1975), *The River Horsemen* (1981), and *Eye of the Father* (1985). Laurence was particularly drawn to the first of these because of its realistic and sympathetic portrait of native characters, based considerably on his experience growing up near a native reserve and his family's funding of a mission on the edge of the Shagonis Reserve in northeast Saskatchewan. The relationship between much of his academic writing and his creative work is emphasized in his publication *Confessional Fictions: A Portrait of the Artist in the Canadian Novel* (1991). He first met Margaret Laurence at a Writers' Union meeting in 1977.

Budge Wilson—b. Halifax, Nova Scotia, 1927—has published ten children's books (the first in 1984). Her collection of adult short stories *The Leaving* (1990) has won a number of regional, national, and international awards. Her books have also been published in the United States, Australia, New Zealand, Denmark, and Finland. Two new collections of stories, *Cordelia Clark* and *The Courtship*, and one of her many children's books, *Cassandra's Driftwood*, appeared in 1994. Long before she began to write herself, she first met Margaret Laurence in Peterborough in 1969.

George Woodcock—b. Winnipeg 1912, d. 1995—grew up in England, and returned to Canada in 1949 to become one of the country's leading cultural critics and literary figures. He published over one hundred books. His literary criticism ranges from *The Paradox of Oscar Wilde* (1950) to *The World of Canadian Writing* (1980) and *The Meeting of Time and Space: Regionalism in Canadian Literature* (1981); his works on history include *The Doukhobors* (1968, with Ivan Avakumovic), *Gabriel Dumont* (1975), and *A Social History of Canada* (1988); his *Collected Poems* appeared in 1983, and an autobiography, *Beyond the Blue Mountains*, in 1987. His most recent books are *George Woodcock on Canadian Poetry* and *George Woodcock on Canadian Fiction* (both 1993) and *Letter from the Khyber Pass* (1993). He edited *A Place to Stand On: Essays by and about Margaret Laurence* (1983) and wrote *Introducing Margaret Laurence's* The Stone Angel, *A Reader's Guide* (1989). He first met Margaret Laurence "around 1958" when she was living in Vancouver.

Dale Zieroth—b. Neepawa, Manitoba, 1946—lives in North Vancouver and teaches at Douglas College in New Westminster, B.C., where he also edits the literary review *Event*. Laurence first wrote to him in 1971 after she read his poem "Father" in Purdy's *Storm Warning* and discovered he was from her hometown. He has published four books of poetry; the first, *Clearing: Poems from a Journey*, appeared in 1973, and the most recent, *The Weight of My Raggedy Skin*, in 1991. His work has also appeared in a number of literary anthologies. He is currently working on an untitled book of poems about office politics and workaholics. He and Laurence met at her cottage on the Otonabee River in 1972.

Margaret Atwood

1. O. Mannoni, *Prospero and Caliban: The Psychology of Colonization* (New York: Frederick A. Praeger, 1964).

2. Betty Friedan, *The Feminine Mystique* (New York: W.W. Norton, 1963).

3. Margaret Atwood, *Procedures for Underground* (Toronto: Oxford University Press, 1970).

4. Jim Polk was Atwood's husband at that time.

5. Margaret Atwood, *Power Politics* (Toronto: Anansi, 1971).

6. Margaret Atwood, *Survival: A Thematic Guide to Canadian Literature* (Toronto: Anansi, 1972).

7. Molson's awards two to four prizes annually "to encourage Canadians of outstanding achievement in the fields of the arts, the humanities or the social sciences to make further contributions to the cultural or intellectual heritage of Canada" (*The Canadian Encyclopedia*. Edmonton: Hurtig, 1985). In 1981 each award was $15,000; the amount has since been increased to $50,000.

8. I have been unable to discover the identity of this Quebec writer.

9. Ding Ling (1907–1988). Her early stories considered the impact of modern life on China's youth and established her reputation. She joined the Communists during the revolution, was exiled in 1957, and came back into favour in the 1980s. Several of her works have appeared in English, including her best-known novel, *The Sun Shines over the Sanggan River* (1984).

10. The 1986 Booker Prize winner was Kingsley Amis for *The Old Devils*. Robertson Davies' *What's Bred in the Bone* and Margaret Atwood's *The Handmaid's Tale* were shortlisted.

Don Bailey

1. Possibly manuscript of *My Bareness Is Not Just My Body* (Fredericton: Fiddlehead Books, 1971).

2. Jane Rule, *This Is Not for You* (New York: McCall, 1970).

3. "margaret laurence" in *My Bareness Is Not Just My Body*.

George Bowering

1. George Bowering, *Flycatcher and Other Stories* (Ottawa: Oberon, 1974).

2. George Bowering, "That Fool of a Fear: Notes on *A Jest of God*", *Canadian Literature* 50 (Autumn 1971), pp. 41–56.

3. Audrey Thomas, *Blown Figures* (Vancouver: Talonbooks, 1974).

4. *Boundary 2: An International Journal of Literature* was first published in 1972 as *Boundary 2: A Journal of Postmodern Literature*.

5. *The Canadian Novel in the Twentieth Century: Essays from Canadian Literature*, George Woodcock, ed. (Toronto: McClelland & Stewart, 1975).

6. Jane Rule, *Theme for Diverse Instruments* (Vancouver: Talonbooks, 1975).

Ernest Buckler

1. Ernest Buckler, *The Cruelest Month* (Toronto: McClelland & Stewart, 1963).

2. Robert D. Chambers, *Sinclair Ross & Ernest Buckler* (Vancouver: Copp Clark, 1975).

3. Ernest Buckler, *The Mountain and the Valley* (New York; Holt, 1952; Toronto: McClelland & Stewart Limited, 1970).

4. A. A. Alvarez, *The Savage God: A Study of Suicide* (London:

Weidenfeld and Nicolson, 1971).

5. Sylvia Plath, *The Bell Jar* (London: Faber and Faber, 1966).

6. Ernest Buckler, *The Rebellion of Young David and Other Stories*, Robert D. Chambers, ed. (Toronto: McClelland & Stewart, 1975).

7. Alan Young, *Ernest Buckler* (Toronto: McClelland & Stewart, 1976).

8. Clara Thomas, *The Manawaka World of Margaret Laurence* (Toronto: McClelland & Stewart, 1975).

9. I have been unable to find this early 1975 review.

10. Margaret Laurence, review of *Sinclair Ross & Ernest Buckler*, *Globe and Mail*, Nov. 8, 1975.

11. Claude Bissell, Buckler's biographer, is not aware of the nature of this illness.

12. Robert Browning, "Rabbi Ben Ezra", *Dramatis Personae*, 1864.

13. Joyce Cary, *The Captive and the Free* (London: Michael Joseph, 1959).

14. Joyce Cary, *The Horse's Mouth* (London: Michael Joseph, 1951).

15. Ernest Buckler, *Whirligig* (Toronto: McClelland & Stewart, 1977).

Silver Donald Cameron

1. John Prebble, *Culloden* (London: Secker and Warburg, 1961).

2. These two articles "Good Morning to the Grandson of Ramases the Second" and "Captain Shawkat and Kipling's Ghost" were eventually published in Laurence's *Heart of a Stranger*. They never appeared in *Holiday*.

3. *The Fire-Dwellers* was serialized in *The Ladies' Home Journal* 86 (1 March 1969): pp. 127–34.

4. "One of the first things he said was that to his mind Margaret Laurence is the biggest talent now working in Canadian letters. 'A good book has a kind of *resonance* about it, you know? [I]t goes on working in the mind long after you've finished it. My God, but *The Stone Angel* had that quality.'" Cameron to ML, September 15, 1968.

5. Mordecai Richler, *The Apprenticeship of Duddy Kravitz* (London: André Deutsch, 1959, and Toronto: McClelland & Stewart, 1969).

6. Mordecai Richler, *St. Urbain's Horseman* (New York: Knopf, 1971, and Toronto: McClelland & Stewart, 1971).

7. Ernest Buckler, *Ox Bells and Fireflies: A Memoir* (New York: Knopf, 1968, and McClelland & Stewart, 1968). Cameron's review appeared in *Queen's Quarterly* 76 (Autumn 1969), pp. 346–347.

8. Mordecai Richler, *Cocksure* (New York: Simon and Schuster, 1968, and Toronto: McClelland & Stewart, 1968).

9. Silver Donald Cameron was the *Mysterious East's* publisher and editor. He calls it "a lively journal of social criticism", which ran from 1969–71.

10. Margaret Laurence, "Ancestral Voices Prophesying", *Mysterious East*, (Dec. 1970); pp. 6–10.

11. Harold Horwood, *White Eskimo: A Novel of Labrador* (Toronto: Doubleday Canada, 1972).

12. Denis Smith, *Bleeding Hearts, Bleeding Country: Canada and the Quebec Crisis* (Edmonton: Hurtig, 1971).

13. The Waffle was "A group established in 1969 as a caucus within the New Democratic Party [of Canada]. . . . It issued a Manifesto for an Independent Socialist Canada that demanded that Canadian public ownership replace American private ownership. . . . Its politics were militantly socialist and nationalist." It also organized provincially. The Waffle dissolved in 1974. *(The Canadian Encyclopedia).*

14. Donald Cameron, "Tim Crawford Meets the Mind Police", *Saturday Night* 87 (Nov. 1972), pp. 15–19.

15. *Conversations with Canadian Novelists*, Donald Cameron, ed. (Toronto: Macmillan of Canada, 1973).

16. The story, "Snapshot: The Third Drunk", appeared in *Atlantic Monthly* and has been anthologized several times, most notably in *Canadian Short Stories, Third Series*, Robert Weaver, ed. (Toronto: Oxford University Press, 1978) and *The Cape Breton Collection*, Lesley Choyce, ed. (Porters Lake, N.S.: Pottersfield, 1984).

17. Hubert Evans, *O Time in Your Flight* (Madeira Park, B.C.: Harbour, 1979).

18. ML reviewed Evans' book in the *Toronto Star*, October 27, 1979.

19. Hubert Evans, *Mostly Coast People: The Collected Poetry of Hubert Evans* (Madeira Park, B.C.: Harbour, 1982).

Marian Engel

1. Eleanor Perenyl, review of Victoria Glendinning's *Vita: The Life of Victoria Sackville-West* (New York: Knopf, 1984) and James Lees-Milne's *Harold Nicholson: A Biography* (London: Chatto and Windus, 1984), in *The New York Review of Books*, Vol. 31, No. 3 (March 29, 1984).

2. Sylvia Fraser, *Berlin Solstice* (Toronto: McClelland & Stewart, 1984), and Timothy Findley, *Not Wanted on the Voyage* (New York: Viking, 1984).

Hubert Evans

1. *Mist on the River* (Toronto: Copp Clark, 1954; Toronto: McClelland & Stewart, 1973).

2. *Endings* (Madeira Park, B.C.: Harbour, 1966). ML must have been referring to this, as the previous book of Evans' poems appeared in 1966.

3. *O Time in Your Flight* (Madeira Park, B.C.: Harbour, 1980).

4. Kate Hamilton worked for The Writers' Union running writers' tours and providing the first members books. Arthur Phelps

(1887-1970) was general superintendent of the Canadian Broadcasting Corporation from 1945 to 1947 and then taught at McGill University until his retirement in 1953. He was the author of *Poems* (1921) and *A Bobcaygeon Notebook* (1922), and of a series of radio scripts on relatively unknown Canadian authors, *Canadian Writers* (1951).

5. *Mostly Coast People: The Collected Poetry of Hubert Evans* (Madeira Park: Harbour, 1982).

Timothy Findley

1. Timothy Findley, *The Last of the Crazy People* (London: Macdonald and Company, 1967).

2. Timothy Findley, *The Butterfly Plague* (New York: Viking, 1969).

3. Jerzy Kosinski, *Steps* (New York: Random House, 1968).

4. Timothy Findley, *Famous Last Words* (Toronto: Clarke, Irwin, 1981).

5. The film of *The Wars*, based on the novel, was released in 1983.

6. I have been unable to find out whether Sinclair Ross has received the Order of Canada.

7. "Old Women's Song", in Laurence's *Dance on the Earth* (Toronto: McClelland & Stewart, 1989).

8. Timothy Findley, *Not Wanted on the Voyage* (Markham and New York: Viking, 1984).

9. Margaret Laurence, "Greater Evil", *Toronto Life* (Sept. 1984), pp. 58–59, 92.

10. Laurence's article, "Constant Hope: Women in the New and Future High Tech Age", appeared in *Canadian Woman Studies*, 6 (Spring 1985), pp. 12-15.

11. "I Am a Camera" was a 1951 dramatic adaptation by John Van Druten of Isherwood's *The Berlin Stories* (1945).

Gary Geddes

1. Gary Geddes, *rivers inlet* (Vancouver: Talonbooks, 1971).

2. Gary Geddes, *The Terracotta Army* (Ottawa: Oberon, 1984), and *Letter of the Master of Horse* (Ottawa: Oberon, 1973).

Graeme Gibson

1. Margaret Atwood, *Surfacing* (Toronto: McClelland & Stewart, 1972). The review of *Surfacing* that appeared in *Quarry* Vol. 22, No. 3 (Summer 1973) was by Helen Sonthoff.

Harold Horwood

1. Harold Horwood, *The Foxes of Beachy Cove* (Don Mills: PaperJacks, 1967, 1975).

2. Rudy Wiebe, *The Temptations of Big Bear* (Toronto: McClelland & Stewart, 1973).

3. Ray Smith, *Lord Nelson Tavern* (Toronto: McClelland & Stewart, 1974), and Clarke Blaise, *A North American Education* (Garden City, N.Y.: Doubleday, 1973).

4. Leo Simpson, *The Peacock Papers* (Toronto: Macmillan of Canada, 1973).

5. Horwood got this Canada Council grant in 1975.

6. Harold Horwood, *Bartlett, the Great Canadian Explorer* (Garden City, N.Y.: Doubleday, 1977).

7. Norman Penner, *The Canadian Left: A Critical Analysis* (Scarborough, Ontario: Prentice-Hall of Canada, 1977); John Porter, *The Vertical Mosaic* (Toronto: University of Toronto Press, 1965); John Fowles, *Daniel Martin* (Boston: Little, Brown, 1977); Tim Buck, *A Conscience for Canada* (Toronto: Progress, 1975); Laurens Van der Post, *Jung and the Story of Our Time* (New York: Pantheon, 1975).

8. Harold Horwood and Stephen Taylor, *Beyond the Road* (Toronto: Van Nostrand Reinhold, 1976).

Myrna Kostash

1. Myrna Kostash, "Women: Groovy Men and Other Myths of Liberation", *Maclean's* 86:84 (Feb. 1973).

2. This is likely a reference to a Women's Studies class Kostash was teaching at the University of Toronto.

3. Margaret Atwood, *Survival* (Toronto: Anansi, 1973).

4. Myrna Kostash, *All of Baba's Children* (Edmonton: Hurtig, 1977).

Robert Kroetsch

1. Robert Kroetsch, *The Words of My Roaring* (Toronto: Macmillan of Canada, 1966), and *The Studhorse Man* (Toronto: Macmillan of Canada, 1969).

Dennis Lee

1. Scott Symons, *Helmet of Flesh* (Toronto: McClelland & Stewart, 1986).

2. Jack Hodgins, *Spit Delaney's Island: Selected Stories* (Toronto: Macmillan of Canada, 1976).

Norman Levine

1. "A Bird in the House" appeared in *Canadian Winter's Tales*, Norman Levine, ed. (Toronto: Macmillan of Canada, 1968).

2. Margaret Laurence, "Crying of the Loons", *Atlantic Advocate* 56 (March 1966), pp. 34–38.

3. Norman Levine, *From a Seaside Town* (Toronto: Macmillan of Canada, 1970).

Hugh MacLennan

1. Hugh MacLennan, *The Other Side of Hugh MacLennan* (Toronto: Macmillan of Canada, 1978).

2. This appears to have been David H. Harrison, who was premier from Dec. 26, 1887 to Jan. 12, 1888.

3. Paul Stuewe, "Better Dead Than Read?", *Books in Canada*, Vol. 7., No. 8 (Oct. 1978).

4. Timothy Findley, "Better Dead Than Read? An Opposing View," *Books in Canada*, Vol. 7, No. 10 (Dec. 1978).

5. F.R. Scott, *Essays on the Constitution: Aspects of Canadian Law and Politics* (Toronto: University of Toronto Press, 1977).

6. Hugh MacLennan, *Voices in Time* (Toronto: Macmillan of Canada, 1980).

7. Elspeth Cameron, *Hugh MacLennan: A Writer's Life* (Toronto: University of Toronto Press, 1981).

8. The Royal Bank Award for Canadian Achievement "honours a Canadian . . . whose outstanding accomplishment makes an important contribution to human welfare and the common good" according to a Royal Bank brochure. The award consists of $100,000 and a gold medal. Other winners include Morley Callaghan and David Suzuki.

Joyce Marshall

1. Joyce Marshall, *Lovers and Strangers* (Philadelphia: J.B. Lippincott, 1957) and *Presently Tomorrow* (Boston: Little, Brown, 1946).

2. Joyce Marshall, *A Private Place* (Ottawa: Oberon, 1975).

3. Gabrielle Roy, *The Road past Altamont*, Joyce Marshall, tr. (Toronto: McClelland & Stewart, 1966).

4. This book has not yet been published.

John Metcalf

1. John Metcalf, *The Lady Who Sold Furniture* (Toronto: Clarke, Irwin, 1970).

2. Margaret Laurence, "Where the World Began: A Small Prairie Town As an Aspect of Myself," *Maclean's* (Dec. 1972), pp. 22–23.

3. Alice Munro, *Lives of Girls and Women* (Toronto: McGraw-Hill Ryerson, 1971).

4. *The Narrative Voice: Short Stories and Reflections by Canadian Authors*, John Metcalf, ed. (Toronto: McGraw-Hill Ryerson, 1972).

5. John Metcalf, *Going Down Slow* (Toronto: McClelland & Stewart, 1972).

6. John Metcalf, "Private Parts: A Memoir", *Canadian Fiction Magazine*, No. 24–25 (Spring/Summer 1977), pp. 109–159.

7. John Metcalf, *The Teeth of My Father* (Ottawa: Oberon, 1975).

Claire Mowat

1. Claire Mowat, "The Mermaid Inn Column", *Globe and Mail*, May 26, 1984.

2. Claire Mowat, *The Outport People* (Toronto: McClelland & Stewart, 1983).

Alice Munro

1. Alice Munro has told me that this magazine was *Harper/Queen's*. I have been unable to discover any details about the date or the title of the article.

Frank Paci

1. Frank Paci, *The Italians* (Ottawa: Oberon, 1978).

2. Paci did not win the award.

3. Frank Paci, *Black Madonna* (Ottawa: Oberon, 1982).

4. Frank Paci, *The Father* (Ottawa: Oberon, 1984).

Al Purdy

1. Al Purdy, *The Woman on the Shore: Poems by Al Purdy* (Toronto: McClelland & Stewart, 1990), p. 69

2. *Margaret Laurence—Al Purdy: A Friendship in Letters*, John Lennox, ed. (Toronto: McClelland & Stewart, 1993).

Janis Rapoport

1. Unpublished attempt at a novel set at Expo 67 in Montreal. "This manuscript now resides at the back of a long, dark drawer" (JR to A. Wainwright, February 23, 1993).

2. Janis Rapoport, *Jeremy's Dream* (Erin, Ont.: Press Porcépic, 1974).

Will Ready

1. Ready's review appeared in *The Hamilton Spectator*, Sept. 17, 1966.

2. Margaret Laurence, "The Drummer of All the World", *Queen's Quarterly* 63 (Winter 1956), pp. 487–504.

3. Will Ready, *The Tolkien Relation: A Personal Enquiry* (Chicago: Regnery, 1968).

4. J.R.R. Tolkien, *The Hobbit* (London: Allen and Unwin, 1966), and *Lord of the Rings* (Boston: Houghton Mifflin, 1966).

5. The 1971 edition of *Contemporary Authors* (Vol. 25–28) cites *The Canadian Imagination* as a work in progress.

6. Work in progress, 1971 *Contemporary Authors* (Vol. 25–28).

7. Kildare Dobbs, "Will Ready Papers", *Maclean's* 86 (Jan. 1973), pp. 38–39, 50.

8. Will Ready, *Losers, Keepers: A Play in Two Acts* (Hamilton, Ontario: Cromlech, 1979).

Mordecai Richler

1. Richler was editing *Canadian Writing Today* (Harmondsworth: Penguin Books, 1970), which contains (pp. 203-209) an excerpt from *A Jest of God*.

2. See Silver Donald Cameron, Note 2, page 251.

3. Mordecai Richler, excerpt from *St. Urbain's Horseman* in *The Tamarack Review* 41 (Autumn 1966), pp. 137–142, 145–150.

4. "Crying of the Loons" in *Atlantic Advocate* (March 1966), pp. 34–38. "Horses of the Night" in *Chatelaine* (July 1967), pp. 46, 70–77.

5. Mordecai Richler, *Cocksure* (Toronto: McClelland & Stewart, 1968).

6. I cannot find "The Running Man" by Leslie Fiedler or anyone else.

7. Leonard Cohen, *Beautiful Losers* (Toronto: McClelland & Stewart, 1966).

8. "Playing Ball on Hampstead Heath" was an excerpt from *St. Urbain's Horseman* that appeared in *Canadian Winter's Tales*, Norman Levine, ed. (Toronto: Macmillan of Canada, 1968).

9. "Horses of the Night" did not appear in *Canadian Winter's Tales*.

10. "This Year at the Arabian Nights Hotel", in *The Tamarack Review*, No. 47, (Spring 1968) pp. 9–18.

Gabrielle Roy

1. Gabrielle Roy, *The Tin Flute*, Hannah Josephson, tr. (New York: Reynal and Hitchcock, 1947, and Toronto: McClelland & Stewart, 1969).

2. Roy, *The Road past Altamont*, Joyce Marshall, tr. (Toronto: McClelland & Stewart, 1966).

3. Sheila Egoff, *The Republic of Childhood: A Critical Guide to Canadian Children's Literature* in English (Toronto: Oxford University Press, 1967).

4. I have been unable to track down any review by ML of Ken Adachi's *The Enemy That Never Was*.

5. Gabrielle Roy, *The Enchanted Summer*, Joyce Marshall, tr. (Toronto: McClelland & Stewart, 1976).

6. "Listen. Just Listen", in *Divided We Stand*, Gary Geddes, ed. (Toronto: Peter Martin Associates, 1977).

7. Gabrielle Roy, *Garden in the Wind*, Alan Brown, tr. (Toronto: McClelland & Stewart, 1977).

8. George Woodcock and Ivan Avakumovic, *The Doukhobors* (Toronto: Oxford University Press, 1968).

9. Published in English as *Children of My Heart*, Alan Brown, tr. (Toronto: McClelland & Stewart Limited, 1979).

10. The Calgary Conference to celebrate the twentieth anniversary of the New Canadian Library was sponsored by McClelland & Stewart, the Canada Council, and the University of Calgary. Invitations were sent out to teachers of Canadian literature and to many prominent Canadian writers. Those attending were to be asked to name the best books on the NCL list, but because of the Council's and the university's involvement they were ultimately asked to name the top hundred, and then the top ten, Canadian works of fiction.

11. Untitled story in *Children of My Heart*, p. 111.

12. "Tal des Walde", published in *Vox Wesleyana*, 1946.

13. Gabrielle Roy, *Courte-Queue* (Montreal: Stanké, 1979)

14. The dialogue between ML and Lois Wilson, then Moderator of the United Church of Canada, appeared in the *United Church Observer* in February, 1980, pp. 10–12.

15. Gabrielle Roy, *The Fragile Lights of Earth: Articles and Memories 1942–1970*, Alan Brown, tr. (Toronto: McClelland & Stewart 1982).

Glen Sorestad

1. Glen Sorestad, *Wind Songs* (Saskatoon: Thistledown, 1975).

2. Glen Sorestad, *Prairie Pub Poems* (Saskatoon: Thistledown, 1976).

3. The Prairie Writers Workshop at Evan Hardy Collegiate in Saskatoon. Sorestad organized this event and brought in Laurence, Robert Kroetsch, Henry Kreisel, Paul Hiebert, Ken Mitchell, Max Braithwaite, Lorna Crozier, Anne Szumigalski, Rudy Wiebe, and a dozen or more other writers over a three-day period. Laurence had one question-and-answer session with about fifty or sixty students and teachers. "Despite Margaret's fears, the session was wonderful and she felt immediately at ease discussing her work with young people" (Sorestad to A. Wainwright, March 15, 1993). She also had a one-hour question-and-answer session after a reading at the University of Saskatchewan before two to three hundred students.

4. Rudy Wiebe, *The Scorched-Wood People* (Toronto: McClelland & Stewart, 1977).

David Watmough

1. David Watmough, *Ashes for Easter and Other Monodramas* (Vancouver: Talonbooks, 1972).

2. David Watmough, *Love & the Waiting Game: Eleven Stories*,

(Ottawa: Oberon, 1975),

3. David Watmough, "Terminus Victoria", *Saturday Night* 91 (May 1976).

4. Patricia Morley's review of *Love & the Waiting Game* appeared in *Queen's Quarterly* 83 (Autumn 1976), pp. 519–20.

David Williams

1. Williams' uncle had sharply criticized his first novel because he considered it contrary to his fundamentalist faith.

2. David Williams, *The Burning Wood* (Toronto: Anansi, 1975).

3. Earle Birney, *Turvey: A Military Picaresque* (Toronto: McClelland & Stewart, 1949).

4. Rudy Wiebe, *Peace Shall Destroy Many* (Toronto: McClelland & Stewart, 1962).

5. Rudy Wiebe, *The Temptations of Big Bear* (Toronto: McClelland & Stewart, 1973).

6. This poem "For My Son On His Twenty-First Birthday, August 1976" appears in *Dance on the Earth*.

7. David Williams, "The Indian Our Ancestor", *Dalhousie Review* 57 (Summer 1978), pp. 309–328.

Budge Wilson

1. "The Metaphor" appears in Budge Wilson, *The Leaving* (Toronto: Anansi, 1990).

George Woodcock

1. W.O. Mitchell, *The Kite* (Toronto: Macmillan of Canada, 1962); ML's review was published in *Canadian Literature* 15 (Winter 1963).

2. George Woodcock, "Various Americans", in *The New Romans*, Al Purdy, ed. (Edmonton: Hurtig, 1968).

3. Margaret Laurence, "Ten Years' Sentences", in *Canadian Literature* 41 (Summer 1969).

4. George Woodcock, *Herbert Read: The Stream and the Source* (London: Faber and Faber, 1972).

5. George Woodcock, *Gabriel Dumont* (Edmonton: Hurtig, 1975); ML's review, "Man of Honour", appeared in *The Canadian Forum* Vol. LV, No. 657 (Dec. 1975/Jan. 1976).

6. George Woodcock, "The Human Elements: Margaret Laurence's Fiction", in his *The World of Canadian Writing* (Vancouver: Douglas and McIntyre, 1980).

Dale Zieroth

1. *Storm Warning*, Al Purdy, ed. (Toronto: McClelland & Stewart, 1971).

2. "Exiles", *Saturday Evening Post* 234 (June 3, 1961), pp. 28–29; "Spell of the Distant Drum", *Saturday Evening Post* 235 (May 5, 1962), pp. 24–25.

3. Sinclair Ross, *As For Me and My House* (New York: Reynal and Hitchcock, 1941, and Toronto: McClelland & Stewart, 1957).

4. *Soundings*, Jack Ludwig and Andy Wainwright, eds. (Toronto: Anansi, 1970).

5. Dale Zieroth, *Clearing: Poems from a Journey* (Toronto: Anansi, 1973).

6. Andrew Suknaski, *Wood Mountain Poems* (Wood Mountain, Sask.: Anak, 1973).

PRINTED IN CANADA